General Education in the Social Sciences

1891-1991

A Centennial Publication of
The University of Chicago Press

General Education in the Social Sciences

*Centennial Reflections on the College
of the University of Chicago*

EDITED BY

John J. MacAloon

THE UNIVERSITY OF CHICAGO PRESS

Chicago and London

John J. MacAloon is associate professor in the Division of the
Social Sciences and the College, the University of Chicago.
An earlier book, *This Great Symbol: Pierre de Courbertin and
the Origins of the Modern Olympic Games,* was also published by
the University of Chicago Press.

The University of Chicago Press, Chicago 60637
The University of Chicago Press, Ltd., London
© 1992 by The University of Chicago
All rights reserved. Published 1992
Printed in the United States of America

01 00 99 98 97 96 95 94 93 92   5 4 3 2 1

ISBN (cloth): 0-226-50002-0
ISBN (paper): 0-226-50003-9

Library of Congress Cataloging-in-Publication Data
General education in the social sciences : centennial
   reflections on the College of the University of
   Chicago / edited by John J. MacAloon.
        p.   cm.
     Includes bibliographical references and index.
     1. Social sciences—Study and teaching (Higher)—
   United States—History—20th century.   2. University of
   Chicago. College.
   I. MacAloon, John J.
   H62.5.U5G46   1992
   300'.71'177311—dc20   91-42118
                                                        CIP

⊗The paper used in this publication meets the minimum
requirements of the American National Standard for
Information Sciences—Permanence of Paper for Printed
Library Materials, ANSI Z39.48-1984.

Contents

Part III   Intellectual Biographies and Institutional Settings

Part IV   Enduring Controversies in Changing Times

Preface

John J. MacAloon

This volume explores the history and contemporary practice of general education in the College of the University of Chicago. Its publication contributes to the centennial celebration of a university known for its long preoccupation with the place of general education in American undergraduate learning. These new analyses of the Chicago experience find their contemporary context in the extensive and often fierce national debate over the collegiate curriculum which began in the early 1980s and continues unabated. Today's most vibrant and contentious issues—common and specialized learning in the curriculum, conceptions of general and liberal education, the design of common core sequences, the relative pedagogical merits of classic texts and contemporary research, Western and non-Western course materials, the place of undergraduate teaching in scholarly careers—have been debated for decades by the faculty of the College. More significantly, these concerns have been practically embodied at Chicago in educational programs of sufficient historical depth to reveal patterns of intellectual and pedagogical continuity amidst changing social and institutional circumstances.

The University's centennial year is also the sixtieth anniversary of one of these enduring educational projects, the "Social Sciences 2" course at Chicago. "Soc 2" (*sōsh too*), as it has long been called, is one of the oldest, probably the most continuous, and—from the standpoint of its transdisciplinary and staff-taught character and roster of faculty—the most distinguished of American experiments in constituting social science for general education purposes. Tracing the evolution of the College within the University of Chicago and of general education within the College, this book recaptures and analyzes the record of Soc 2 as an exemplary general education enterprise.

The volume is thus experimental in two related ways. While the festschrift is a well-established academic genre, it appears never to have been devoted to the contributions of a particular college course rather than to those of an individual scholar, department, or school of thought. Yet, for faculty and students alike, the course is the chief temporal, spatial, social, and evaluative unit of American undergraduate pedagogy. By focusing on the Soc 2 course, the authors of these essays have tried to produce an account firmly rooted in the phenomenology of actual undergraduate teaching and learning.

Our aim differs from that of standard institutional history in a second way. Just as we regard courses as neither passive dependencies nor as mere servomechanisms of abstract structural arrangements and educational visions, so too we refuse the common convention of discussing courses as if no particular human beings were responsible for them. This book seeks a true-to-life portrayal of the encounter of flesh-and-blood persons—their situations, personalities, perspectives, and projects—with the established intellectual agendas and academic routines that compose what is called "the course."

In this volume, we experiment with the view that the biographies of a course and of a college are most compellingly captured in their multifarious and selective incorporations into the autobiographies of a succession of faculty and students who have sojourned with them. Our hunch is that the continuities and discontinuities which emerge through this strategy of memory and memorial stand out rather more starkly than those derived from typical general histories of the higher learning in America. Thus, we have made no effort to quell the dissonances and contradictions of recollection, judgment, and voice that cross-cut these highly personal evaluations of the Soc 2 experience. The course has survived, indeed prevailed, because it has always been a sustained and committed argument, not a monument of any kind. Today, as in the past, everything is contested among the faculty, save perhaps the judgment once expressed by Soc 2's most picaresque former instructor, the ex-thief and Borstal boy, Mark Benney: "I think that had I known . . . that such a course as Social Science 2 was being offered anywhere in the world I would have strained all my resources to take it. It was ironical that I found myself . . . both taking and teaching it."

The contributors to this volume are present and former Chicago students or faculty, instructors in or close observers of the College and the course, and equally apportioned between current Chicago faculty and scholar-teachers who pursue their careers at other institutions. In these essays, their experiences in different decades are deployed to illuminate one other and to probe the persistent claims of social science to status as a distinctive mode of intellectual production worthy of a place in modern common learning.

Since useful histories are always inquiries into particular creations in particular settings, no apology seems necessary for the authors' focus on the University of Chicago. Still, we would not have considered publishing the book if we had not been convinced that it would interest a variety of readers never connected with Chicago or Soc 2. No American college is so self-contained that its experience is rendered incomparable with the intellectual and pedagogical struggles at other institutions of higher learning. Over the past decade, Soc 2 faculty have regularly been called upon for consultation by other colleges initiating or reviving core curricula, and colleagues at these institutions have urged us to make the Chicago experience more widely accessible. At the same time, it is vanity to imagine that the record of any one institution could substitute itself—as a historical index, much less as any sort of paragon—for developments elsewhere. Among the explicit comparisons lacing these essays are the educational models and antimodels faculty and students brought to and took from Chicago and the transformations such translocations inevitably entailed. As the first intensive ethnohistory of a single course over six decades, the book aspires to create baseline conditions for a more systematic comparative geography of social science pedagogy in the future.

The decade-long process of exploration culminating in this volume began with a symposium on Soc 2 held on campus in November 1982. Successive deans of the College, Jonathan Z. Smith and Donald Levine, gave the symposium their full support, and President Hanna Gray inaugurated the meeting in Cobb Hall's Quantrell Auditorium. Wendy Olmsted's participation—as master of the New Collegiate Division and director of the Forum for Liberal Learning, which cosponsored the conference—was emblematic of the wide endorsement received from faculty throughout the College. Special contributions were made by Susanne Rudolph and Lloyd Rudolph. Professors Sylvia Thrupp of the University of Michigan and David Bakan and Paul Antze of York University returned to campus to make important contributions, as did the extramural authors in this volume and many former Soc 2 students and faculty in the Chicago area. Scores of alumni from around the country wrote in response to news of the gathering. The entire event was made possible through the generous support of Maurice F. Fulton and Muriel G. Fulton, College alumni whose understanding gave the first clue of the nerves to be struck by concerted reflection on the Soc 2 tradition.

Current dean of the College Ralph Nicholas—like his two predecessors a stalwart of Soc 2 teaching—and John Boyer, master of the Social Sciences Collegiate Division, have greatly assisted in preparing this volume. Its publication has been supported by a Ford Foundation grant to the University of Chicago College for the improvement of social science education. We are grateful for the helpful suggestions of two anonymous reviewers and to the editorial staff of the University of

Chicago Press, particularly Penelope Kaiserlian and John Tryneski, the latter himself a Soc 2 alumnus. Various administrative debts are owed to Roberta MacGowan and Katherine Karvunis and to social sciences course secretary Diane New, who typed the manuscript. Finally I should like to thank my current Soc 2 cochairmen, Bertram Cohler and Moishe Postone, for assuming extra burdens while I completed my editorial duties.

General Education in the Social Sciences

Introduction

John J. MacAloon

The creation of this book takes place under the influence of two compelling ironies of American higher education, one local and one national. From its foundation in 1892, the University of Chicago has made scholarly research and graduate training its main aims rather than functions adjunct to the work of an established college. And yet, in few American research universities has the program of undergraduate instruction been so continuously central to the history, composition, and culture of the overall enterprise as the College has been at the University of Chicago. Comprehending this curious situation means reckoning with the larger irony that American universities and colleges, institutions publicly charged with preserving the past and conveying a living sense of it to younger generations, are notably profligate with their own histories.

The College in the University

For many who have passed through Chicago or have contemplated it from afar, the College *is* the University. For others whose primary connections have been with Chicago's graduate departments, professional schools, or research institutes, the presence of the College has been invariably felt through its claims on institutional resources, its association with notable scholarly achievements, and the sharing of classrooms, laboratories, and coffee shops with Chicago's special brand of audacious and intellectually peripatetic undergraduates. Today the College enrolls more students than either the graduate divisions or the professional schools; in other periods it has been the smallest of the three units of University teaching and research. At times the College has been the focus of local controversy and national attention; at other times it has quietly gone about its business. For many Chicago faculty over several generations, the College has provided a center of institutional identity, intellectual excitement, and pedagogical vocation; for others, resistance to its siren calls and self-righteous demands has been a main fact of professional life. Always and insistently, the College has been there.

One might expect that this notable record of endurance and countervailing struggle, particularly within a profoundly conservative institution with a strong corporate identity like the University of Chicago, would be well understood by now. However, the University has not been immune to the general casualness with which American institutions of higher learning have treated their own historical endowments. Previous analyses of the College, nearly all more than twenty years old, are virtually unknown among today's faculty, students, and alumni. No less than other educational communities, the College suffers from the absence of an effective "history of the present." In seeking to help alleviate this situation, the contributors to this volume have been acutely aware of the need for new strategies of memory and reflection to penetrate the barriers of amnesia which persistently afflict American colleges.

Universities and Their Histories

While the rare ritual occasion—a centennial celebration, for instance— may create a burst of concerted reflection on a university's heritage, a routine "presentism" soon enough returns. Institutional history is rapidly reconfined to the archivist's office, the odd dissertation, the potted briefs in recruitment and fund-raising brochures, and the anecdotage of the faculty club or alumni gathering: a matter for specialists, in other words, not a day-to-day requirement of group living. Most revealingly in these edifices of honored curiosity, the local history of teaching and learning is rarely deemed a subject fit for formal classroom study. Moreover, especially in university colleges, there is a hidden corollary to the informal maxim that those who can't do research teach: those who can't do either (or who aspire to administrative posts) cultivate the institution's heritage. As a result of these attitudes, the bodies of intellectual achievement conceived to be worthy of serious contemplation are either distant in space and time, language and conception, or else purely private matters of individual biography. The institution itself—the proximate community of accumulated experience—is treated as if it were, or ought to be, a neutral, merely instrumental medium through which individual persons and the collective projects of humankind gain access to one another. Such is the common-sense logic that colleges and universities create for their inhabitants by cavalier practices with regard to their own patrimonies.

It is not difficult to adduce reasons for this state of affairs. At the deepest level, the context-free logic of modern science itself is inscribed in these practices, as is the cult of the new in the valuation of research and scholarship. Institutions devoted to establishing human continuities and connections are hardly immune to the general culture's perduring ethos of progress and individualism. Indeed, the contradictions between official institutional values and the practical reproduction of the dominant culture may be all the more acute within them. Then, too, there are factors of social identity and the rhythms of academic production in the contemporary university. Extramural faculty identifications with the discipline and research specialty and intramural allegiance to the department may rival and, in conditions of high mobility, regularly supplant, identifications with the whole university. Neither the multiyear rhythm of research and publication nor the annual turnover of courses and students readily matches the temporal frameworks by which institutional history must be reckoned. On the student side, unless directly provoked, few undergraduates easily shed the featureless American notions of "college" and the "good school," and graduate students, usually more identified with their departments than their universities, rarely possess the breadth of view needed for such perception. With the passage of time, alumni gain increasing perspective on their educational experience, but typically as a frozen cross-section of the institution's total career. These and other factors conspire to deliver the accumulated struggles and achievements of generations of university citizens as a superficial, uninspiring, and nearly useless vernacular history.

Destructive consequences, and not just irony, flow from this situation. Besides inadvertently reinforcing the general American attitude that—as Henry Ford has come to be quoted—"history is bunk," colleges severely restrict their own capacities to contextualize and to manage their contemporary practices of teaching and learning. Without access to thoughtful records of the curricular debates and initiatives of the past, faculty groups more readily fall prey either to the latest intellectual and pedagogical fashions or to the dead weight of routine legitimated as "tradition." The sterile debates which ensue frequently betray generational conflict. Younger faculty propose changes they take to be innovative and in line with the latest intellectual advances and social conditions of pedagogy. Senior faculty respond that the proposals are old hat, tried and found wanting twenty or forty years ago. Without an independent record against which to measure such opinions, it cannot be rationally decided who really are the progressives and who the conservatives. Moreover, without the publication of analyses which go beyond abstract formulas or individual memoirs, institutions cannot really learn from one another's experience. Colleges considering alternative curricular models are forced to deliberate in splendid isolation, or else to rely on the authority or anecdotes of pilgrims and consultants from other places.

The collaborators in this volume seek to demonstrate the practical value of sustained reflection on several decades of educational experience at one important American college. Taken ensemble, these essays are intended to provide both an extended reference point for future debate on the undergraduate curriculum at Chicago and a useful touchstone for colleagues at other institutions. As social scientists and educational philosophers, we further hope that the book will help to remedy an existing scandal to our disciplines. We teach that all knowledge is socially embedded, and we regularly endeavor to historicize the texts, concepts, and arguments that compose our courses. Yet at Chicago we have been no better situated than other American undergraduate educators to provide our students with materials rich enough to compel them to think seriously about the course and the college as media for the selection and transmission of knowledge that are historically constituted, particular, and far from neutral. The struggle to fulfill these intentions in ways more effective than conventional educational writing has led to the innovations of interpretive strategy in this book.

The Course as Sinew and Visage

We proceed from the assumption that no one experiences the whole of a complex institution of higher learning. "The College," however much it is reified as a proper noun, is not a natural unit of anyone's experience. Relatedly, "the curriculum," as Ralph Nicholas points out in his Afterword to this volume, is not a disembodied and self-existent thing, though College faculty themselves are accustomed to thinking of it this way. Outside commentators likewise regularly refer to the "Chicago curriculum" as if it were an autonomous entity rather than a complex process abstracted and simplified through use of conventional language to describe it. But actual college life teaches us all differently.

At any given moment, the natural unit of engagement and preoccupation for students and faculty alike, the main locale where the intellectual and pedagogical "rubber meets the road," is not the curriculum or the College, but the course. That the course stands as the fundamental unit of collegiate spatial and temporal organization, of student-teacher interaction, of academic labor, evaluation, and memory, could hardly be more obvious. And yet, educational conferences and publications rarely focus on the course as the critical entity for consideration. In defiance of educational life itself, particular courses, when discussed at all, tend to be treated as mere dependencies, instances, or illustrations of overarching curricular models, pedagogical styles, or intellectual agendas. Part of the frustration with educational histories and reform initiatives surely lies in this contradiction between college life as lived and college life as imagined and publicly discussed.

Our experimental focus on the course in exploring the record of the College in the context of the contemporary national debate on college education was encouraged both from within and from without. In the late 1970s and early 1980s renewed attention to undergraduate learning focused on the decline of common "core" subjects, which was perceived as a consequence of the potency of the distribution-requirements model and of 1960s activism. (The role of college marketing strategy was less frequently discussed.) This emphasis on common learning renewed national interest in the University of Chicago's College, where general education requirements had been maintained through the preceding decades. In 1980 the Carnegie Foundation for the Advancement of Teaching, under the leadership of Ernest Boyer, surveyed the general education requirements of a representative sample of 309 two- and four-year colleges and produced an analysis of the stated purposes of general education in three main historical periods of revival. Because of the College's enduring commitment to a core curriculum for all students, the University of Chicago was chosen by Carnegie as the appropriate site for a national conference of faculty, administrators, and educational leaders, summoned to hear these results and to debate Carnegie's own proposals in "A Quest for Common Learning."[1]

Wishing to be proper hosts, we resolved to keep the College's claims to attention as inconspicuous as possible at this meeting. To our chagrin, visitors immediately began requesting information on the Chicago curriculum. In response, we provided a general outline of Chicago's baccalaureate requirements: year-long common core sequences in the biological sciences, physical sciences, the humanities, and the social sciences, and additional coursework in civilizational studies, mathematics, and foreign language, required of all students; the concentration programs; and the electives. This "architectural" material turned out not at all to satisfy our interlocutors from around the country. They wanted the actual outlines and syllabi of our specific general education

1. Ernest L. Boyer and Arthur Levine, *A Quest for Common Learning* (Washington: Carnegie Foundation for the Advancement of Teaching, 1981). The report calls for reorganizing curricula in a wide variety of institutions around the themes of shared use of symbols, membership in groups and institutions, producing and consuming, relationships with nature, senses of time, and values and beliefs. This agenda sought to take advantage of the breaking down of conventional boundaries among the academic disciplines which many regard as the hallmark of the contemporary intellectual scene.

courses. No amount of protest as to how decontextualized and inchoate these simple course outlines would appear caused our guests to desist. Faculty knew what faculty wanted: discussions of general intellectual themes and abstract curricular designs were all well and good, but teachers teach and live in *courses*.

This reminder was quite striking, as was our inability to provide more context than a catalog paragraph or two for any of our major general education courses. The College itself lacked any compelling "thick description" of the contemporary life of these courses, much less written accounts of their rich and instructive histories. These lacunae were having significant local consequences as well. For example, as Michael Schudson notes in his essay in this volume, those of us who joined College core course staffs in the 1970s—Soc 2 in our case—were left to our own devices to pick up in bits and shards the archeology of the enterprise into which we had entered. As undergraduates in the 1960s, many of us had been curricular activists and were, as young instructors, only too eager to take up roles in what we were told was an important long-term drama in American undergraduate education. We were keen to contribute new scenes to the continuing drama of the pedagogical evaluation of social science trends, and we tried to embody in ourselves the same consonance between teaching and research values that generations of notable forebears were said to have achieved. In the odd conversation and in staff meeting asides, in the code our elders spoke with one another, we were given laconic hints of the depth of the Soc 2 project and of the centrality of its mission to an extended family with whom we were expected to feel identification. But no means were available to permit us to read the story of the extended family for ourselves, to come face-to-face with more distant relatives, including our elders' elders, and to hear them tell their own tales.

As often happens in such circumstances, real history had become condensed and hidden in potent symbols of an earlier golden age. In Soc 2's case, it was the almost unbelievable roster of present or soon-to-be luminaries in American social science who composed the course staff in the 1940s and 1950s: Robert Redfield, Milton Singer, Maynard Krueger, David Riesman, Daniel Bell, Reinhard Bendix, Joe Gusfield, Sylvia Thrupp, Barrington Moore, Bert Hoselitz, Ben Nelson, Philip Rieff, Lewis Coser, Helen Mims, Reuel Denney, Rosalie Hankey Wax, Robert Keohane, Christian Mackauer, Morton Grodzins, C. Wright Mills, Murray Wax, Livio Stecchini, Martin Meyerson, and still others. We ourselves came to recite the litany, but it was impossible to learn very much about how and by whom the lake had been created that attracted all these swans, about the role that teaching the course played in transforming not a few of them from academic ducklings, or about the social scientific agendas within that group which ran counter to the "culture and personality" orientation associated with their work in present memory. Without the capacity to access the debates and practices of even the Soc 2 floruit of the forties and fifties, much less of the oddly more hidden cohorts of the sixties and early seventies (whose names once known turned out to be equally recognizable to us), day-to-day labor in the course in the mid- to late seventies often felt to its younger members less like the great tradition than the little community. We could not easily draw upon the special moral resources of a multi-generational collective project—a true lineage of social science teacher-scholars—to help overcome the enervation of this kind of teaching, the professional and institutional obstacles to maintaining the course, and the endless interpersonal squabbles over what and how to teach. These effects were reduplicated when it fell to us in our turn to socialize and incorporate junior faculty into the course in the eighties, most with no previous association with the University or the College, and at a time when the temptation to "modularize" the common core had to be fought off to place Soc 2 on a trajectory toward enrolling almost 60 percent of Chicago undergraduates, as it does today.

Our struggle to make the history of Soc 2 a resource for the contemporary course rather than a nostalgic impediment to its vitality follows a paradigm in the historical representation of the College as a whole: the rise and fall of the so-called Hutchins College. Particularly in its later period, when an autonomous College faculty mounted a fully required four-year general education curriculum, the Hutchins College has stood as the axial period of College history for insiders and outsiders alike. Dramatic enough even before they became legend, the Hutchins years retained much of their national cachet and local charisma through the 1970s and 1980s. In contrast to the courses mounted and the staffs that made them work, this famous moment in American educational history has generated a great deal of published commentary on its overall vision, curricular form, and notable personalities.[2] (Which is hardly to say, given the framing ironies discussed earlier, that line faculty and administrators at Chicago have necessarily read any of this literature.) But the revisionist process of reembedding the Hutchins College, and, in particular, its ideals and practices of general education,

2. Harry S. Ashmore, *Unseasonable Truths: The Life of Robert Maynard Hutchins* (Boston: Little, Brown, 1989); Mortimer Adler, *Philosopher at Large: An Intellectual Autobiography* (New York: Macmillan, 1977). Other commentaries are cited in the essays that follow. This project of reflection continues with two further volumes published in 1991 by the University of Chicago Press for the centennial celebration: Mary Ann Dzubak, *Robert M. Hutchins: Portrait of an Educator,* and William H. McNeill, *Hutchins' University: A Memoir of the University of Chicago, 1929–1950.*

in the much longer and larger history of the College has barely begun.[3] This volume contributes to that process directly, but still more so by using the history of Soc 2 to explore the sometimes dependent, sometimes dialectical, and sometimes nonexistent relation between teaching and learning in particular courses and the overarching curricular visions dominating the College in different periods.

Over the last twenty years and still today, not only in Soc 2 but in general education settings across the College, younger faculty have not always been able to tell when the recollections and opinions of senior colleagues who were themselves undergraduates in the Hutchins College—such as Don Levine, Bert Cohler, and David Orlinsky in the case of Soc 2—were reflecting the actual experience in these courses or the general dramas of that era. As this book demonstrates, the project, at this university, of constituting social science for general education purposes encompassed, rather than was encompassed by, the golden age both of Soc 2 and of the College. For example, David Orlinsky's revelations of the dependency of the Hutchins College on the earlier New College Plan and of the creation of Soc 2's ancestor course by Louis Wirth, Jerome Kerwin, and Harry Gideonse in the 1930s have helped release today's Soc 2 faculty from any lingering sense of imprisonment in the imagery of a faithful remnant. Furthermore, they have cleared the way for a closer scrutiny of the intellectual progress of the course since 1953, and of the specific social science challenges for the future (taken up in the final section of this book).

The methodology employed in this volume is useful also in addressing another, more widespread difficulty in current educational discourse: theoretical discussion concerning the knowledge most worth having without much reference to the substantive bodies of knowledge available to be had. At least some of the gap between the values of professional researchers and general educators, a key theme in this book, is attributable to the offhand way the latter sometimes speak of the achievements and problems of the scholarly disciplines. This is a book about general education in the social sciences, not about the history of social scientific theory and research as such. At the same time, to discuss Soc 2 without sustained reference to the staff's contentions about which bodies of social research are worthy of inclusion in a general education, and to their laborious selections and codifications of these materials for teaching purposes, would be to miss the historical message of the course entirely. As these essays show, contemplation of the syllabi of long-term multidisciplinary courses like Soc 2 offers a useful mode of evaluating the internal continuities and discontinuities among various lines of re-

3. Donald Levine, "Challenging Certain Myths about the 'Hutchins College'," *University of Chicago Magazine* 77 (2; Winter 1985): 36–39, 51.

search and scholarship in the social sciences, and their impact upon the reading public. For example, some readers may be surprised to learn from these essays that many of today's most pressing critical issues in social science education—a "canon" of social science classics versus contemporary research, modernity and its alternatives, "multiculturalism" and "American identity," Western and non-Western cultural materials—have been struggled over for decades by the staff of Soc 2.

Moreover, the popular notion that social scientific research hurries forward in a professional vacuum while general education comes along slowly behind, as a kind of pedagogical flower arranging, is gainsaid repeatedly by the record of Soc 2. *The Lonely Crowd,* by David Riesman and his colleagues, is only the most famous, and Peter Homans' *The Ability to Mourn: Disillusionment and the Social Origins of Psychoanalysis* is only the most recent of the important social science books inspired in significant measure, according to their authors, by Soc 2 teaching and weekly staff discussions.[4] The authors of the essays in this volume provide their own commentaries—and the evidence of their own careers—as to the falsity, under the right institutional conditions, of the dichotomy between scholarly research and undergraduate teaching. Mutual education by faculty about developments in the various disciplines has always been the real intellectual and professional payoff of general education teaching in the staff-course model. Where teaching is itself educative and intellectually challenging for faculty, it becomes of its own accord a mode of scholarship and research. This is no less true today, when American social science as a whole is being propelled by developments in the domestic and global social orders into its own sea change.

Soc 2 has remained a remarkably integrated "text": from the ancestor Wirth-Kerwin-Gideonse survey course of the 1930s; through the consolidation in the early 1940s of Social Sciences 2 as an interdisciplinary and staff-taught examination of "the possibilities and limitations of studying human nature in a scientific spirit"; through the celebrated course of the 1940s and 1950s, with its focus on the relation between an individual's personality and his culture, "a problem which naturally interests a student at this stage of his life"; to the course of the 1990s. While the Soc 2 text has been continuously annotated, amended, and reordered in response to changes in social scientific frameworks of understanding, new developments in and among the disciplines, variations in how Americans live their lives and what problems they face over time, and the shifting intellectual resources and concerns of faculty and students, a core of commitments already evident in the

4. David Riesman et al., *The Lonely Crowd: A Study of the Changing American Character* (New York: Doubleday, 1953); Peter Homans, *The Ability to Mourn: Disillusionment and the Social Origins of Psychoanalysis* (Chicago: University of Chicago Press, 1989).

1930s remain central to the course today. Constituting social science as a distinctive intellectual enterprise; doing so on a multi- or trans-disciplinary basis; focusing on the problem of modernity by tracing the joint transformation of economic, social, and political institutions from preindustrial or "folk" society, through the vicissitudes of the Industrial Revolution, to the problems of the contemporary urban industrial and global orders; exclusive use of primary sources, with a balance between classic texts of the seminal theorists and contemporary research; doing so in a mix of lecture and small discussion-section formats; and, as in other College general education courses, devoting keen attention to students' acquisition of facility in reading, argumentation, and prose communication: this has been the enduring text of Soc 2. The melody has been repeatedly altered or elaborated in counterpoint with earlier versions of the tune: structuralism could (and did) replace evolutionism; culture might (and did) become an independent rather than a dependent variable; the human self could be (and has been) reconceived as a system of meanings rather than of instinctual needs; the West could lose its hegemony over the rest of the world (and has indeed lost some); industrialism, modernity, and democratic pluralism could (and might yet) shift to postmodernity and multiculturalism. No such change, however, ever occurred once and for all, since staff consensus has always been an evanescent thing, renegotiated year by year, quarter by quarter, even week by week. Institutional and intellectual necessities require holding together a staff of diverse and frequently discordant social scientific views, and every paradigm rejected as current scholarship immediately presents itself as a candidate for reinclusion in the syllabus as part of the history of social theory. But, for all this melodic change and periodic cacophony, the harmonies of the course have endured across sixty years. Understanding how this remarkable continuity has been achieved in the face of the structural, political, and psychological difficulties of commitment to this style of instruction is a principal purpose of this volume.

The Expedition Undertaken in This Volume

In the effort to expose, explore, and comprehend this experience of dynamic continuity, utterly rare in the national record of social science general education, the authors seek to let all the variables loose on stage without privileging in advance any number of them. We see institutional, curricular, social-historical, intellectual, disciplinary, generational, political, personality, pedagogical, and moral factors in the autobiographies of the course as a complex of contexts for one another rather than as determinate causal chains "explaining" Soc 2's survival, significance, and present vitality. Moreover, while respecting its achievements, the contributors have sought to record the conditions and circumstances which over the years have led to faculty defections from the course. Some people departed because they perceived an inflexibility and rigidity of approach, often with regard to the pride of place accorded the social science classics. Others, by contrast, left because the course seemed to them too accommodating to diverse currents of disciplinary interest, sacrificing coherence for consensus and making the students conform to faculty agendas rather than the faculty to student needs. Still others found the temporal and human-relations demands of a staff-taught course with a labor-intensive teaching style simply too burdensome after a while. Always, but especially after the change from a separate College faculty to today's regime of joint appointments with the graduate departments, there were the competing demands of departmental teaching, graduate student supervision, and faculty research and publication. These struggles make the fact that Soc 2 has reproduced itself with a remarkable continuity still more worth pondering over.

This volume opens with David Orlinsky's historical review of general education at Chicago. His essay is the first sustained study since 1963 of the changing structural situation of the College in the University, the varied and competing educational visions which have dominated it, and the shifting pedagogical cultures of general, liberal, and specialized learning, whose dialectical syntheses or uneasy junctions have led to the curricular practices of any given period in College history. Against this backdrop of the College's long history and its present organizational form and curricular requirements, former Dean F. Champion Ward's "Requiem for the Hutchins College" recounts the College's most dramatic, pivotal moment. The intimacy and human feeling running through Ward's description and analysis should indicate to readers the abiding moral seriousness with which "the issue of the College" has ever been taken at Chicago.

Having set the College in the context of the University, the volume proceeds to set Soc 2 in the context of the College and of social science. In chapter 3, Donald Levine presents a portrait of what might be recognized as the synchronic logic of Soc 2, shared in common with other core courses in the social sciences and the humanities. He outlines a view of what makes a modern social science text "classic," and why such texts have perennially been featured in the course. The trope of the "campfire conversation" well represents the mode of theoretical comparison and application of grand social theory to contemporary events which has served as the paradigmatic discussion format and writing assignment for generations of Soc 2 students. In the priorities given to *explication de texte* and to small group discussion over lecture, the course design has been congruent with an understanding of liberal learning as an increasingly informed capacity for conversation, for "good talk" as James Redfield likes to put it. At the same time, the tensions between liberal education in its etymological sense, for which any quality texts might do, and general education, in which systematic exposure to a domain of learning is the goal, rise up in Levine's campfire light.

This double agenda in Soc 2 is taken up explicitly in chapter 4. David Orlinsky provides a diachronic account of a Soc 2 significantly altered over time in both its institutional framings and its social science content, yet also sufficiently stable to enable the regular reproduction of such initiatory educational experiences as Levine invokes. Orlinsky's recovery of the 1930s ancestry of Soc 2 not only deepens the history of social science general education at the University but offers an antidote to histories which leave the impression that no research scholars associated with the Chicago schools of sociology and political science took any interest in undergraduate general education.[5]

In chapter 5, Michael Schudson adds historical flesh to these X-ray images of Soc 2's skeletal system. Schudson develops the key theme of memory, organizing his essay not as professional oral history, but as "reflections guided by and responding to the recollections of many others." Through this strategy, Schudson brings to dramatic life the course's main pedagogical organs (the staff meeting, the reading list, the classroom, the lecture, the examination, the essay), lines of filiation among successive generations of students and faculty, and the extension of its replicatory energy outward from Chicago to, for example, Swarthmore, Hawaii, Harvard, and the University of California, and often back again. Schudson adds detail to the visages social science presented to the faculty in various periods, and the profiles they in turn chose to offer to the students. Personal memories of the competition among course sections and teaching styles, the hot and cold wars between the graduate departments and the College loyalists, the emotional tensions between senior and junior staff members, and the conflict between theory and empiricism which is the inevitable lot of every social scientist compose the nervous system of the Soc 2 community, and the cases of nerves among its

5. For example, Martin Bulmer in his informative book *The Chicago School of Sociology* (Chicago: University of Chicago Press, 1984) rightly emphasizes the difference between Chicago and other institutions like Harvard in privileging, in the 1920s and 1930s, research and graduate student training over undergraduate teaching. However, in failing to give any indication whatever of the significant commitment of figures like Louis Wirth and Robert Redfield to the undergraduate program (Kerwin and Gideonse are not mentioned in his book), Bulmer fails to capture the irony of College/graduate department relations which, as I noted in opening this introduction, have long typified Chicago.

individual faculty members. Schudson divines a dominant streak of ontological and intellectual pessimism in Soc 2, a complete countercurrent to the positivist optimism in which social science was born in Europe and America, a triumph, one might say in reference to Soc 2's iconic roster, of Weber and Freud over Marx and Durkheim. Certainly, Schudson shows how the very satisfactions of the course can engender simultaneous feelings of frustration and longing, a real malaise for faculty who have lived and worked within it.

Robert Ginsberg remembers, as a sixteen-year-old Soc 2 student in 1953–54, becoming aware of that moral tension. "What struck most deeply," he writes in chapter 6, "was not the theories and methodologies of the social sciences, which were clever intellectual constructions, but the human content colored with suffering and embedded with values." His memoir is one of several which came to us in an unsolicited outpouring of response by former Soc 2 students to the *University of Chicago Magazine* article describing the 1982 symposium.[6] Some, like Ginsberg and Gordon Burghardt, wrote detailed recollections as perceived through the lens of subsequent academic careers in other disciplines; dozens of others from various walks of life penned more laconic but no less heartfelt and reflective notes. Ginsberg's essay points up the gaps between the faculty's and the students' perceptions of the course. Soc 2 staffs have always torn themselves up over the intellectual coherence and conceptual architecture of the syllabus, yet I suspect, as does David Riesman in his essay, that the great majority of Soc 2 students over the years have, like Ginsberg, taken "little notice of the overall structure of the course." What he experienced and recalls "are not the great units, but the great readings, discussions and problems," not the "instructor's ideal vision" of the course but its "concrete assignments." Yet few could wish for more than the realization that decades later a student had kept the thirty-five-cent copies of books assigned and yellowed course papers with faculty comments still worthy of reflection—now ready to hand for use in an autobiographical essay. And there is always a secret symmetry. What faculty member looking at Ginsberg's page of Soc 2 student notes can fail to recognize something of herself or himself as a young undergraduate? Exactly how much does it matter that students "missed the forest for the trees," when through such concrete arboreal encounters they are enabled over the course of years to discover and articulate for themselves the existence of forests?

From an assemblage of memories of ancestral shades and far-flung

6. James Graff, "The Debate Goes On: A Tribute to Forty Years (More or Less) of Social Sciences 2 and the Value of General Education," *University of Chicago Magazine* 75 (3; Spring 1983): 6–12.

persons, Ginsberg's paper shifts the book into the fully autobiographical voices of the next section. Lewis Coser, Joseph Gusfield, and David Riesman reflect on their recruitments in the post–World War II period, when the College hired its own faculty with an extraordinary freedom to seek out learned persons and to judge their classroom and collegial potential by the values of the intellectual public as well as those of the academic guild. A European émigré, Coser was especially struck by the comparatively unbureaucratic character of the University of Chicago he entered. As an institution without any semblance of an FTE system, where each individual faculty member is a budget line and can scarcely be prevailed upon by anyone to teach what she or he is not interested in, Chicago retains much of this character today. Hiring decisions and criteria, however, are much more conventional and discipline-based now. Stories of the recruitment of that extraordinary Chicago cohort of social science scholars represented by the authors of part 3 raise severe doubt as to whether such a system, particularly in the form of hiring established "stars," is as reliable a way of fostering scholarly attainment as simply assembling a company of the brightest and often unconventional young intellectuals. This is a question confronting not only Chicago but many American universities today.

In his essay, Joseph Gusfield thoughtfully compares the two modes of intellectual production that he calls "graduate craft" and "undergraduate imagination." He reminds us that the antagonisms between the graduate departments and the undergraduate college in research universities like Chicago are above all failures to recognize the complementarities of these modes of the intellectual life. Most American institutions of higher learning today proclaim the merits of joining general and specialized learning in free-standing colleges through the mating of core requirements with work in a major. Gusfield's paper makes us painfully aware of how little real thought has been given to understanding the grounds on which such a marriage should be based.[7] He further brings to attention a little-discussed service that staff courses like Soc 2 have regularly provided in the creation of the sort of young scholar-teachers whose rarity is so often lamented today. Like others after him, Gusfield began teaching Soc 2 while an advanced graduate student. In few departments today are graduate students seriously encouraged to think of themselves as social scientists (much less

7. In the recent public debate about undergraduate education, attention has begun to turn from preoccupation with core curricula and issues of "the canon" in the early and mid-1980s to the major and its proper relation with liberal education. Two recent Association of American College Reports—*Integrity in the College Curriculum: A Report to the Academic Community* (1985) and *Liberal Learning and the Arts and Sciences Major* (1991)—when read together set out these challenges with particular clarity.

as public intellectuals) beyond their identities as psychologists, econo-
mists, or anthropologists ignorant or even patronizing of the intellectual traditions of neighboring fields. Young professionals who may
reject this socialization are nevertheless tightly focused on their sub-
fields and dissertation research projects in their final years of training.
Teaching in multi- and interdisciplinary staff courses like Soc 2 goes a
long way toward unlearning this institutional parochialism. Engaged in
teaching materials from outside their specialties, in face-to-face collaboration with colleagues from other disciplines, and in contexts where
the cruder forms of disciplinary hegemony are highly interdicted,
young academics are prepared to become more flexible teachers, more
resourceful scholars, and more catholic citizens of the universities and
colleges in which they will spend their lives.

Like Joe Gusfield, David Riesman has sought to encourage these virtues throughout his career. In chapter 9, he recounts his move from law
to social science, his recruitment to the College, his College years, and
the conditions of his leaving for Harvard, where he endeavored to
transplant Soc 2. No person has been more deeply associated with the
collective memory of the course and with its inspiration of works of
scholarship intended to have public as well as academic impact.
Riesman's essay amply portrays what is required for an absolute commitment to a student-centered, sensitive but unsentimental, understanding of the teaching vocation. He offers his own reflections on the
empirical/theoretical debate in curricula, the graduate school/college
relation, and the merits of various teaching formats and styles. Few
American educators have so long and thoughtfully struggled to address
attention to the problems of liberal democracy, a national vision of comparative instructional models, and the conditions in particular institutions for men and women to relate to one another as whole human
beings.

Riesman's joining of these commitments in an autobiographical portrait of a life in the academy, together with his judgments on Robert
Maynard Hutchins, inspired Harold Wechsler to reflections in chapter
10 on the relation between the two figures. Wechsler's essay further reminds us that scholars have not only intellectual parents, but natal families as well. Soc 2 has always sought to challenge students to see the
ways in which their own choices—of politics, of intellectual and career
interests, of social vision—are constituted by (or react to) the choices
made before their time by parents, grandparents, and the social communities from which they derive.

Bertram Cohler's research has focused on this relationship between
life history and social history, the acquisition of life stories in multi-
generational contexts, including their unconscious dimensions. His es-

say leads off a final trio of papers devoted less to exploring Soc 2 as such than to employing it as a platform from which to address perennial challenges in the design of social science general education courses everywhere. In "Why Read Freud?" Cohler transposes the question of the instructional value of fundamental texts into a consideration of a course's "subjective curriculum." He argues that readings must always be chosen not only for their intellectual merit but also for their fit with the developmental challenges, interests, and anxieties of students who take the course at a particular life stage about which psychologists and educators know a great deal. Cohler suggests that ignoring the emotional and sociomoral lives of students, conceiving of them as blank slates for the inscription of the professional interests of faculty—most of whom are at quite another life stage and possess very different cohort experiences—is at best illiberal and at worst exploitative.

Soc 2's current organization around the themes of work and authority in the first quarter, meaning and community in the second, and gendered selves and cultures in the third owes much to Cohler's chairmanly insistence on a considered response to the psychological preoccupations of first- and second-year college students. The course's present layering of social scientific concerns with the problems of modernity set in the 1930s, the relation between culture and person of the 1940s and 50s, the symbolic and hermeneutic turn of the 1960s and 70s, and the 1980s preoccupation with issues of gender and otherness is defended by the staff on grounds of mutuality between intellectual substance and student-centered pedagogy, a particular way of solving the tension between general and liberal education. At the same time, Cohler's essay contains the grounds for its own critique, alerting readers to the problems faced by faculty everywhere in knowing and judging what really is on the minds of students much younger than they and differently situated in history, and on their own minds as well.

A second perennial issue is the role that current policy questions and modes of thought relevant to professions like law and medicine should play in core course construction. In many institutions public policy debates are emphasized in initiatory courses, and whole disciplines like sociology may be presented to beginners exclusively as ways of addressing contemporaneous social problems. Historical and theoretical texts and materials are selected solely on criteria of their relevance to current public issues and professional school agendas. While several contributors point out the greater primacy afforded policy matters in past decades at Chicago, the general tendency in core courses of recent years has been to deploy texts and materials that have constituted whole intellectual domains and fundamentally distinct ways of looking at the world, and then to apply them in ancillary texts, classroom discussions, and writing assignments to current events and public quandaries. The first approach has the merit of treating social science as a living thing and a public good, while running the risks of reinforcing the presentism of students and creating the impression that social theory is but a refined form of journalism and the classroom a slightly more dialogic op-ed page. The second approach is more likely to promote the historical sense, intellectual respect, and a liberating challenge to the students' cultural common sense. At the same time, it risks leaving students with the impression that social science consists entirely of the purely intellectual productions of "dead Germans and Frenchmen" or politically alienated Americans who prefer to spend their time in other societies: that, in other words, social scientists have solely an "academic" relation to the difficulties of the present American social world.

Marc Galanter's essay takes up this problem in exploring the relation between basic social science learning and professional legal education. By this point in the volume, readers will have noticed that this is a persistent, if underexplored theme in the history of the College and of Soc 2, embodied in Hutchins' progress from law school dean to promoter of classical curricula, in Gusfield's and Riesman's abandonment of the law for sociology and social science general education, and in the off-stage hundreds of students who have passed through Soc 2 on their way to law school. Galanter is interested in the fit, or its absence, between legal conceptions of society and consequent discursive routines of legal professionals and those of social scientists, instantiated by his first experience of India where, like Gusfield, he found that little he'd been taught seemed to apply. Galanter goes on to outline the new hybrid field of social inquiry on law, which he has done much to pioneer. He reflects on the contribution that teaching in Soc 2 made to his commitment to developing a new intellectual discipline.

In chapter 13, McKim Marriott takes up the crucial issue of Western and non-Western points of view in social science coursework that would be truly liberal—that is, liberating—for students in American colleges, and truly general with respect to portraying human conceptions of reality. His essay begins by returning us to Don Levine's image of a conversation among classic European social theorists applying their respective sciences to events across time and global space. Marriott satirizes this trope of the "traveling seminar" as a species of "intellectual telecommunications" which imperially obliterates distances between cultures and histories in the very act of claiming to illuminate and compare them. Developed from his anthropological—like Gusfield's sociological and Galanter's legal—encounter with India, Marriott's critique is more radical than the usual (and today, especially vociferous) demands to include

19

materials from non-European cultures in the syllabus. Marriott notes that this has for a long time been the practice of Soc 2 and the non-Western civilization sequences at Chicago, but that it solves nothing if such "data" are subjected only to the same Eurocentric, universalistic conceptions of science (or the humanities), built upon categories of analysis whose abstraction simply disguises their dependency on a particular Western ontology. It is hardly enough, Marriott argues, to treat the practices and historical trajectories of other cultures merely as "anomalies" for Western science to grapple with and temporarily to humble itself over. Only ethnosciences, which afford other cultures the equal privilege of theorizing as well as of being theorized and compared, offer any true possibility of liberation from Euro-American parochialism and scientific imperialism. Marriott proceeds to outline what a "hydrodynamic" behavioral science for Hindu India, an "aerodynamic" social science for Japan, and a "photodynamic" social science for Morocco would contribute to the project of developing a "wide range of alternative sciences . . . which can grasp and reason with all of mankind's diverse ways of perceiving and constructing reality."

Marriott's proposal leaves certain key questions open; for example, the degree to which it really is possible in a regime of translation into and discourse in English to bring beginning students into living encounter with alternative worlds and systematic indigenous theorizing within them. His brief acknowledgments that these alternative visions may better map the experiences of "some persons in the modern West" and "help in understanding our own changing selves" leave open the possibility that the problem lies at least as much in an overmonolithic construction of Western ontology, personology, and social theory. For example, Soc 2 teachers of Freud's texts today find ready to hand in them all the materials necessary to construct an alternative reading suggesting that the problem right along was parents' wishes toward and appropriations of children (which Marriott marks as a feature of Hindu ethnopsychology), and our students, to say the least, have little difficulty in following us in this. Perhaps a more developed account of the implicit and explicit dimensions present in all cultures is necessary to articulate these alternative models. But the strong force of Marriott's critique further suggests how severely limited, even conventionally ethnocentric, currently fashionable "cultural studies" approaches to "otherness" really may be.

Finally, Ralph Nicholas reflects on the meaning of Soc 2 and several of the broader issues raised by the essays in this volume. It is fitting that he should have the "Afterword," not only as the dean presiding over the College's celebration of the centennial, but as the person most responsible for Soc 2's current intellectual program. A distinguished anthropologist of South Asia and undergraduate educator, Nicholas was lured back to Chicago, where he had trained as a graduate student, specifically to revitalize Soc 2. His success in that mission carried the course into the 1980s, and the intellectual coherence and educational capital he helped it attain were chief factors in its successful confrontation with the institutional challenges it faced in that decade.

Nicholas provides an elegantly simple summary of the efforts in this volume to comprehend the remarkable longevity, vitality, and influence which give Soc 2 a record probably unparalleled in American higher education. As a teaching and learning community, Soc 2 has always reflected the predominant interests and concerns of the wider society "in times of world war and peace, of domestic repression and liberty, of tranquility and turmoil." This has been its guiding principle and its practical engine of change. At the same time, as its principle of continuity, the Soc 2 community has shared an intellectual legacy "based on the conception that a whole human being—a person with a sense of self—is both product and participant in a distinctive social and cultural system, a system of interaction and meaning which give form and significance to human life." Through six decades, Soc 2 faculty have collectively combined their fast commitment to the proposition that every student needs to comprehend this general idea with a studied selection—from the myriad forms of human society and culture—of those whose comprehension may hold the greatest significance for contemporary public life.

As these essays show, the process has never been easy. Each new generation of Soc 2 faculty has had to contend with its own complex of institutional challenges from within the University, intellectual politics within the social sciences, and the shifting political conditions and concerns of American public life. Today the Soc 2 staff—dominated as it is by anthropologists, cross-cultural psychologists, historians, and scholars of comparative religion—endures the delicious though frustrating irony of being labeled relativist radicals by nativist defenders of the "great Western tradition" and ethnocentric conservatives by proponents of "postmodern multiculturalism"—while being regularly summoned to assist faculty at other institutions newly interested in welding together a serious encounter with cultural diversity and the abiding aims of liberal education. As we approach the twenty-first century, and the University and the College enter their second century, periods which promise great change both in the social sciences and in America's position in the world, new intellectual and pedagogical ironies will arise for the Soc 2 staff, joining the twin ironies which, as noted at the outset, continuously color the University of Chicago and the American academy in general. Perhaps the ironic condition is both a sign and the source of Soc 2's endurance and significance. In any case, it is hoped that the memories and memorials presented in this volume will help postpone indefinitely the writing of *in memoriam* to the legacy of Soc 2 and to those general education projects elsewhere that could profit from its experience.

Part I

The College in the University

1

Not Very Simple, but Overflowing: A Historical Perspective on General Education at the University of Chicago

David E. Orlinsky

The Historical Landscape

General education has been a distinctive feature of the College of the University of Chicago through most of its hundred years. At times general education has been the whole of the undergraduate curriculum, and at other times its role has been more circumscribed. At times the general education curriculum was the coherent achievement of a true community of scholar-teachers who made it a major focus of their sustained collective effort, and at other times it has been little more than a congeries of diverse courses loosely rationalized in terms of standard college catalog rhetoric. Major changes over the years have largely reflected changing conceptions of general education and the changing value placed on it by the University. Yet recognizable themes and patterns have also endured or recurred. The founding president of the University, William Rainey Harper, might be pleased to find that the College, half given over to general education originally, has a similar formal requirement in its centennial year (though certain contents of the program might amaze him). In this chapter, I give a condensed account of institutional and curricular arrangements of the past century, as a frame in which the reminiscences and reflections that follow about one important and well-loved general education course can be appreciated and understood.[1]

Two important histories of general education in the College have previously appeared. In 1950, Reuben Frodin published an informative essay, "Very Simple, but Thoroughgoing," as a chapter in *The Idea and Practice of General Education*. (My homage to Frodin and my difference in perspective are indicated by this essay's title.) In 1962–63, Russell Thomas, with the collaboration of Richard Storr and Knox C. Hill, updated Frodin's account with an essay on "The Evolution of the

---

1. For the sources I have made use of in this essay, please see the Acknowledgments at the end (p. 74).

College and Its Curriculum" published in the short-lived *College Curriculum Bulletin*.[2] Reflections on selected aspects of Chicago's general education history, particularly during the Hutchins presidency, have also appeared in dozens of other publications (cited inter alia in the present essay and elsewhere in this volume). There are several reasons for a new historical effort now.

Thirty years have passed since the last sustained history was written, and the College has undergone substantial change in that time. But there is reason to do more than simply add a description of recent decades to Frodin's and Thomas's accounts. The perspectives from which those authors wrote were conditioned by their perceptions of contemporary events and their expectations of circumstances likely to ensue—events and expectations that look quite different now in light of what actually occurred. The optimistic tone of Frodin's chapter and the whole of *The Idea and Practice of General Education* was expressed by F. Champion Ward in his introduction to the volume: "At the University of Chicago, the long struggle of the College to control, define, and construct an intelligible and effective curriculum has passed through its uphill stage. A period of fruition has been entered upon, and a national concern has been added to the local preoccupations of the recent past." Barely three years later, Ward and his colleagues found themselves "struggling to salvage some part of the University's curriculum of general studies and some degree of authority over what remained." Imagining, in 1950, that "in the nation, general education is at last in vogue . . . [bidding] fair to become the operative educational theory for the remainder of this century" had proved an "act of hubris . . . soon avenged."[3] (In the next chapter of this volume, Ward returns to the story with the added perspective of another twenty-five years.)

By contrast with Frodin's account, Thomas's history reflects and reports the confusion and demoralization in the College during the years 1954–63 and "the loss of anything approximating a uniform conception of general education. . . . Administration of the programs was difficult and their rationale was hard to explain to students."[4] Thomas's

2. Reuben Frodin, "Very Simple, but Thoroughgoing," in *The Idea and Practice of General Education*, ed. F. C. Ward (Chicago: University of Chicago Press, 1950), 25–102. Russell Thomas, "The Evolution of the College and Its Curriculum," in *College Curriculum Bulletin*, ed. J. Mayfield (University of Chicago, 1962–63). Thomas's views were later expanded in his *The Search for a Common Learning: General Education 1800–1960* (New York: McGraw-Hill, 1962), though this paper was not included in the volume.

3. F. C. Ward, "Principles and Particulars in Liberal Education," in *Humanistic Education and Western Civilization: Essays for Robert M. Hutchins*, ed. Arthur Cohen (New York: Holt, Rinehart, and Winston, 1964), 120–37.

4. Thomas, "The Evolution," 6.

work appeared in the first public communication of a College Curriculum Coordinating Group (whose membership included current University president Hanna H. Gray), called into being "to help this faculty discover what [it wants] in a four-year undergraduate curriculum." Reflected in this charge and this text is a dolorous sense of beginning all over again that, in turn, looks quite different in light of the new challenges and reforms of the late 1960s and 1970s, and the general education revitalization of the 1980s, when the College leadership included persons who, as students and young instructors, had lived through the events and atmospheres that colored the histories of Frodin and Thomas.

But even for such individuals, personal memory and reflection are today not enough. Recollection unassisted by historical research is partial and idiosyncratically organized, uncorrected by new facts to be discovered and current perspectives through which to render such facts intelligible. There must be an analytic understanding of the complex circumstances in which the College has existed and continues to exist, the problems to which it has attempted to respond, and the deeper reasons for what men and women have done and undone here.

History inevitably is *interpreted* history. The concepts of institutional structure, academic ethos, and progress-through-conflict, which I have found useful in understanding the College, may seem all too likely choices for a social scientist, but this perspective on the College as an institution with a complex changing structure and an evolving plural culture seemed rather to impose itself on me as I struggled to comprehend the not very simple, but overflowing, variety of events that comprise the College's history. With the concepts of institutional structure and academic ethos, I shall try to show what led to the programs that emerged in each period and demonstrate how these in turn affected the organization and vision of the College within the University.

The Interpretive Perspective

Institutional Structure

The institutional structure of the College as a unit of the University has both internal and external aspects. Internally, of course, the College requires a specific organization of faculty, administration, student body, and supportive staff, to carry on the varied functions of College life. This must be understood in relation to the external situation of the College, which is jointly defined by three intersecting structures. One of these defines the place and purpose of the College within the University as a whole. A second defines the place and purpose of undergraduate work in the student's total educational career. The third defines the place of college teaching among faculty duties.

The place and purpose of the College within the University have been defined in three significantly different ways over the past century by presidents Harper, Hutchins, and Levi. Harper's original vision was that colleges should have a gate-keeping function, selecting and preparing students to become active members of the University community. Hutchins' view of the College's function was that it should be a separate unit providing the general education requisite for future citizens. Levi's idea was to have the College become a microcosm of the University at large, an intimate space where faculty representing specialized fields could communicate with undergraduates and each other, restoring a measure of wholeness to the body of knowledge.

The mission of Harper's University was the advancement of scholarly and scientific research, together with the graduate education of young scholars and scientists to pursue such research. The mission of undergraduate education within that context was to provide an entry to the University for those students who found their calling in intellectual work. Harper's initial plan for undergraduate studies—published in 1891, eighteen months before the first classes met in Cobb Hall—was a radical departure from the traditional form of higher education in America.[5] It called not for a single College but for multiple Colleges, separately organized and administered, conceptually justified and complexly defined by level of studies and area of specialization.

There were to be three Junior ("Academic") Colleges—of Arts, Literature, and Science—offering "Associate" certificates on the student's

5. University of Chicago, *Official Bulletin*, no. 2 (Spring 1891). In *The Search for a Common Learning,* Thomas described the curricular schemes then prevalent in American higher education. The most familiar scheme in nineteenth-century colleges was the classical liberal arts curriculum, centered on the study of Latin and Greek for the disciplines of the trivium, mathematics for the disciplines of the quadrivium, and Christian theology and ethics. This scheme was increasingly displaced after 1870 by the elective curriculum advocated by President Eliot of Harvard, as a way of accommodating the newer fields of knowledge and thereby "liberalizing" the traditionally prescribed classical liberal arts curriculum. After its popularization, abuses of the elective system were more and more frequently criticized, and Harvard replaced it with the "concentration-and-distribution" system after A. Lawrence Lowell, its leading proponent, was inaugurated as president in 1909. Later schemes exemplifying "liberal education" and relevant to the College include the common core curriculum, in one version that presents "orientation" or "survey" courses to sample the major fields of human knowledge and in another version that seeks a similar goal through the presentation of integrated, comprehensively designed "general" courses; the Great Books–liberal arts curriculum, such as Hutchins himself advocated at Chicago and saw developed instead at St. John's; and what Thomas terms the dual course of study, in which about half the student's work is common core and the other half a specialized concentration.

completion of two years of undergraduate study. Harper saw the mission of the Junior Colleges to be completion of the general education that students should normally have received in college preparatory academies and secondary schools. It was also to be an opportunity for students to gain sufficient self-knowledge to discover whether they personally desired and were fitted for specialized training of the sort that the University intended to provide.[6]

Three corresponding Senior ("University") Colleges were to offer bachelor's degrees in arts (A.B.), philosophy (Ph.B.), and science (S.B.) upon successful completion of two further years of departmental study. The Senior Colleges were seen as introducing mature students directly into the work of the University's graduate departments and professional schools.[7] So strong was Harper's imprint that four decades passed (1892–1930) before the "Colleges" officially became "the College" under a single dean.

The second definition of the place and purpose of the College was established in 1930 by President Hutchins' administrative reorganization of the departments into the four graduate divisions (Humanities, Social, Biological, and Physical Sciences), whose mission was the pursuit of specialized research and training, and an undergraduate division ("the College"), charged simply but very specifically to "do the work of the University in general higher education." The College at that time was defined as comprising the first two years of postsecondary education, and for some time yet the baccalaureate was not conferred by the University until a student had completed two further years of divisional work.

In this incarnation, the College occupied the same space that had been filled previously by the Junior Colleges. However, the function of

6. "The proposition for a three-year course is based on the supposition that the entire work of the college course is really university work. This is a mistaken supposition. The work of the freshman and sophomore year is ordinarily of the same scope and character as that of the preceding years in the academy or high school. . . . The real university work [is] done in the junior and senior year of the college course. . . . The average man is not prepared to take up university work until he has reached the end of the sophomore year. No greater mistake is being made in the field of higher education than the confusion which is coming to exist between college and university methods of work." William Rainey Harper, *The Trend in Higher Education* (Chicago: University of Chicago Press, 1905), 339.

7. "The university is the place for men who have come to know themselves, and who have learned what they can do and what they cannot do, to study in the line of their chosen calling. For, strictly speaking, university life begins only when a man has discovered the subject or subjects which are to be connected with his life-work. No man has any business to enter the university until his life-work has been determined. And to this end some remedy must be found for the confusion as to the respective functions of college and university which now exists almost universally in our country." Ibid., 324–25.

the College no longer was mainly one of recruiting and preparing students for university work. It was rather to provide all students, those who would go on to be specialists and those who would not, with "a common stock of fundamental ideas" that would permit communication among specialists and create a basis for effective participation in a democratic society.

"Under an intelligible program of general education," Hutchins wrote in *The Higher Learning in America,* "the student would come to the end of the sophomore year with a solid knowledge of the intellectual disciplines. He would be able to distinguish and think about subject matters. He would be able to use language and reason. He would have some understanding of man and of what connects man with man. He would have acquired some degree of wisdom." Hutchins' aim was to "get order in the higher learning by removing from it the elements that disorder it today, and these are vocationalism and unqualified empiricism."[8] This aim was achieved, substantially if imperfectly, in two stages: the first, largely by inheritance, in the College of 1931–42; the second, in the College of 1942–53.

The third major definition of the College's structural place and educational purpose was initiated in 1965 by Edward Levi, then University provost. The College had not been exclusively concerned with doing "the work of the University in general higher education" for a decade, although its place as a separate undergraduate division had not been decisively reformulated. Levi proposed that the College be reorganized into a set of collegiate divisions, corresponding in the main to the graduate divisions and sharing their faculties, linked together through an interdivisional College Council presided over by the dean of the College and administered in concert with the collegiate division masters. The College was thus transformed organizationally from a distinct division into a microcosm of the University.

Levi desired to regain the "sense of community and identification" that had been "one of the real glories of what is now called the Hutchins College." But he thought this goal could be realized more effectively if the College could be made, not an insulated common curricular experience for all, but the meeting ground and theater of common interest for the faculties of the graduate divisions. He hoped that the graduate divisions would provide the College with the stimulation and legitimation of a great research institution, and that the College in turn would exert a unifying and "generalizing influence within the institution, a way of communicating among the disciplines."

This pattern resembles Harper's original design, but those separate

8. Robert Maynard Hutchins, *The Higher Learning in America* (New Haven: Yale University Press, 1936), 91, 112–14, 117.

"area colleges" of arts, literature, and science did not become actual academic communities. Levi really expected that his new organization would "not work if these colleges [collegiate divisions] do not in fact become communities with something of an existence of their own . . . where communication is established between faculty and students, where ceremonies and events reaffirm the ideals of the community, and where the concern of the faculty . . . for the education of their students will give rise to those informal pressures that guide and induce faculty participation."[9] This third definition of the place and purpose of the College within the University, imperfectly achieved but ever improved, is still the reigning one.

Beyond the mission assigned to the College within the University, two other variables have critically shaped the changing institutional structure of the College. One is the sequential place occupied by the "college years" in a typical student's career. The traditional American expectation has been that twelve years of primary and secondary education (elementary, junior, and senior high school) should be followed by four undergraduate years (grades 13–16), culminating for most individuals with the award of a bachelor's degree. Yet this was not always the pattern followed at Chicago, where there were no fewer than six periods in which different conceptions of the "college years" prevailed.

Under Harper's initial plan, the Junior Colleges (grades 13–14) had a required curriculum and capped the student's secondary education at a level equivalent to the German *Gymnasium* or French *lycée*. In the Senior Colleges (grades 15–16), students with the aptitude and calling were introduced directly to elective university-level work, with the expectation that they would continue beyond the baccalaureate. This European model in the long run proved ill-adapted to the needs of American students, and the pattern imposed in 1892 eroded over subsequent decades.

By 1920 the Colleges functioned as a conventional four-year program (grades 13–16) in all but name, as recognized by the appointment of a single dean. They remained this way until Hutchins' administrative reform of 1930, when "the New College Program" was designed and the undergraduate division was converted to an innovative two-year College (grades 13–14) providing a distinctive general education. Dating this period would be relatively easy (1931–42), except that in 1937 a four-year general education program (grades 11–14) was introduced as a concurrent experiment with students entering the College directly from the University High School. In 1942 the experimental four-year general education program culminating in award of

9. Edward Levi, "General, Liberal, and Specialized Education," in his *Point of View* (Chicago: University of Chicago Press, 1963), 83, 86, 95, 98.

the bachelor's degree was made the norm by Hutchins, to the scandal of the educational establishment and not a few Chicago faculty and alumni. Since early admission was offered after the sophomore year of high school, the college years were in effect redefined for all as grades 11–14. This "glorious revolution" was rescinded in 1953, two years after Hutchins left the University. Since then the college years at Chicago have coincided with the general American norm (grades 13–16).

This variation in the grade levels of college students has inevitably induced a complementary variation in the role accorded to college teaching by the University's faculty. Whenever grades 13–14 have been integrated with secondary or purely general education, there has been a tendency for college teaching assignments to be given to a separate and dependent faculty, often consisting of advanced graduate students or postdoctoral fellows. On the other hand, when grades 13–14 have been aggregated to "senior college" years and specialized education, departmental faculties have been more directly involved. Thus, during the initial period, those who taught in the Junior Colleges were viewed as advanced secondary teachers, like the masters of the sixth form in English public schools. They were expected to devote all their time to teaching and supervising their students' work. Instruction in Senior College courses was often given by departmental faculty, whose teaching was viewed as incidental to their primary responsibilities as scholars and scientists, that is, the training of students to become active members of the research professions.

The correlation between college grade levels and college teaching, however, has been only approximate. There have been occasions, as in the innovative survey courses of the 1920s, and the New College Plan of the 1930s, when leading professors in the University have devoted time to lecturing undergraduates. This is illustrated, for example, by the founding and teaching of Soc 2's ancestral course by the distinguished research scholars Louis Wirth, Jerome Kerwin, and Harry Gideonse. A different exception to the pattern occurred during the period 1942–53 and after, for about another decade, when the College faculty was separate from the departmental faculties but also independent of them, appointed and promoted without reference to departmental work.

The structural conflicts and tensions in a university with an autonomous college faculty is an important theme in several of the essays of this book. However, the main structural tension for faculty in the period of the "Levi College" (from 1965 to the present) has come from the favored model of joint appointments between the College and the graduate divisions and departments, which created cross-cutting pressures on most faculty members to teach simultaneously at several levels: both general and specialized undergraduate courses, as well as basic graduate courses and advanced doctoral supervision. To paraphrase Marx, the same professors were now expected to be college teachers in the morning, graduate faculty in the afternoon, and productive researchers at night.

This is the situation in the University today. Its strength is a closer attachment of the work of the College to that of the University through the medium of a more unified faculty. Its challenge has lain in an increasing dependence on, in Edward Levi's words, "those informal pressures that guide and induce faculty participation," particularly with respect to the labor-intensive, nondepartmental general education courses.

Academic Cultures

The culture of an institution consists of the general symbolic *themes,* or motifs, which delineate its identity, inform its collective sense of purpose, and animate its rhetoric, together with the symbolic *schemes,* or programs, which particularize those general themes into plans or blueprints for institutional organization. One symbolic theme can be given expression in varied schemes, and one symbolic scheme can represent a combination of themes. Themes are frequently articulated in bipolar contrasting pairs. Schemes can be relatively "pure" or simple types, or they may be mixed or compound types. As regards the institutional culture of the College and the University at large, the dominant themes define the spirit, or ethos, of the place; symbolic schemes are reflected in the design of its curriculum.

The University was founded to be primarily if not exclusively a center of advanced scholarly and scientific research.[10] The spirit animating this development was frankly described in 1927 by a committee of the University faculty as "the University Spirit," by which they understood "the combination of the desire and ability to participate in the advancement of knowledge or in the application, as it advances, to the development of human welfare." This committee found the Colleges "not adequately pervaded by this Spirit," due in part to "the notorious fact that curriculum and other intellectual interests rate low in the students' opinion as compared with social, athletic, and 'activity' inter-

10. For historical and comparative background, see Thomas, *Search for a Common Learning;* Charles Wegener, *Liberal Education and the Modern University* (Chicago: University of Chicago Press, 1978); Laurence Veysey, "Stability and Experiment in the American Undergraduate Curriculum," in *Content and Context,* ed. Carl Kaysen (New York: McGraw-Hill, 1973), 1–64; Bruce Kimball, *Orators and Philosophers* (New York: Teachers College Columbia University, 1986).

ests." The symbolic theme that encompassed the latter activities and contrasted sharply with the University Spirit might be called the student-life ethos or, as it was formerly known, the "Varsity Spirit."

Historically at Chicago, the University Spirit has been associated most directly with President Harper and the people he brought with him to found the University. As President Hutchins proclaimed in his inaugural address, their "emphasis on productive scholarship . . . has characterized the University from the beginning and must characterize it to the end." Every president has sounded this same note on ceremonial occasions, indeed, whenever need has been felt to reassert the distinctive collective identity of the institution. Its opposite, the student-life or Varsity Spirit, is little more than the familiar collegiate youth culture of the late-nineteenth- and twentieth-century academic community in America. In the early years of the University (and in more recent times as well), "students . . . chronically complained that the University lacked many of the amenities of college life and that the faculty stressed intellectual achievement at the expense of all other kinds of accomplishment."[11] While the faculty committee of 1927 may have decried its presence, those who have had responsibility for recruiting prospective students, maintaining enrollments, and improving the quality of student life have perennially had to struggle with the widespread perception of its absence at Chicago.

Another pair of contrasting themes that have figured prominently in the ethos of the University of Chicago may be called, respectively, the "Liberal Arts Spirit" and the "Progressive-Pragmatic Spirit." The Liberal Arts Spirit envisages the University as a community of scholars committed to maintaining, enlarging, and transmitting the great tradition of intellectual and artistic achievement. It is militantly, even moralistically, intellectualist and often antipractical in its thrust. The Progressive-Pragmatic Spirit, on the other hand, emphasizes the vital role of universities as integral parts of democratic industrial society, and stresses their function in preparing students to adapt successfully as citizens and workers living in such a society. Concern is directed to professional and vocational training, broadly or narrowly conceived, and to maintaining "relevance" vis-à-vis troublesome social and political issues in the community.

The Liberal Arts Spirit is particularly associated at Chicago with President Hutchins and the people he brought with him, although it has a venerable history in European and in American education. The modern version of the Liberal Arts Spirit (as enunciated by Hutchins,

11. Harold Wechsler, *The Qualified Student: A History of Selective College Admissions in America* (New York: Wiley, 1977), 221.

Adler, McKeon, Buchanan, and Barr) was in some respects congruent with the University Spirit that Hutchins reaffirmed in his inaugural address, yet in other respects it clashed violently with it. Both the University Spirit and the Liberal Arts Spirit celebrate the life of the mind, but the former does so by emphasizing science, specialized scholarly research, and the continual advancement of knowledge, whereas the latter does so by emphasizing the humanities, the interrelatedness and integration of diverse fields of study, and the continuing relevance of traditional learning embodied in the classics of Western civilization to present-day life. To those imbued primarily with the University Spirit, exponents of the Liberal Arts Spirit often seemed reactionary dilettantes. On the other hand, to those imbued primarily with the Liberal Arts Spirit, adherents of the University Spirit have appeared to be narrowly departmental, blindly empirical, and virtually anti-intellectual in outlook. War between these camps broke out shortly after Hutchins' friends arrived, and it raged throughout the 1930s and intermittently thereafter, with great consequence for the history of the College.

The Progressive-Pragmatic Spirit at the University of Chicago is most directly associated with the presence of John Dewey and his followers, whose excesses were a favorite target of Hutchins' rhetoric and who fired not a few barbs back at Hutchins and his "medieval" ideas. During his term as head of the departments of Philosophy and of Education and after he left the University, Dewey was a major intellectual influence at Chicago. His associates, G. H. Mead, J. R. Angell and J. H. Tufts, were faculty eminences at Chicago, and their ideas likewise pervaded many departments. Dewey's philosophy merged with the University Spirit and formed what William James christened "the Chicago School of Thought." The Progressive-Pragmatic Spirit was well characterized by Amy Kass as "the conviction that traditional learning was inadequate to a proper understanding of society and incapable of assimilating and promoting social and cultural progress. Time-honored theories were eagerly attacked. Belief in the existence of immutable truths was ridiculed. Philosophers, physicists, chemists, and mathematicians, as well as social scientists and even humanists, vied with one another to break through barriers, to efface outlines, and to supersede current professional training. The devotion to 'progress,' scientific and social, required special training in facts, methods, and techniques."[12]

The interpretation of the College's history that is advanced here

12. Amy Apfel Kass, "The Liberal Arts Movement: From Ideas to Practice," *The College* 25 (October 1973): 1–26.

turns in large part on the visible conflicts and the subtler interpenetrations of these motifs: the University Spirit versus the Varsity Spirit, the Liberal Arts Spirit versus the Progressive-Pragmatic Spirit. To understand general education as it evolved at Chicago, it is vital to recognize its roots in the pre–Liberal Arts era, when the University Spirit and (especially) when the Progressive-Pragmatic Spirit contributed to the formation of the general education ideal. Many of the curricular innovations commonly associated with the "Hutchins College" of 1942–53 had in fact persisted or been consciously adapted from earlier practices in the College.

The Process of Curricular Change

Each of the discernible stages in the history of the College seems to represent the formation of a synthesis (or at least an attempted resolution) of competing claims on and for undergraduate education. These claims emanate from diverse sources: the ideal interests of persons imbued with one or another educational ethic or academic culture and the material interests of persons with a stake in certain structural and organizational arrangements. These, in turn, are mediated by the loyalties of persons to a traditional or familiar curricular design.

Out of contention and contrariety, which may predominate for a time, something intelligible eventually seems to emerge. If the synthesis provides a real resolution, so that the interests of all influential parties are reasonably satisfied, a period of stability will ensue— broken, eventually, either by some shift in external circumstances or by some change in the active parties or their perceived interests. Where, on the other hand, the attempted resolution is an incomplete synthesis, resulting from the "political" exclusion or suppression of some legitimate interests, disequilibrium will persist or return soon enough, often through the unexpected triggering of an opposite extreme. This quasidialectical view of the College's history is borne out, I think, by a more detailed account of the complex interplay of structural conditions and symbolic commitments in the three main periods and schemes of general education at Chicago.

Mr. Harper's "Junior Colleges": General Education *Faute de Mieux*

President Harper and his associates came to Chicago not to found a college but to embody the University Spirit in a new institution. The prospect of combining the "desire and ability to participate in the advancement of knowledge" in a center of graduate research and study made it worth their while to leave eminent and comfortable positions elsewhere. Given Harper's view of the undergraduate student's career, work in the University Spirit could not be expected on average until the junior year (grade 15), when the student was a young adult of about twenty who already had chosen his lifework. The structural and organizational division of undergraduate work between the University or Senior Colleges and the Academic or Junior Colleges, with separate deans, administrations, and curricular principles, embodied Harper's convictions. Indeed, Harper would have preferred to remove the Junior Colleges physically from the Quadrangles, and to have the work of the freshman and sophomore years added to that of the University's suburban high school affiliate, the Morgan Park Academy.

The work of the Junior College was conceived from the beginning to be general education but was thought to be closer in spirit and in method to secondary education than to true university work. Requirements for admission to the Senior Colleges were formulated by aggregating the student's academy or high school credits with his Junior College credits, stating minimum levels in each required subject in terms of the combination. What students had not studied in high school or academy, they would have to take in the Junior Colleges. Thus, for example, a student who had taken four years of Latin in secondary school was held for only one more year of Latin in college, while a student with only three years of high school credit in Latin was required to take two years of the subject in Junior College. The Junior Colleges thus established a pattern for Chicago-style general education in later periods: a prescribed set of required subjects for all students, and the principle of adjusting these requirements at the college level to take due account of the strengths and weaknesses of the individual's secondary preparation. However, the work of the Junior Colleges was *not* animated by the University Spirit. The president and no doubt most of the faculty viewed the Junior Colleges as an alien and uncongenial presence in their University, undertaken only because there were not sufficient academies and junior colleges nearby to do this work for them.

The original undergraduate program, then, was a "synthesis by segregation" between the divergent needs and claims of secondary (general) and university (specialized) education. The ethos ideally animating work in the upper division was already that of the University Spirit. In the lower division, however, there was no comparable *positive* ideal, only a recognition of the necessity that the University needed to recruit and prepare its own students for more advanced studies. The original undergraduate program also attempted a synthesis between the competing claims of classical humanistic and scientific education, a paramount struggle in the American college curriculum through much of the nineteenth century. The solution, however, was a purely organizational and (therefore less successful) one: the establishment of three "area colleges" with separate curricula in arts, literature (later for a period subdivided into literature and philosophy), and science, leading to separate baccalaureate degrees.

The limits of this resolution by separation quickly became visible in the extensive requirements of the Junior Colleges and the absence of faculty consensus about them. As the logical foundation for all subsequent educational activities, "the question of prescriptions in the Junior Colleges possessed particular urgency," as Richard Storr notes. Yet "in practice, the ideal of inquiry did not plainly indicate what broad learning the University should require as a foundation for investigation. . . . From the time when the University opened, professors had disagreed vehemently over the ingredients of the culture upon which true university study should rest. The argument raged right up to the time of the decennial celebration and had not been settled then."[13]

The battle focused on the amount of Latin to be required of students in the S.B. and Ph.B. programs, with W. G. Hale, head of the Latin Department, defending the centrality of his subject as the main vehicle of liberal general culture, and T. C. Chamberlin, head of the Geology Department, leading the fight to gain more time for scientific studies in the S.B. program. (Students in the College of Science were required to show a total of three years of Latin as general preparation.) President Harper sought to mediate the unsettled difference with a new synthesis that interestingly foreshadowed later developments in liberal education. In his *President's Report, 1898–99* and in his later essay "Latin versus Science," he urged

> what may perhaps be called an intermediate policy [which] would accept as its fundamental principle the contention of the conservative wing that an essential element in the education of every man, and especially in that of the scientist, is a study of the great heritage we have received from the past. The policy would be in agreement, however, with the contention of the radical party, that this end is not conserved simply by a study of the Latin language. It would propose that in the case of students who are familiar with French and German, and after a reasonable amount of language work exhibit a real inability to do such work with ease and profit, there be required, instead of the specified number of courses in Latin, a specified number of courses in the study of the history, the institutions, and perhaps the liter-

13. Richard Storr, *Harper's University* (Chicago: University of Chicago Press, 1966), 311.

ature of the past. . . . In accordance with the proposition here suggested, every student would be required to gain a certain familiarity with the life and thought of the various nations which have contributed most to our modern civilization.[14]

Changes in the curriculum of the College occurred in 1905 and again in 1912, tending to cause undergraduate instruction to approximate that of a conventional four-year college utilizing the popular concentration-and-distribution scheme of studies. In 1905, the rigidly prescribed courses of the Junior College curriculum were replaced with more flexible "group" requirements, and "concentration" was sought in the Senior Colleges in a further requirement that at least six quarter courses be selected from one department. Latin disappeared as a requirement for any degree except the A.B., and the general foreign-language requirements for the Ph.B. and S.B. were also somewhat reduced. The 1912 curriculum, which with only minor modifications prevailed until 1931, sought

> to secure by the end of the second year a reasonable proficiency in both the written and spoken use of the mother-tongue, a reading knowledge of French or German, and some familiarity with at least four of the following great divisions of knowledge, i.e., (1) Philosophy, History, and Social Science, (2) Modern language other than English, (3) Mathematics, (4) Natural Science. At least four [quarter] courses must have been pursued in each of these four divisions prior to the third year of the college residence. It is also provided that the student carry through his entire Freshman year at least one subject which he has pursued extensively in the high school. . . . The latter part of the course is designed to permit a measurable amount of free election, while it none the less requires concentration in at least two lines of work, one to the extent of nine major courses, and the other to the extent of six such courses. . . . These sequences. . . . are arranged, as far as possible, to represent not only coherent, but definitely progressive, development in a given field of knowledge.[15]

These struggles over the definition of general and liberal learning and the relationship of both to later specialized work in the University Spirit necessitated structural and organizational changes as well. The separate administrations of the Junior and Senior Colleges had largely been reduced to mere formalities. In 1920, direction of undergraduate studies was consolidated under a single executive officer, the dean of

14. Harper, *The Trend in Higher Education*, 289–90.
15. University of Chicago, *The President's Report, 1910–11*, 34.

the Colleges of Arts, Literature, and Science, assisted by subordinate officials who supervised the work of students in the several colleges. The first dean of the consolidated Colleges was David Allan Robertson (A.B., 1902), the first Chicago graduate to serve in this office.

The "New College Plan" and the "Hutchins College": Two Positive Conceptions of General Education

By 1920 the College had drifted into a state that alarmed many members of the University. Enrollments had gradually increased for twenty-five years, and after the armistice jumped to nearly two thousand in the Junior Colleges alone.[16] Furthermore, as Frodin later noted, "The departments had turned the Junior College into a training ground for their graduate students; [by 1923] approximately a hundred graduate students were teaching elementary courses, and the annual turnover in the staff of these courses was 40 percent." Frodin wryly added that while President Judson complained at the time of the "tendency . . . to siphon off funds from more advanced work" due to increased College enrollments, thereby undermining support of the University Spirit, he did so without "mentioning the large tuition revenue that came from these students."[17]

The University Spirit had been further undermined by an enhancement of the Varsity Spirit on campus, notably through the rise of fraternities and intercollegiate football. Ernest Hatch Wilkins, dean of the College during the years 1923–25, described this collegiate atmosphere as one of "overexcitement about football which prevails through the autumn, increasing as the season advances, not limited to the days of the games, infecting more and more of student time and thought, and culminating in the weeks of the big games at the end of the season. This overexcitement manifests itself directly in the neglect of college work." Besides students' failure to attend class, do assigned readings, and submit papers on time, Wilkins attacked the inversion of normal educational values brought on by the Varsity Spirit. Students developed a scorn for peers who did well in their academic labors, and settled themselves for passing grades regardless of their potential abilities.[18]

Under cover of attacks on the Varsity Spirit and in the felt absence of any positive intellectual ethos at all, critics of the Progressive-Pragmatic Spirit who associated it with a narrow utilitarianism themselves became

16. Wechsler, *The Qualified Student*, 218.
17. Frodin, "Very Simple," 41, 37.
18. Ernest H. Wilkins, *The Changing College* (Chicago: University of Chicago Press, 1927), 119–21.

more vocal.[19] The merely political solutions of the previous years, with their incomplete syntheses among contending themes in Chicago's academic culture, had resulted in a disequilibrium so extreme that Chauncey Boucher characterized it in the following way:

> During a considerable period, while the University of Chicago was winning eminence in graduate education and research, much of the undergraduate work was grossly neglected; even worse, the College came to be regarded by some members of the family as an unwanted, ill-begotten brat that should be disinherited. Nearly all agreed that we had reached a situation that necessitated a decision either to abandon the College or to develop it to a position of strength in its field comparable to that of our graduate schools in their fields.[20]

Upon taking office in 1923, President Burton chose the latter course. He appointed Wilkins—a professor of Romance Languages trained at Amherst and at Harvard—as dean of the Colleges, and impaneled a Commission on the Future of the Colleges, whose other moving figure was Henry C. Morrison, professor of education and a specialist in the curriculum of secondary schools. The commission's report, issued in April 1924, was never directly implemented by the faculty, but it had a very important influence on subsequent developments, including Burton's 1925 pamphlet on *The University of Chicago in 1940*, Hutchins' inaugural address of February 1930, and his plan for the reorganization of the University proposed in October of that year.[21]

The Commission Report defined the positive, intellectually serious purpose of undergraduate instruction as the provision of higher general education. The report distinguished three broad phases in an individual's education: (1) a primary stage of preparatory studies "devoted to the acquisition of the primary adaptations which make systematic study possible;" (2) a secondary stage of "general education, which insures the proper adjustment of the individual to the environment in which he is to live;" (3) a tertiary stage of university training "devoted to

19. In this context, Frodin cited Dean Robertson's rationale for undergraduate education from *The President's Report, 1920–21* (p. 23): "The general function of the Colleges is to provide training for efficiency in labor for one's self and for society, and for the enjoyment of leisure by one's self and in society. Efficiency in labor . . . is ordinarily developed for the purpose of securing the largest and easiest pecuniary reward for efforts. . . . Even courses which are not contributions to a technical skill in making a living may appeal to selfish interest in success."

20. C. S. Boucher and A. J. Brumbaugh, *The Chicago College Plan*, 2d. ed. (Chicago: University of Chicago Press, 1935), 1.

21. Frodin, "Very Simple, 42.

the acquisition of power in some special field of intellectual activity." The first stage, according to the report, is normally accomplished in grades 1 to 6, while the second stage should extend from grades 7 through 14. Instead of the conventional division into junior high school, high school and junior college, the commission proposed that these eight years be divided equally between high school (grades 7–10) and college (conceived as grades 11–14), in the so-called "6-4-4 plan." Higher general education (grades 11–14) was to be pursued in what the commission proposed to call "the College," which would be established in its own quadrangle on the south side of the Midway.

The general education which the commission had in mind was designed, in Wilkins' words, "to insure the proper adjustment of the individual to the complex and changing environment in which he is to live, and to give him such ideals as will equip him to criticize and transform that environment."[22] Clearly the spirit animating this positive conception of general education is the Progressive-Pragmatic Spirit associated with the work of John Dewey and diffused, in synthesis with the University Spirit, throughout sectors of the faculty as the "Chicago School of Thought." The report diverged radically from the University Spirit, however, in emphasizing the importance of teaching as a standard of faculty work, in contrast to the usual criterion of original research. "The success or failure of the College as an educational institution will depend primarily on the teaching ability and the personality of the men and women employed as teachers. . . . The College is not an institution for research, and the teachers though they may well be potential scholars, should be free from any constraint to accomplish anything but success in teaching."[23]

The Commission Report further particularized its ideal of general education in "three types of power necessary to a proper adjustment of the individual to modern society": independence in thinking in the major fields in which civilized societies of the past and present have done and are doing their thinking; in appreciation of the fine arts and their absorption into the individual's life; and in moral living. There followed a set of criteria for subjects viewed as necessary to equip students for independent pursuit of truth, beauty, and goodness, together with highly detailed specifications for the physical plant, and the social, academic, and administrative organization in which this sort of education might best proceed.

22. E. H. Wilkins, "Theory of Education," in *Report of the Commission on the Future of the Colleges* (University of Chicago, 1924), 1, emphasis added. Wilkins' ideas were later elaborated in his *The Changing College* and *The College and Society* (New York: Century, 1932), written while president of Oberlin College.
23. Wilkins, "Theory of Education," 8.

Many of these specific recommendations would later come to be regarded as hallmarks of the "Hutchins College" of 1942–54; unification of the first two years of college with the last two of high school, entry to college at about age 17 leading to a bachelor's degree upon the completion of general education; a college faculty independent of departments, appointed by the president on the recommendation of the dean, and organized in interdisciplinary groups adapted to their teaching function; adjustment of the common curricular requirements to the student's established competencies; encouragement of the student to progress at his own pace; and evaluation of the student's "progress toward the attainment of intellectual, aesthetic, and moral independence" on "evidential grounds" other than accumulation of grades and course credits.

By echoing Harper (and foreshadowing Hutchins) in seeking to distinguish graduate work and professional training from general education, the commissioners clearly anticipated opposition from the graduate departmental faculties. This the authors sought to counter with a number of practical arguments.

> Through the establishment of The College (as proposed) many
> conspicuous advantages accrue to the University proper in devel-
> oping, on the level of attainment reached in The College, all the
> possibilities of research and of training for professional careers.
> In the first place, a large amount of space in the laboratories, li-
> braries, and classrooms on the main campus will be released for
> further and more comfortable elaboration of the aims of the
> University. In the second place, the establishment of The College
> ensures the presence in the University of a large number of stu-
> dents admirably qualified for advanced work. . . . We urge the
> careful consideration, by those members of the University who
> are primarily devoted to the promotion of research and of pro-
> fessional training, of the product likely to result from such a pro-
> gram of general education. We contend that the issue will be
> men and women whose qualifications . . . will raise them far
> above the level of the students who, under present conditions,
> emerge from our so-called Junior College into the No Man's
> Land of the Senior College as a preliminary to entrance upon
> graduate work.[24]

Despite these appeals to both ideal and material interests, the Commission Report was discussed without decision. President Burton's untimely death in 1925 foreclosed the prospect of support from the

24. Ibid., 14.

University's highest office. His successor was Max Mason, a physicist committed to "a university in which participation in scholarship is pleasant, looked for, and appreciated by the undergraduate body. . . . With the research background of this institution there seems to be clearly indicated a type of performance in education which it is our specific duty to try—education by participation in research."[25] In his Convocation statement of June 1926, Mason expressed hope for conditions under which the "College will stimulate, as it is stimulated by, the work in graduate teaching and research."

Wilkins persisted in seeking faculty approval of the 1924 report, but powerful faculty members committed to advanced research, aware of President Mason's sympathy, came forward to denounce existing undergraduate education on other grounds and to suggest a philosophy quite different from that offered by the Commission on the Future of the Colleges.[26] Frodin gives the flavor of the debate and notes its immediate outcome:

> Julius Stieglitz, Chairman of the Department of Chemistry, spoke for the scientists when he proposed that the existing junior college be improved "with decidedly enlarged opportunities for underclassmen to receive inspiration by work under, and contact with, men who, by their research work, are contributing to the boundaries of human knowledge." At the same time, however, the Dean of the Graduate School, Gordon J. Laing, was saying: "Not even in the best [university] is the graduate work on the scale or the quality that would be possible if the institution were entirely free from undergraduate entanglements." The conflicting philosophies with regard to the place of general education in a university were not to be easily settled. Wilkins tried vigorously to get the faculty of the Colleges to adopt a position which would clarify administrative, faculty, and curriculum matters in this regard, but the resulting document—adopted in January, 1927—was a compromise report which left the existing situation largely unchanged.[27]

In an oblique fashion, the split in the faculty between general educationists and research scientists echoed the debate a quarter century earlier over the requirement of Latin in the curriculum, and it would recur a quarter century later in the struggles over the "Hutchins College" program. In the stalemate of the mid-1920s, little more could be

25. University of Chicago, *The President's Report, 1925–26,* xiv.
26. Wechsler, *The Qualified Student,* 223.
27. Frodin, "Very Simple," 44.

achieved than such administrative expedients as a committee to oversee the raising of College admission standards.

Despite the frustration of the broader goals of his administration, Dean Wilkins nonetheless introduced some important developments. Chief among them—both from a national point of view and as reflecting a main theme of this book—was the interdisciplinary "survey" or "orientation" course to replace the departmental introductory course for students not intending to concentrate in a field. Wilkins was keenly attuned to national developments on this front:

> In 1922 Committee G of the American Association of University Professors brought out a report containing a survey of all the orientation courses then known to be in existence, together with definite recommendations. . . . The first of these courses was that introduced in Amherst [Wilkins', and also Scott Buchanan's, alma mater] in 1914 (by President Alexander Meiklejohn) on "Social and Economic Institutions." The two which have had the widest influence are Columbia's "Introduction to Contemporary Civilization" and Dartmouth's "Evolution," both established in 1919. . . . Committee G recommends the division of the orientation program into two sections: the first tracing the story of life from the origin of the earth up to the point where man is defined as man, and covering in general the fields of the physical [and biological] sciences; the second dealing with the main achievements and the main present problems of man as man, and covering in general the humanistic [actually, chiefly the social scientific] fields. To these two sections correspond two courses: the first on "The Nature of the World and of Man," to be given in the freshman year; the second on "Man in Society," to be given in the sophomore year.

Writing in 1926, he sought to position Chicago in light of these national developments and to claim for the College a position of leadership:

> This plan is now followed exactly at the University of Chicago—with the addition of a third and similar course on "The Meaning and Value of the Arts." . . . These courses represent a courageous attempt to achieve a modern educational synthesis—to repossess the tremendously enlarged province of all knowledge. . . . But it is not enough to know one's world—one must be able to deal with it. We must therefore refine and exercise the instrument of thought. . . . We have thus a second type of initiatory course, less general than the other as yet, devoted to this

purpose. . . . Chicago now offers a . . . course, under the title
"Reflective Thinking," to the students who have already had
"The Nature of the World and of Man" and are still to have "Man
in Society."[28]

The course on The Nature of the World and of Man, organized by
Professor H. H. Newman of the Department of Zoology, extended over
two quarters as an elective sequence. It became very popular, and resulted in a notable book of the same title. The other courses, according
to Frodin, "were offered but failed to meet with enough faculty support
to become established in the curriculum."[29]

Wilkins' writings show deeper and more serious thinking about the
undergraduate curriculum at the University of Chicago than anyone
since President Harper had displayed, and they stimulated a number of
his successors (who often did not openly acknowledge his efforts).
Frodin justly comments that "the impetus created by his proposals and,
in particular, by the success of 'The Nature of the World and of Man'
greatly assisted curriculum reform in the following years."[30] Out of the
wasteland of a narrowly utilitarian view of college work and an anti-
intellectual Varsity Spirit, there had emerged a thesis advanced by Dean
Wilkins and his associates, under the aegis of President Burton. That,
in turn, evoked an antithetical reaction by leading graduate faculty
members animated by what they described as the University Spirit,
under the aegis of President Mason. The practical synthesis of the University Spirit and the Progressive-Pragmatic Spirit was brought about
by Wilkins' successor, Chauncey Boucher, who served as dean of the
College from 1925 to 1936, through the time of Hutchins' arrival at
Chicago.

The New College Plan

Max Mason shared the doubts of many American educators of the
time concerning the "academic bookkeeping" of course units and credits as the basis for awarding degrees. Seizing on this, Dean Boucher prevailed upon the president to appoint a strong Senate committee, with
Boucher himself as chair, to review the Chicago credit system. In its
May 1928 report, the committee recommended the substitution of
comprehensive examinations both for admission to the Senior Colleges

28. Wilkins, *The Changing College*, 3–5.
29. Frodin, "Very Simple," 44. Another of Wilkins' innovations as dean was the introduction of an orientation week for freshmen preceding the opening of the autumn quarter, following the example instituted first at the University of Maine.
30. Ibid.

and for the award of baccalaureate degrees. Three such examinations would be required for the latter, one in a major and two in minor fields, taken whenever the student felt ready. The Junior College requirements were to be five comprehensive examinations: English composition and literature; foreign language; natural science and mathematics; social science; and an elective representing the early stage of a student's potential specialization. The Junior College faculty would determine the character and length of coursework preparatory to these examinations, to be administered by a Board of Examiners whose establishment was also recommended.[31]

These recommendations were held in suspense following the announcement of President Mason's resignation on the day before the Senate meeting scheduled for their discussion. The interregnum lasted more than a year, during which consideration of the new plan by specially appointed faculty boards for the Junior and Senior Colleges led to no practical outcome. After Robert M. Hutchins was named University president, Dean Boucher presented the Senate committee report to him and found "that he was thoroughly in sympathy with [its] objectives."[32]

President Hutchins' speeches and actions during his first year in office (1929–30) give ample evidence of a substantial acquaintance with the history, organization, personalities, and ideas of his newly adopted University, including the work of the Wilkins and Burton commissions. In 1930, Hutchins proposed the reorganization of the University into its present divisional structure, with a two-year College as a separate undergraduate division (replacing the former Junior Colleges) to "do the work of the University in general higher education." Completion of College work was to be recognized by the award of an "Associate" certificate, followed by a bachelor's degree after two further years of specialized study in one of the graduate divisions (Humanities, Social, Biological, or Physical Sciences).

Following the Wilkins Commission recommendations, this new College was indeed devoted exclusively to general education and to upgrading the intellectual quality of undergraduate work. Its curriculum followed almost exactly the recommendations of Boucher's 1928 Senate committee. Only the following changes were made: the required comprehensive examinations were extended to seven, retaining social sciences, dropping foreign languages, and in place of the proposed "natural sciences and mathematics" and "English composition and literature" examinations, specifying examinations in biological sciences,

31. Ibid., 46–47.
32. Boucher and Brumbaugh, *The Chicago College Plan*, 7.

physical sciences, English composition, and the humanities; and making two the number of examinations covering a second full year's work in any of the four general areas. For each of the courses, a syllabus was to be published containing appropriate bibliographical material, selected readings, and sample examinations. The 1930 plan required that, in Boucher's words, "immense amounts of time, careful study [and] pointed discussion [be] devoted [by groups of faculty] to the weighing of objectives, the selection and organization of appropriate subject matter, the selection of reading and demonstration materials, and the selection of methods of instruction."[33]

The price paid for initiating this positive program of general education was contraction of the College to a two-year curriculum and the ceding of control over the bachelor's degrees to the graduate divisions. In return, divisional faculty participated in shaping the new courses, and "a new organizational device, the staff, came into being for each of the general courses; there were to be no departments."[34] (As I recount in chapter 4, the "Soc 2" course finds its ultimate origin in this "trade-off.")

There was an enthusiastic response to this "New Plan" among students and faculty alike, and a quickening of intellectual emphasis in the College ethos. The synthesis provided a real resolution, reasonably satisfying the interests of all influential parties. An extended period of equilibrium might have been expected to set in, but—as even those most casually acquainted with the University of Chicago and the history of American higher education well know—that is not what happened.

Many aspects of the story of Hutchins and his closest colleagues have been discussed in numerous sources, including Harry S. Ashmore's recent biography of Hutchins and others cited below and elsewhere in this volume.[35] In addition, two new University of Chicago centennial publications focus on the Hutchins years at Chicago and complement

33. Ibid., 38. In addition, in a further effort to signal the separation of the University from the Varsity Spirit, all nonacademic activities devoted to the welfare of students, together with student advising, were transferred to a newly established University officer, the dean of students.

34. Frodin, "Very Simple," 53.

35. In addition to other references cited herein and elsewhere in this volume, see for example, Amy Kass, "Radical Conservatives for Liberal Education" (unpublished Ph.D. diss., Johns Hopkins University, 1973) and "The Liberal Arts Movement: From Ideas to Practice," cited above; Benjamin McArthur, "A Gamble on Youth: Robert M. Hutchins, the University of Chicago, and the Politics of Presidential Selection," *History of Education Quarterly* 30 (Summer 1990): 161–86; Harry S. Ashmore, *Unseasonable Truths: The Life of Robert Maynard Hutchins* (Boston: Little, Brown, 1989); Mortimer Adler, *Philosopher at Large: An Intellectual Autobiography* (New York: Macmillan, 1977).

this book.[36] As a consequence, I make no effort here to summarize the whole drama of the Hutchins years—for example, I say nothing about the ideas of the president and his allies on graduate education—but rather focus on undergraduate general education and those factors and events most significant from this point of view. In brief, the New Plan of 1930–31, initially supported by Hutchins, was destabilized and transformed by two general factors. The first was the effort, beginning in 1932, to expand the College program to four years; the second, the president's conversion to, and fierce advocacy of, the Liberal Arts Spirit.

Hutchins, and still more, the faculty groups he followed in this matter, drew on the 1924 Commission Report in support of efforts to expand the College program to four years. They accepted the suggestion that the first two years of college (grades 13–14) should be combined with the final two of high school (grades 11–12) to compose a comprehensive four-year curriculum devoted exclusively to general education. The two-year College was unsatisfactory, the president argued, "because it was difficult to frame a unified curriculum in an institution which must lose [to the departments and divisions] 50 percent of its student body every year." Though Hutchins' new proposal for a four-year College passed the University Senate and the Board of Trustees in 1933, significant opposition appeared immediately among segments of the College as well as the graduate faculty. "The College curriculum committee took the position that the faculty had, within the preceding two years, worked out an entirely new curriculum which had just been put into operation." According to Frodin, a number of College faculty staffs also feared their status would be reduced to that of high school teachers under Hutchins' new proposal.[37]

The proposals were temporarily shelved, but between 1934 and 1937 the College Curriculum Committee, in concert with the University High School faculty, shifted its attention from structural concerns with the division of the "college years" and of college teaching responsibilities to consideration of "the ideal four-year curriculum." The process accelerated when Boucher resigned in late 1935 to take up the presidency of West Virginia University and was replaced as dean by Aaron Brumbaugh, professor of education and College dean of students. In early 1937, the Curriculum Committee headed by Brumbaugh brought in a report outlining a new four-year program devoted to general education, with time available to pursue special interests, techniques, and subjects

36. Mary Ann Dzubak, *Robert M. Hutchins: Portrait of an Educator* (Chicago: University of Chicago Press, 1991); William H. McNeill, *Hutchins' University: A Memoir of the University of Chicago, 1929–1950* (Chicago: University of Chicago Press, 1991).

37. Frodin, "Very Simple," 54–55.

required for advanced work. The proposal, accepted in March by the College faculty, called for a common program for all students in the four-year College, preparing them for fifteen comprehensive examinations through specific coursework.

> A three-year course in the humanities . . . including material from history (ancient, medieval, modern European, and American), the fine arts, and literature; a three-year course in the natural sciences . . . offered in two variations: two years of biology and the existing General Course in the Physical Sciences, or two years of physical science and the existing General Course in the Biological Sciences; a three-year course in the social sciences; . . . a study of reading, writing, and criticism; . . . a one-year course in philosophy . . . designed to encourage active critical reflection and interrelations of subject matters previously considered; two departmental elective courses; . . . and, finally, mastery of mathematics and a foreign language equivalent to two high-school entrance units each.[38]

President Hutchins' role in developing this organizational and curricular prototype of what was later to become known as the "Hutchins College" seems to have been limited to providing initiatives (and an active new dean) for the College faculty to follow. The plan itself seems largely to have been the work of the several curriculum subcommittees of the (formerly Junior) College and of the University High School faculty—among whom there were more than a few distinguished individuals—taking their lead from the arguments and proposals of the earlier faculty committees who reported before Hutchins arrived on the scene. To appreciate how little direct influence President Hutchins had on the content of this experimental four-year curriculum, one must see it in the context of his pursuit, during the period 1930–37, with Mortimer Adler, Richard McKeon, Scott Buchanan and others, of the Liberal Arts Spirit. This was, of course, the second feature which disequilibrated the synthesis represented in the New Plan of 1931.

Adler and McKeon, both trained in philosophy, had been graduate students at Columbia University during the mid-1920s, and were instructors in John Erskine's famous General Honors Course in Columbia College, where they first taught the "Great Books." They met Scott Buchanan (educated at Amherst, Oxford, and Harvard) at the People's Institute, an adult-education program serving the immigrant population of New York's Lower East Side. Their interactions, in part embodied in lectures addressed above all to one another, slowly gave birth to

38. Ibid., 59–60.

an idea for a "new kind of scholarship, one cut loose from the more specialized research fostered by universities." By focusing on methods of
inquiry, whether in literature, social theory, or religious thought, and
on the ideas underlying various subject matters, "they thought this kind
of research could contribute important material to the process of assimilating scientific thought to traditional culture."[39]

Between 1927 and 1929, in conjunction with his work at Columbia
on the psychological foundations of the law, Adler met and began to
collaborate with Hutchins, then dean of the Yale Law School. Hutchins'
own research at Yale, done in collaboration with Donald Slesinger, dealt
with implications for the law of evidence of modern empirical research
in psychology and the social sciences. With Milton Winternitz, dean of
Yale Medical School, Hutchins had also been instrumental in founding
the interdisciplinary Institute for Human Relations. These interests
helped overcome the fact that Hutchins, who ran an antiphilosophical
law school and was less concerned with efforts to unify knowledge than
with rendering legal studies more scientific and socially relevant, had
little prior reason to engage himself with the Adler-McKeon-Buchanan
collaboration. But shortly after his Chicago appointment, Hutchins, in
one of the more famous and fateful vignettes in modern American educational history, confessed to Adler that "I'm the president of a great
university, but I haven't thought about education." Adler was happy to
lead him, by way of the Great Books, to the philosophical interests he
shared with McKeon and Buchanan. Adler further hatched a scheme
whereby Hutchins should appoint all three to the Chicago faculty in order to create "a new Department of Philosophical Studies . . . independent of but related to all existing departments at the University . . . [as]
a way to integrate learning."[40]

When they became known at Chicago, these schemes excited immediate suspicion, particularly among the faculty of the philosophy department. Unable to gain the position he sought, Adler was appointed
to the Law School and in 1930 joined Hutchins in co-teaching a Great
Books seminar.[41] The provisional appointments Hutchins had offered
to Buchanan and McKeon were rescinded and the plan for a Department of Philosophical Studies was shelved. In 1934, Hutchins managed
to bring McKeon to Chicago as a visiting professor in the Department
of History. A year later, a permanent appointment was secured for him

39. Kass, "The Liberal Arts Movement," 17–19, 30–31.
40. Ibid., 1, 36–38.
41. Ibid., 2–4. A somewhat different account is given by Darnell Rucker in *The
Chicago Pragmatists* (Minneapolis: University of Minnesota Press, 1969), 25. Rucker claims
that "Adler was appointed to a position one-third in philosophy, one-third in psychology,
and one-third in law." Adler's own account is closer to Kass (*Philosopher at Large*, 145–48).

as dean of the Division of Humanities and professor of Greek, and later he did indeed become a professor of philosophy. With Adler and McKeon present, and with a few years experience teaching Great Books seminars at various levels, Hutchins in 1936 published *The Higher Learning in America,* the first major statement of his version of the Liberal Arts Spirit.

To appreciate the shock waves this set off on campus, we must remember that neither the substance nor the spirit of the Liberal Arts Movement, as Kass calls it, had penetrated the "ideal" four-year general education curriculum put into effect in the mid-1930s. Moreover, the Brumbaugh synthesis took its place as a special program beside the main two-year New Plan curriculum and resembled it too, insofar as the same blending of the Progressive-Pragmatic Spirit and the University Spirit animated its work. The actual programs had been the collective work of the University faculty. Hutchins' prompting had brought the basic feature of the 1924 plan once more to the faculty's attention, and his sponsorship helped assure that something was done. In this sense his role was essential, but it was also also quite limited. As Harry Gideonse, chairman of the Social Sciences Courses in the College, co-founder of the course celebrated in this volume as "Soc 2," and later an eminent president of Brooklyn College, put it: "Mr. Hutchins' administrative office at the University of Chicago might easily lead—and has led—to a confusion of his personal views on [education] with the actual program now pursued at the University of Chicago." Gideonse published *The Higher Learning in a Democracy,* his scathing critique of what he viewed as Hutchins' retrogressive, antiscientific, and antidemocratic neoscholasticism, precisely to clear up the confusion generated by *The Higher Learning in America.*

> "Books . . . put in the place of things"—this is . . . perhaps the final comment upon an educational proposal to substitute the classics of the Western world for scientific training in our modern society. To have it come from the University of Chicago—which has always stressed the method of science since its birth—adds to the confusion of the higher learning in America.

Gideonse doubtless spoke for the majority of the faculty who, like him, had spent six years developing and implementing the 1930–31 New Plan when he added: "The University enjoys an enviable reputation as an institution not afraid to try the new. But this involves the correlative need to preserve such gains as have been made and not to give up known and tested practices until a reasonable chance exists that a superior practice is at hand to be tried."[42]

42. H. D. Gideonse, *The Higher Learning in a Democracy* (New York: Farrar & Rinehart, 1937), 4, 23–24.

A second grouping of faculty, according to Frodin, took Hutchins' proposals "as immediate goals to be effected at the first opportunity, with little attempt to relate them to existing conditions." This body of opinion centered on the Committee on the Liberal Arts, chaired by Dean Richard McKeon, which Hutchins had established with the aid of funds contributed by wealthy admirers in response to *The Higher Learning in America*. In addition to McKeon, the committee included Adler, R. S. Crane, Norman Maclean, Henry Prescott (who had chaired the 1924 Commission), and Arthur Rubin; three of McKeon's students from Columbia (including Paul Goodman); William Gorman and James Martin (who had assisted Adler and Hutchins in an ambitious Great Books course in the Law School—in which Harry Kalven and Edward Levi had been students); and, brought from the University of Virginia, Scott Buchanan, Stringfellow Barr, and two of their graduate students. Dean McKeon "was to be the Committee's spokesman to the University faculty."[43]

Rather than insulating it, the committee's financial independence only increased faculty insurrections against its perceived nepotism. Internal problems proved even greater, as Adler, Buchanan, and McKeon found their disagreements overwhelming. According to Kass, "Although [they] agreed on the nature of the problem to be resolved and on the necessity to restore the tradition of the liberal arts, they disagreed on what to study, about how to read, how to interpret, and how to teach the tradition. . . . To pursue their common goals, they had to go their separate ways."[44] By the end of 1936, the committee had disbanded, and in the spring of 1937 Barr and Buchanan were appointed president and dean, respectively, of St. John's College in Maryland, with Hutchins as its Board chairman. Adler continued to teach at the University, while devoting more and more of his time to adult education in the University Extension program and to editing, with Hutchins, *The Great Books of the Western World*. McKeon's many activities included the setting up within the Division of the Humanities of four degree-granting interdepartmental committees. These included the Committee on the Analysis of Ideas and the Study of Methods, which he chaired: its courses sought to explore the unitary underpinnings of the various specialized fields and included the study of the great books. A home for their version of liberal arts studies was thus found within the University, a development with later consequences for the College.[45]

43. Frodin, "Very Simple," 57; Kass, "The Liberal Arts Movement," 8.
44. Kass, "The Liberal Arts Movement," 25–26.
45. Other interdepartmental graduate committees were the Committee on Language and Communication, the Committee on the History of Culture, and the Committee on Comparative Studies in Art and Literature, each devoted in its own way to

Finally, Frodin also identified, among faculty reactions to Hutchins' theories, "a third group [which had] been keenly aware that Hutchins' leadership and ideas . . . made possible a College within, and of, the University of Chicago in which a program of general education could be developed [in the Liberal Arts Spirit]; it [was] this group which, stimulated by him to work out a meaningful program . . . built [yet another 'New Plan' for] the College."[46] From this third group came the synthesis that repolarized the ethos of the College into a blend of the Progressive-Pragmatic Spirit and the Liberal Arts Spirit, on the one hand, as against both the postgraduate University Spirit and the Varsity Spirit, on the other.

The "Hutchins College": Rise and Fall of a Comprehensive Curriculum

In autumn 1941 Hutchins selected Clarence Henry Faust as dean of the College to succeed Brumbaugh, who became University dean of students. Faust, who had taught for eleven years in the College and the Department of English, let it be known in his first meeting with the College Policy Committee that he favored a complete reconsideration of the objectives of the College, centering on a more positive definition of the purposes and functions of general education. Like McKeon, a spokesman for Hutchins in College affairs, Faust argued for a completely prescribed curriculum of general courses in a merged four-year program. Shortly thereafter the United States entered World War II, and early in 1942 President Hutchins proposed that the time was "propitious to award the Bachelor's degree to mark the completion of [the four-year] general education [grades 11–14] offered by the College. This would enable the student to reach a definite educational goal before entering military service." Consonant with his proposals in *The Higher Learning in America,* Hutchins added that "the building of significant programs to the Master's degree in the three-year period of study in the divisions would materially improve the quality of specialized training."[47]

In the Senate—constituted of professors of full rank—the battle over the President's proposals was intense. Sentiment in the humanities and the social sciences tended to favor the change; in the natural sciences, particularly the physical sciences, to oppose it; and in the professional schools, to be rather evenly di-

---

preventing the fragmentation of the humanistic enterprise. See Kass, "Radical Conservatives," 158–61.

46. Frodin, "Very Simple," 57.

47. Ibid., 62–63; Kass, "Radical Conservatives," 162, 165.

vided. . . . After discussion and debate at two extended meetings, the Senate voted on January 22, 1942, by a vote of 63 to 48, "that the Bachelor's degree be awarded in recognition of the completion of general education, as redefined by the College faculty." At the same time, the power to award the degrees of Bachelor of Arts and Bachelor of Philosophy was taken away from the Divisions of the Humanities and Social Sciences and from the professional schools, while for the "continuation of the national emergency" the Divisions of the Biological Sciences and the Physical Sciences could award the degree of Bachelor of Science.[48]

Struggles continued over the nature of the curriculum both within the College and in the University Senate. During the winter quarter of 1942, the College Policy Committee voted six to five that only one degree should be awarded and that three electives should be included in the curriculum. Faust came to accept that, to achieve the combination of the four-year College and the two-year College, the possibility of taking some electives would have to be provided. It was agreed to set up two degree programs, one without electives leading to the A.B. degree and the other including two electives leading to the degree of Ph.B. Either eight or fourteen comprehensives would be required, depending on whether a student had finished two or four years of high school. The College actions were reported to the Senate, which, by taking no action, permitted the changes to become effective. By a vote of 48 to 32, however, the Senate referred back to the College faculty the plan to award two bachelor's degrees, expressing once again the split in the Senate over the use of the traditional degree names. The College faculty met again and reaffirmed its action on the programs leading to two degrees. An attempt was again made in the Senate to overturn this faculty action, but a motion to rescind the approval of January 22 failed by the narrowest margin, and the programs outlined were ready for implementation.[49]

The full four-year program for early entrants originally required three years each of physical and biological sciences (two of either plus one of the other), social sciences, humanities, and English; plus a year-long philosophical course on "Observation, Interpretation, and Integration" (replacing the earlier fourth-year integration course called "Method, Cosmology, Values"). Dean Faust became acting chairman of the College humanities sequence;[50] Maynard Krueger chaired College

48. Frodin, "Very Simple," 64–65.
49. Ibid., 65–68.
50. Frodin credits Faust with the design of the three-year sequence in humanities

55

social sciences; Clifford Holley, Leo Nedelsky, and John Mayfield taught the two elementary years of physical and biological sciences, respectively; Russell Thomas and others taught the first two years of College English; Dean McKeon, extending the approach developed in the graduate Committee on Ideas and Methods to the College, chaired the "O.I.I." course. The two-year program for students entering after high school graduation required the established one-year courses in the physical and biological sciences (which were used as third-year courses in the four-year program), two years each of humanities and social sciences, one year of English composition, and the "O.I.I." course.

Frodin comments that "On the surface . . . the 1937 and 1942 curriculum specifications were not dissimilar. It fact, it may fairly be said that the 1942 action was merely a rationalization of the previous reforms." The new legislation marked the deepening effort to synthesize the Progressive-Pragmatic and the Liberal Arts Spirits, but in structural terms what the revolutionary 1942 legislation really aimed at was, in Thomas's words, "the abandoning of the concept of a two-year college and the implementation of the concept of a four-year college [that] would graduate students with a bachelor's degree . . . at what would normally correspond to the end of the sophomore year in a traditional college. Nominally the curriculum requirements of the new four-year college resembled those of the experimental program. Substantively there were great differences [felt] almost immediately . . . [as] the principles which controlled the organization of the new sequences were quite different." The newly reprincipled sequences were "prescribed courses dealing comparatively with related but distinct subject matters and methods," as Faust's successor, Dean F. C. Ward, later remarked of the "Aristotelianism" of this curriculum. It aimed "to keep principles and particulars in tandem, to provide a grasp of both the unity and diversity of the world of knowledge, and to instill in students balanced habits of relevant judgement."[51]

The final struggles to secure the integrity of the new Liberal Arts general education college took place in 1945 and 1946. One focus was the effort to reorganize the three-year science requirement which, like the proverbial Chinese menu, allowed the student to select "two from column A and one from column B" or vice versa. The other focus of contention was the effort to eliminate the Ph.B. program, which al-

---

(p. 69), while Kass attributes the design of these courses to McKeon (pp. 174–76). Further investigation of this important period is clearly needed.

51. Frodin, "Very Simple," 68; Thomas, "The Evolution," 4; Ward, "Principles," 127–28. See also Joseph Schwab, "The Natural Sciences," in *The Idea and Practice of General Education,* 163–65.

lowed students to substitute two examinations on specialized (typically science) electives for two examinations covering general course areas.

The science course conflict arose between proponents of the highly successful survey course sequences, taught since 1931 and widely imitated around the country through publication of their innovative textbooks, and faculty who sought a more philosophical approach to science as a method and mode of inquiry. The former group sought to preserve the "comprehensive" aspect of general education in its synthesis with the University Spirit, while the latter group—centered on Joseph Schwab, Benson Ginsburg, John Mayfield, Thornton Page, and Aaron Sayvetz—were willing to sacrifice some coverage in favor of the "Aristotelian" principle of balancing general with liberal education. These proponents of a philosophically and historically organized natural science sequence further argued that the existing courses artificially separated the biological and physical sciences. They were in turn attacked for advocating an antiquarianism, for wishing to teach scientific discoveries and experiments which had been superseded by later work, and for failing to respect the difference between teaching science itself and teaching about science.[52] The College faculty, however, approved the experiment and voted to accept a comprehensive requirement covering three years work in the natural sciences, while attempting to effect some degree of compromise by retaining the existing two-year sequences for high school graduates. Both sequences were taught between 1945 and 1950.

Antagonisms over the proper conception of the undergraduate curriculum and the rivalry of academic cultures embodied in them had immediate consequences for institutional structure, especially regarding the place of College teaching in the University faculty member's career. By 1947, the College was experiencing more difficulty in finding competent staff for the natural science sequence than for the other general-education sequences. Scientists in the graduate departments were not reticent about expressing their low opinion of the scientific qualifications of those teaching in natural science and refused to support joint appointments for College scientists until substantial modifications produced a curriculum more to their liking. Younger divisional scientists willing to put aside their curricular doubts to do their duty for the College faced an additional impediment. Dean Ward recalled a typical meeting "at which the dean of the physical science division joined me in exhorting members of the faculty to teach in the College. A young

52. Christopher Jencks and David Riesman, *The Academic Revolution* (Chicago: University of Chicago Press, 1977), 496.

chemist next to me listened with solicitude but did not enlist. 'I'd like to help you,' he murmured, 'but my faculty pays off for research.'"[53]

A similar political configuration came into play over the related issue of the Ph.B. degree. In 1945, Faust proposed to undo the 1942 compromise by abolishing the Ph.B. degree, with its elective substitution of two departmental sequences for two general College courses. He argued that it was undesirable to perfect examinations which placed students in a three-year humanities sequence, then allowed them to substitute a course in chemistry for a year's work in humanities. Predictably, divisional scientists teaching in the elective courses led the opposition, pointing out that the already low proportion of College faculty with divisional connections (40 percent) would surely drop below 30 percent if the elective sequences were done away with. The scientists were joined by many of the graduate foreign-language faculty and by such luminaries as R. S. Crane of the English Department. Nonetheless, the College faculty decided upon a required program by a vote of 65 to 43. Elective courses could be taken in any field, along with the required general courses but not as substitutes for them.[54]

A significant, and in the long run quite destructive, accompaniment to the story was a de facto political purge from the College of senior divisional faculty members. A rules revision, also passed in February 1946, declared that only those teaching in the College for at least three of the four academic quarters were eligible to stand for election or to vote in College elections or on any mater of College policy. As the geneticist Sewell Wright pointed out in his resolution in the Council of the University Senate aimed at forcing the College to rescind its ruling, twenty-five divisional faculty, the majority of senior rank, were thus disenfranchised, leaving less than a third of the jointly appointed faculty with professorial standing. Though the Council of the Senate voted down the Wright resolution, it did vote 30 to 10 to request the College to rescind its action eliminating the Ph.B. degree. Hutchins, who had assumed the office of chancellor of the University the previous year, exercised his first and only veto against this motion, which in turn brought its reaffirmation by the Council ten days later. Facing a constitutional crisis and the prospect of Board of Trustees action on a purely educational question, both the chancellor and the Council rescinded their actions. A joint Council-College discussion resulted in five amendments

---

53. F. C. Ward, "Principles," 125; Stanley Severson, "The Defeat of General Education at Chicago" (unpublished M.A. thesis, Department of Sociology, University of Chicago, 1972), 19, 42–43.

54. Frodin, "Very Simple," 78–79, 81; Severson, "The Defeat," 8–9.

by the College Policy Committee to the action of February 6 that were
eventually accepted by all parties:

> (1) the postponement for one year of the effective date of the ab-
> olition of the Ph.B.—until 1947; (2) the addition of a one-year
> course entitled "General Physics" as an alternative mode of prep-
> aration for the examination in the physical sciences—a "plus"
> course for students going on in the Division of the Biological Sci-
> ences (including the School of Medicine); (3) plans for offering
> the third year of the humanities program in certain foreign lan-
> guages . . . ; (4) agreement to study the problem of including
> general history in the requirement . . . for the Bachelor of Arts
> degree; and (5) provision for joint residency in the College and
> an upper Division while fulfilling College requirements.

As Stanley Severson remarked, "The College had won a notable but
precarious victory." In it, and in the action on the Natural Science sequences, lay important seeds of the counterrevolution that was to come
in 1953–54.[55]

At the time, however, the achievement of College faculty authority,
autonomy, and community on the structural side and the synthesis of
the Progressive-Pragmatic and Liberal Arts Spirits on the cultural side,
ushered in "that period of fruition" lauded in 1950 by F. C. Ward, the
philosopher who in 1947 succeeded Clarence Faust in the College
deanship. Since several essays in this volume reflect on the College of
this period, beginning with Dean Ward's own "Requiem" in the next
chapter, a few summary testimonies may suffice here. Frodin's own was
eloquently straightforward. "The course of study," he said, "is simple:

First Year	*Second Year*
Social Sciences 1	Social Sciences 2
Humanities 1	Humanities 2
Natural Sciences 1	Natural Sciences 2
English	Mathematics

Third Year	*Fourth Year*
Social Sciences 3	History of Western
Humanities 3	Civilization
Natural Sciences 3	Observation, Interpretation,
Foreign Language	and Integration

55. Frodin, "Very Simple," 7, 79–81; Severson, "The Defeat," 10.

The achievement of this curriculum and other aspects of the plan of the College at the University of Chicago has required a thoroughgoing reform in ways of meeting many of the problems of higher education. The issues dealt with are always old, and always new."

By contrast with Frodin's emphasis on overarching curricular issues and frameworks, David Riesman (whose extended treatment of his Chicago experience appears later in this book) emphasized the freedom of the "great diversity [to be found] in the College at Chicago."

> The physical sciences staff attempted something different from the biological sciences staff, and each of the three year-long sequences in the social sciences was taught by a different staff with different pedagogic aims. These staffs were by no means uniformly hostile to the academic disciplines. . . . Not all the staffs shared the reverence for the classics. What they did share was a belief that pedagogic issues were of vital importance. They were willing to argue about such issues and to collaborate in a staff-taught course with colleagues of strong views and different persuasions, despite the compromises this necessitated.[56]

In *The Reforming of General Education*, Daniel Bell, another distinguished alumnus of the College and Social Sciences 2 faculties, likewise stressed the intellectual and pedagogical excitement of the staff courses over administrative visions.

> After the war, Chicago recruited a young faculty of undeniable brilliance and subsequent renown, whose lectures (given more to impress each other in the barnyard competition) were of extraordinarily high caliber. . . . In the construction of the course sequence, the interests of the staff more often determined the content than did the intentions of the administration, and since the large staffs brought together persons of diverse backgrounds and trainings, the debates about the courses were lively and provocative. The courses, as I can testify from personal experience, were extraordinarily intellectual adventures for the teaching staff; and perhaps this was its prize, if unintended, virtue, for what a teacher finds exciting he can communicate best to his students.[57]

56. Jencks and Riesman, *The Academic Revolution*, 495.
57. Daniel Bell, *The Reforming of General Education: The Columbia College Experience in its National Setting* (New York: Columbia University Press, 1966), 32, 35.

Still further evidence for the central importance of the staff-taught general education course model (and thereby, for the organizing rationale of the present volume) was given to Severson by his informants, several College faculty members of that era.

> Men from all three of the major divisions of the College spoke, when interviewed, of the [weekly staff] meetings' effect as a generator of high faculty morale and solidarity. A representative comment was made by a man who had served on the Social Sciences staff: "The whole thing was a tremendous opportunity to present our own view, to engage in discussions. It was a very good education for the faculty, an extremely high level sort of class for all of us." This man, in his attempt to convey the "effervescence" and high degree of communal feeling, said in a tone touched with amazement, "Why, we even visited one another's discussion meetings, though we didn't have to."[58]

The Durkheimian "effervescence" referred to by many witnesses is one reflection of the process of collective meaning-creation that was sustained, characteristic of a community in the throes of self-discovery and self-assertion. The fusion of the existing Progressive-Pragmatic Spirit with the Liberal Arts Spirit defined an exuberantly intellectual ethos, one that had great effect on the student body. In a peculiar way, this intellectual seriousness replaced the old Varsity Spirit as an integrative focus of campus life. As Jencks and Riesman remarked:

> Whether one looked at the intense student culture or the record of alumni in graduate and professional schools (where most went), the College made a more impressive showing than almost any other undergraduate institution with similar students. The achievements of the College's alumni were not, however, usually the sort a development office welcomes. Their verbal sharpness, not uncommon bohemianism, and frequent pedagogic and political radicalism all alienated parents, the Chicago business community, Chicago alumni of a more staid era, and many graduate school professors.[59]

Even Robert Nisbet, writing critically of Hutchins from his position as vice-chancellor of the very different University of California, in 1964 had this to say about "the celebrated College of the University of

---

58. Severson, "The Defeat," 22.
59. Jencks and Riesman, *The Academic Revolution*, 496.

Chicago" which he saw as having been "ushered in with near Crom-wellian disregard of protocol":

> What made the College notable and seem millenial was the in-spired conjuncture of teachers and students. Rarely have those who would teach been surrounded by so many who would rap-turously learn. . . . Bliss indeed was it to be alive and very heaven to be young. No other enterprise in any university in this country has ever aroused support so passionate, memory so devoted, from its students.[60]

Do these findings mean that Hutchins was unimportant to the syn-thesis achieved in the College that has come to bear his name in collec-tive memory, or more broadly that the vision and coherent definitions of educational purpose by key administrators are largely irrelevant to what transpires? Not at all. To be sure, the "Hutchins College" most emphatically was not Hutchins' personal creation, nor did it conform very closely to his program for teaching the liberal arts through study of the Great Books of the Western World. The "Hutchins College" was, by all accounts, the creation of men and women whom the president chose to listen to and learn from before he arrived, or selected and directly or indirectly protected while he was at Chicago. Hutchins was the gadfly, the instigator, the patron and shield of the College, and in many ways its living symbol, for students as well as faculty. When Chancellor Hutchins left the University for the Ford Foundation in 1951, the Col-lege lost its protector. As Jencks and Riesman have more broadly re-marked: "Looking at the record of the past half-century, a dispassionate observer would probably have to conclude that major innovations within established universities have depended on strong-minded ad-ministrators like Hutchins and Lowell. Once these administrators were gone, the pioneers they brought to clear the departmental jungle were usually driven out too, and the undergraduate landscape reverted to its naturally fragmented and postgraduate ecology."[61]

Hutchins had tried to illuminate, and the College faculty to create, a proper path for general education in a democratic society. To do this well required the resources of a great university, but to do it successfully within the university entailed the creation of an enterprise significantly different from and potentially in conflict with the University Spirit. To do it by means of administrative power, often autocratically exercised in the name of moral and intellectual rectitude, virtually guaranteed that the potential conflict would become actual, and that those in the Uni-

60. Robert Nisbet, "Hutchins of Chicago," *Commentary* 2 (July 1964): 52–53.
61. Jencks and Riesman, *The Academic Revolution,* 500.

versity who lost the conflict would be alienated and perceive themselves oppressed, as a conquered nation awaiting its time of liberation and revenge. Conflicts like this recurred between Hutchins and major sectors of the University's senior faculty, and often enough they concerned the College and its curriculum.

Yet the labels of folk memory are not without their deeper logic. At the most elemental level of experience, Hutchins was the charismatic protector, totemic emblem, and primal father of the College. In that sense, it *was* the "Hutchins College." But the primal father had his enemies, and an archetypal ritual drama was soon to be played out. The College, the father's favored son (as in the biblical Joseph legend), bore the brunt of this reaction when it came. Searching for a different metaphor, Morton Grodzins, political scientist and Soc 2 faculty member, denounced the reaction in the University Senate as "a post-Hutchins Thermidor." F. C. Ward gives a compelling account of the events, from his standpoint as a central figure in the drama, in the next chapter. I content myself here with the bare bones of chronology, conditions, and overall analysis of the fall of the "Hutchins College."

The triggering cause of the University's reexamination of its undergraduate program was a crisis in enrollment. The College's 1946 decision to award only the A.B. degree had been based in part on a faulty enrollment projection. The proportion of students entering the College before completing high school had been 18 percent in 1941 and 40 percent in 1945. The proponents of a fully required general education program expected the figure to continue to rise, but in fact it never passed 40 to 45 percent, and by the early 1950s it had begun to decline, as did enrollments all across the University. The influx of World War II GI's, which for a time masked the enrollment problems, had largely ceased, and the postwar "baby boom" cohort was barely out of diapers.

Students who entered the College after grade 10 had room for two electives in their programs. They could meet at least some divisional requirements while taking the full general education curriculum. Now there were fewer and fewer such entrants. The main body of students, increasing in proportion, could barely complete the general education program in three years even if they took no electives.

Financial strains, engendered in part by reduced enrollments, led to restrictions on faculty hiring, sharpening the conflicts between the divisional and the autonomous College faculties. By 1953 many departmental faculty members had linked the enrollment crisis to their dislike of the College program, suggesting that it was the cause of the large declines in the College and in the A.M. programs. College loyalists, on the other hand, blamed poor publicity and recruitment, not the undergraduate curriculum, and held divisional, not College requirements responsible for declining enrollments in the divisional masters' programs.

Early in 1953, the College began to explore a joint S.B. degree with the Biological Sciences Division as one possible solution to the crisis. This negotiation between two separate academic units allowed the Council of the University Senate to appoint a subcommittee chaired by E. T. Filbey to consider broader changes in the A.B. program. This initiated, on a technicality, an unusual review of the autonomous College faculty by the Council, on which professors of the graduate and professional schools were in the majority. When it became evident that its initiatives would not satisfy the subcommittee, the College faculty voted against any change in the undergraduate program. The Council subcommittee in turn called for a four-year baccalaureate program, with responsibility for course requirements being divided equally between the College and the graduate departments. In a tumultuous meeting in May 1953, Dean Ward led the College forces in a fight to retain control over more than the first two years of the undergraduate program. The amendment was defeated, the recommendations of the Filbey Report were passed, and neither faculty nor student petitions succeeded in forcing a reconsideration.[62]

There were, of course, a number of other structural factors which made abolition of the College's four-year general education program seem an obvious solution to a majority of the University's faculty. Jencks and Riesman point to rivalries between the graduate departments and the collegiate general educationists over whose candidates would be selected to fill ever-fewer budget lines. They further argue that:

> The College at Chicago demonstrated that its unique combination of administrative and curricular independence was better at recruiting and training candidates for graduate school than were the more orthodox undergraduate programs of other major universities. Yet even Chicago's chemists, historians, et al., never accepted this finding, despite the impressive statistical evidence marshaled to support it. Perhaps we should say that especially Chicago's graduate faculties did not accept this finding, because they were irritated by the argumentative students and the assertive faculty of the College, in a setting that, by major university standards, was quite small and intimate.[63]

As Ward, Gusfield, and Riesman further discuss in later chapters, there was indeed a clash in style and in ethos between the College and the graduate divisions. The style of established scholars and research-

---

62. Severson, "The Defeat," 10–16.
63. Jencks and Riesman, *The Academic Revolution,* 499.

ers tends to be disciplinary, and thus generally conservative of the principles and methods by which their fields are founded. The style of the College tended to be dialectical in the extreme, and therefore radically challenging toward all claims to knowledge. The ethos of the graduate faculty was dominated, as it had always been, by the University Spirit, with its high opinion of the value of specialized inquiry and research. The ethos of the College, during the period 1942–53, was dominated by a synthesis of the Liberal Arts Spirit that Hutchins and others had brought to Chicago, and the Progressive-Pragmatic Spirit that Dewey had left here. And so, propelled by past defeats and pent-up resentments over Hutchins' leadership, and many of them doubtless certain that they were saving the University from a distortion of its founding vision, the forces of the University Spirit carried the day.

Mr. Levi's "Collegiate Divisions"

The years 1954–63, as Thomas's history indicates, were ones of confusion and demoralization in the College. After the disestablishment of the comprehensive general education A.B., joint degree programs had to be established between the College and the divisions and, in most cases, between the College and each of the several departments within a division. The result was the loss of anything resembling a uniform conception of general education. The College drifted, in slow stages, toward becoming a traditional four-year American undergraduate institution with an extensive distribution requirement.

At the same time, the curriculum continued to be built around many of the same staff-taught general education courses retained from the Hutchins College, some—like Soc 2—harking back to the 1930s. However, the balance provided by a comprehensive curriculum was lost, creating a confusing patchwork of political compromises that defied rational description and often confounded even the College's student advisers. Throughout the 1950s, for example, students in the physical sciences and some humanities departments took as little as a year and a half of general education, while students in the social sciences were held for twelve of the fourteen existing courses (unless excused by placement tests). Social Sciences 1, 2, and 3 continued to exist, but no longer were all students required to pass either the placement examination or the comprehensive examination for all of these courses.

Because curricular practices were so confusingly varied, President Kimpton in 1958 appointed an Executive Committee on Undergraduate Education in an effort to restore some kind of order. Not surprisingly, the 2 + 2 formula emerged once more. From 1960, all students were required to take two years of general education (that is, eight of the old year-long integrative sequences, of which only ten now remained), and to devote two years to specialized study, one in a concentration program typically mounted by a department, and one year of "free" and "guided" electives.

Each of the three-year sequences in humanities, natural sciences, and social sciences was eventually required to contract into a two-year program. Thus, in 1959–60, Humanities 1 was eliminated from the sequence in that field, as was Natural Sciences 3 from its three-year sequence. In the social sciences, each of the year-long sequences was contracted into two quarters, allowing one quarter of Social Sciences 3 material to be included with two quarters of Social Sciences 1, and a second quarter of Social Sciences 3 material to be included with two quarters of Social Sciences 2. As detailed in later chapters, these shufflings of heretofore carefully integrated material meant the sometimes painful emigrations of persons as well. Some prominent members of Social Sciences 3 (e.g., Maynard Krueger) joined the staff of Soc 1, while others (e.g., Gerhard Meyer and Donald Meiklejohn) joined Soc 2. Social Sciences 1 + 3 was relisted as Social Sciences 111–112–113 ("American Democracy: Its Development and Present Policy Problems." Social Sciences 2 + 3 was relisted as Social Sciences 121–122–123 ("Culture and Freedom"). Though these courses remained well-taught by dedicated staffs operating largely within the former ethos of the Progressive-Pragmatic and Liberal Arts Spirits, the elegant simplicity so admired by Frodin and symbolized by the old course numbers had disappeared.

A concerted campaign was also begun to integrate the autonomous College faculty into the graduate departments by establishing a pattern of joint appointments. This policy was in many ways well-intentioned. It sought to eliminate perceptions of status differences among groups of faculty and to remove the organizational conditions which had led to the struggles of the previous period. At the same time the policy very gradually had the effect of destroying the self-sustaining continuity of the course staffs, and thus of threatening the staff courses themselves as the main constituents of the general education curriculum. With the loss of independent powers of appointment, College officials and course staffs found themselves increasingly at the mercy of negotiations with departments for filling the faculty needs of the general education curriculum. The temptation to alter the content of the courses themselves toward current disciplinary and departmental interests in order to attract faculty participation grew accordingly.

The uniformity of curricular distribution that Kimpton's Executive Committee established soon proved to be something less than the intellectual order so sorely felt to be lacking in the late 1950s and early 60s.

Thus, in 1964, Provost Edward Levi took the reins of the College by becoming acting dean and, in 1965, presented a new conception of the College. Harper had seen the Junior Colleges as gateways to true university work begun in the Senior Colleges. Hutchins had reorganized the University into four graduate divisions and one undergraduate division, the College, which had the pursuit and practice of general education as its special mission. Levi, by reorganizing the College into collegiate divisions, essentially made it a microcosm of the University at large.

The College's new mission was to represent, at the undergraduate level, the breadth of what the University of Chicago was founded to be, and in fact always had been—a comprehensive center of creative scholarship and advanced research. At the same time, Levi desired to retain for the College, on these very different grounds, that unifying function that Hutchins sought. The College was no longer to be conceived as a self-contained and insular curricular universe but as the intellectual and pedagogical meeting ground of the otherwise separated faculties of the graduate divisions. The graduate divisions would provide the College with the stimulation and legitimation (not to mention the recruiting power) of a great research institution, while the College would provide the means of communicating among the disciplines.[64] The collegiate divisions, corresponding in the main to the graduate divisions and sharing their faculty, were to be the structural means for achieving this conception. To accomplish this, the collegiate divisions were to be linked together by means of an interdivisional College Council presided over by the dean of the College, and were to be administered by the dean in concert with the collegiate division masters (who were made associate deans of their respective graduate divisions).

To offset further the centrifugal character of this design upon students and to allow them some time to choose a concentration and thereby a collegiate division "community," the Levi plan mandated that one of the two years of general education in the College be a "common year" of studies intended mainly for first-year students. The content of this common year was left unspecified in the 1965 Levi memorandum. Initially, an innovative design for a common year curriculum focused on the "Liberal Arts of Inquiry" was developed by a committee consisting of the new dean of the College, Wayne Booth, and the new masters of the collegiate divisions (Arthur Heiserman, Ray Koppelman, Donald Levine, Robert Platzman, and James Redfield). They proposed a program of six quarter courses of general education for entering students as part of the common year and two quarters in each of the three re-

64. Edward Levi, "General, Liberal, and Specialized Education," 83–86, 95–98.

maining years, leaving the balance in each year for concentration and elective courses. This plan was tabled by the faculty as impracticable for the College as a whole, though it did result in an experimental one-year course that for a time was a distinguished contribution to the general education curriculum.

The larger problem of what to do with the common year was later resolved by an ad hoc committee under the chairmanship of Norton Ginsburg, the associate dean of the College. The committee proposed that all students in the College be required to take a year-long general course in each of the four large collegiate divisions (Humanities, Biological Sciences, Physical Sciences, and Social Sciences), reconstituting a distributive core curriculum that was somewhat reminiscent of the New College Plan of 1931. The content of the courses required for all College students was left to the determination of each collegiate division, as was the content of the second year of general education (four additional year-long courses that came to be known as the "second quartet") required of students concentrating in the several collegiate divisions. The immediate consequences of this plan for the common year (or "common core" as it is now called), in the social sciences as in other fields, was to further compress each of the two-year general education sequences into a single year-long course, or to rearray formerly sequential offerings as alternatives to one another.

The Levi plan was developed and implemented under Dean Booth and Dean Roger Hildebrand in the late 1960s and early 1970s, during a period of radical turmoil on campus that often made curricular matters seem irrelevant. The basic part of the general education curriculum became a survey of the broad divisional disciplines, tacitly reverting to the overall pattern of the 1930s. However, in the established core courses, especially in the social sciences and the humanities, faculty successfully maintained the 1940s synthesis of the Progressive-Pragmatic and Liberal Arts Spirits. In the 1980s, faculty labored to articulate a new rationale for the synthesis, which Donald Levine describes more fully in a subsequent chapter. The general education curriculum has continued to incorporate the aims of comprehensive exposure to established bodies of knowledge, familiar from the general education model, and intensive exposure to exemplary texts, in the spirit of the Liberal Arts ethos. But the overarching purpose shifted to acquainting students with generic types of intellectual discipline, the major forms of reasoning, inquiry, and expression, which the divisional disciplines were conceived to contain and represent.

Older conflicts reproduced themselves as well during this period. Though periodic attempts were made to generate core courses mounted jointly by physical and biological scientists, the old natural science

courses disappeared. Most College students fulfilled their core requirements in departmentally mounted course sequences which looked disciplinary and preprofessional to faculty proponents of the Liberal Arts
Spirit, but which were defended by their organizers as being science itself, not "about science," and well-taught to boot. Lately two innovative
six-quarter integrated natural science sequences—"Evolution in the
Natural World" and "Form and Function in the Natural World"—have
returned to the core curriculum. Also reminiscent of the survey courses
of the 1930s, these sequences are, however, "designed for first- and
second-year students planning to concentrate in the humanities and social sciences," and therefore are not fully general in the sense of being
required of all students.

Levi's scheme of collegiate divisions and his overall organization and
rationale for the general education program persist today, though over
the 1970s and 1980s there were additional charges. For example, the
remaining integrative general education courses fragmented or disappeared. Each of these courses had been collaborative efforts evolved
and sustained over a number of years by a continuous and coherent faculty group that devoted most of its time to that extraordinarily difficult
task. Since the College and departmental faculties have been almost
completely integrated, there are too few faculty left today with the time
or inclination to mount and teach such labor-intensive courses. The
only experience "capping" the tripartite curriculum of general education, concentration, and elective courses for most students in the College has become the conventional B.A. essay.

The College Curriculum Now

As academic attention returned from radical social and political action
to its more traditional concerns in the late 1970s, administration of the
College came largely into the hands of men and women with a deep
concern for and, in many instances, a long personal experience with
general education at Chicago. Undergraduate enrollments took an up-
swing and then surged in the mid-1980s. This was propelled first by the
large post–World War II birth cohort, a general increase in college attendance among American youth, increased federal aid, and, later, as
these factors reversed themselves, by the commitments of President
Hanna Gray and College Dean Jonathan Z. Smith to revitalized undergraduate recruitment, preservation of a "need-blind" admissions policy, increased University financial aid, and greater national visibility for
the distinctive character and record of the College.

These efforts have been maintained during the subsequent College
deanships of Donald Levine and Ralph Nicholas (both former chair-

men of Soc 2). The Levine administration notably added a new commitment to the quality of nonacademic student services and the synthesis of these with curricular student life at Chicago. These areas of collegiate experience had long been sundered, and often neglected, under the old and powerful antagonism between the University and Varsity Spirits. The net result of these factors and initiatives was an increase of the undergraduate population from 2,401 students in 1975 to 3,478 students in 1990.

With College enrollments equaling or surpassing those of the graduate divisions and professional schools, efforts were made to reconsider and rearticulate the place of the College in the University, within the framework of the Levi scheme. At Dean Smith's request, President Gray empaneled a commission on the governance of undergraduate education chaired by Barry Karl, professor of history. The Karl Commission made several recommendations for improving both the College faculty's sense of itself as a corporate body and the integration of collegiate divisional concerns with those of the congruent graduate divisions. Notable among these recommendations, enacted during the subsequent deanship of Donald Levine, was a restructuring of the College Council around representation of the Collegiate Division Governing Committees, attained through a mixture of direct election and appointment. This attempt to make the collegiate divisions politically operative bodies in the large context of the College as a whole was intended both to parallel the situation of the graduate departments as small political units within the divisional context, and to further the sense of community Levi thought essential for the collegiate divisional model to succeed.

A subsequent committee chaired by J. David Greenstone, political science professor and former master of the Social Sciences Collegiate Division, sought to legitimate the growth of the College that had already occurred while setting a desirable upper limit on undergraduate enrollment. The Greenstone Committee report thus endeavored, with mixed success, to reassure both divisional and the College faculties— the former concerned that the College's new-found strength might represent a renewed threat to the University Spirit and the latter worried that administration interest in undergraduate tuition income might increase enrollment beyond the capacity of the faculty to teach the curriculum, half of which consisted of required general education courses conducted mainly in small discussion groups.

Clearly, the patterns of institutional structure and academic ethos underlying these recent tensions are hardly new at the University of Chicago. However, the elimination of a separate College faculty in the Levi College has made for a new situation with respect to the place of college teaching in the University faculty member's career. The regime of joint appointments between the College and the graduate departments has meant that faculty looking out for departmental interests and those protecting the College's interests are, generally speaking, the same persons. This means that the tensions generated by conflicts among multiple faculty responsibilities are expressed less between groups of faculty, but are rather internalized within each faculty member's position. Additional contextual factors in the 1980s—a modest reduction in overall faculty size, decreased federal research support, impending changes in retirement laws, and the hiring of fewer assistant professors (that faculty segment which in recent years has been expected to teach the general education courses)—have tended to exacerbate the organizational challenges for faculty inherent in the Levi College plan.

A new program of three-year postdoctoral teaching positions was initiated in the late 1970s in the Humanities and Social Sciences Collegiate Divisions to help remedy the gap between section requirements and faculty availability in the general education core courses. These Harper and Mellon Instructorships have brought, and continue to bring, to the University a small number of excellent young scholar-teachers who have helped to vitalize the core courses. The program, while compensating in part for the smaller numbers of assistant professors hired, has, unfortunately, also reconstituted a kind of "second class," College-only group within the faculty, and, because the appointments run for only three years, they have not alleviated the problem of continuity which ensued from the breakup of the autonomous general education staffs in the 1950s and 1960s.

Further steps taken to remedy the staffing problem include research-support awards for faculty teaching in the labor-intensive core courses and a modest increase in the number of advanced graduate students interning in, and later teaching independent sections of, the major general education courses. The most recent faculty committee directly concerned with institutional aspects of the general education program, chaired in 1989 by Roger Hildebrand, former dean of the College, reminded the faculty that Chicago graduate students have long taught in the College. (This writer was privileged to be one of these in 1960–62.) The Hildebrand report further sought to reassure its readers that with proper training and supervision for participants this practice could simultaneously serve the interests of the departments, in providing teaching experience for graduate students, and of the College, in providing a supplement of energetic and dedicated core-course instructors. Once again, the logic of these analyses and recommendations, for both partisans and resisters, flowed from the Levi vision of the College as a microcosm of the University, the latest of the three major attempts to resolve the twin commitments at Chicago to the University Spirit and to a coherent and equally outstanding undergraduate program.

Curricular activity has likewise accelerated in recent years. A reactivated College Curriculum Committee has increasingly functioned as a point of articulation between the College faculty as a whole and departmental and collegiate division initiatives. For example, Curriculum Committee recommendations for College Council approval or disapproval of new concentration programs, or changes in existing ones, represent continuing efforts to insure that the College retains ultimate authority over the baccalaureate degree as a whole. Recent initiatives specific to the general education program have included the 1982 symposium on the Soc 2 tradition, which began the process that culminated in this volume. In 1986, a national conference on the teaching of Western Civilization took place on campus to mark the publication of the nine-volume *University of Chicago Readings in Western Civilization.*[65] The creation of new natural science core sequences has already been mentioned. Establishment of new courses in other collegiate divisions, and the transformation of existing "second quartet" general education sequences, notably in non-Western civilizations and foreign-language instruction, have periodically renewed debate among smaller faculty groups.

Under the title "Project 1984: Design Issues," the first systematic review in many years of the undergraduate curriculum as a whole was carried out through a new Center for Curricular Thought, established by Dean Levine and directed by John MacAloon and Jonathan Smith, a former dean of the College. Eleven task forces involving 138 faculty and students investigated and reported on instructional domains ranging from mathematical and quantitative studies to creative work in the arts, from the senior year to the electives, from college writing to historical and cultural studies. In self-conscious contrast to the horizontal, layer-cake view encouraged by the existing curriculum—a common core of general education courses, followed by concentration and the electives—Project 1984 tried to design a vertical model (suggesting in this respect the untried Liberal Arts plan of the mid-1960s), focused on sequencing and integration in a student's program throughout the four years. Rejecting any abrupt passage from general to specialized studies (a concept familiar from the days of Harper's original plan for Junior

65. Julius Kirshner and John Boyer, eds., *University of Chicago Readings in Western Civilization,* 9 vols. (Chicago: University of Chicago Press, 1986–87). On the Soc 2 Symposium, see James Graff, "The Debate Goes On: A Tribute to Forty Years (More or Less) of Social Sciences 2 and the Value of General Education," *University of Chicago Magazine* 75 (3; Spring 1983): 6–12.

and Senior Colleges), the faculty/student panels of Project 1984 sought to explore the development of specific intellectual and expressive aptitudes over the whole course of the undergraduate years.[66]

The task-force reports generated significant interest in this alternative vision, which, however, has yet to become as widespread in faculty thinking as the synthesis of the University Spirit and collegiate learning reestablished after the fall of the Hutchins College program. Significantly, the most substantive results so far of the Project 1984 review, rather than any undermining of the three-layer curriculum, have been confined largely to the general education component. After much faculty debate, the "Levine reforms" of 1985–86 brought the so-called "second quartet" coursework firmly into the required curriculum. Rather than the patchwork of previous collegiate division requirements, all Chicago undergraduates, in addition to their common core work, must now fulfill requirements in a foreign language, quantitative studies, civilizational studies, and nonverbal arts to earn the bachelor's degree.

The College thus arrives at its centennial with a forty-two–course requirement for the bachelor's degree, to be met by classroom work or placement examination: twenty-one general education courses consisting of a year's work in each of the four common core areas—humanities, social sciences, biological sciences, and physical sciences—a further year's work each in civilizational studies (Western or non-Western) and in a foreign language, two quarters' work in quantitative studies beyond precalculus, and a one-quarter requirement in the nonverbal arts; then a total of twenty-one quarter courses in the concentration program and free electives.

Like the Harper Junior/Senior College Plan, the New College Plan, and the Hutchins College, the Levi College of today represents the enduring struggle to synthesize the University Spirit, the Progressive-Pragmatic Spirit, and the Liberal Arts Spirit. External and internal structural conditions throughout the College's history have entered into dialectical relation with these educational visions and ethics, resulting in periods of greater or lesser consensus and stability. Though organizational difficulties vex the College program today—notably in connection with the place of undergraduate teaching in faculty careers—there is little sign at the present time of major instability in the overall Levi College scheme. The majority of Chicago faculty appear to be satisfied with, or at least to have acquiesced in, the present curriculum, divided more or less equally between general and specialized edu-

66. *Project 1984: Design Issues, Reports of the Task Forces* (University of Chicago, College Center for Curricular Thought, 1984).

cational requirements. For many, the general education component meets the criteria of comprehensiveness and commonality to an acceptable degree, while providing sufficient opportunity for learning in the Liberal Arts Spirit. For others, however, some of whom came of age under the Hutchins College, the diversity of courses, subject matters, and learning styles available for student choice under the heading of general education suggests something rather more like exalted distribution requirements than a true common curriculum, at least by Chicago's historical standards.

How and when such disagreements might grow sufficiently to generate a breakdown and transformation of the present arrangements cannot be predicted, but the history analyzed here suggests that the College probably has not attained its ultimate incarnation. The intellectual commitment and creative energy concentrated there guarantee the reanimation of old ideals and the formulation of new syntheses.

In the mean time, we shall do well to consider, in the chapters that follow, the testimony of key figures in the history I have recounted. In addition to Champion Ward, who served as dean at the zenith of curricular commonality and integration in the College, all have contributed to the continual recreation of a staff-taught general education course that has remained a vital enterprise for sixty years. While the College cannot be understood apart from its place in the University, nor particular instructional programs apart from their embeddedness in an overall curricular design, *this* particular course is one that has left a great mark on the faculty and students who have passed through Chicago. Through these writers' intensive analysis of and reflection upon the venerable general education course known as Soc 2, at different periods and from different perspectives, we may well receive deep insights concerning the ongoing enterprise of realizing educational ideals in an ever-changing historical landscape.

Acknowledgments

The investigations that led to this essay began early in the 1980s, when the dean of the College, Jonathan Z. Smith, invited me to chair the College Curriculum Committee. Smith wisely asked that the committee not retreat into contemplation of ideal programs, but instead seek ways to revitalize discussion of the general education program among College faculty at large. In fulfilling my charge I began to realize that these discussions of general education, to be effective, had to be informed by a sense of history, that a major key to the future of general education in the College lay in a fresh understanding of its past. This realization was brought home to me when my colleague on the committee, Professor William Pattison of the Department of Education, showed me documents he had recently found in his department's archive detailing amazingly similar work by the College Curriculum Committee on the same subject some fifty years earlier, in the mid-1930s. I wish to thank him and others for their stimulating collaboration and for discovering and assembling many of the primary and secondary documents employed here to define and describe the several stages of the College's history. Notable among these are Professors Harold Wechsler and Amy Kass, Michael Ryan and Daniel Meyer of the Joseph Regenstein Library, and Willard Pugh. I also wish to acknowledge a debt of gratitude to David Severn of Monett, Missouri, who has shared his long memory of the College and his passion for accuracy with me through a four-year correspondence. Last and most importantly, I have to thank Professor John MacAloon for applying his considerable expertise in editing and completing this manuscript, and above all for sketching in the most recent history of the College. I am also grateful to the Spencer Foundation of Chicago for a small grant that helped me to spend a year on this research. Of course, no one but me is to be held accountable for the lapses of documentation and understanding, and the blemishes of style, sure to be found in this chapter.

Readers will have noted the many limitations of this essay. One anonymous reviewer remarked that at certain points I seem to show "a distinct lack of familiarity with the secondary literature on higher education in the twentieth century." That is sadly true; my scholarly competence lies elsewhere. Although I have done my best to find and accurately report on basic sources, I write about general education as a generally educated person, not as a specialist. I am also acutely aware of three other limitations. One is the concentration in this chapter on the general education programs at the expense of specialized undergraduate studies. Another is its focus on formal curriculum, to the grievous neglect of the social and political issues that have periodically inspired and agitated campus life; e.g., the "red scare" of the 1930s, and the civil rights and antiwar movements of the sixties and seventies. A third is the more detailed treatment of the first seventy-five years of the College's history, in contrast to the quick summary of more recent events. The task set for me, especially in the context of this volume, was to provide the "bare bones" of institutional organization and the "genetic information" encoded in the College's cultural patterns, as well as some of the "guts" of recurrent conflict. In consenting to provide the framework within which to attach the particular record of Soc 2 to that of the College as a whole, I have been reassured to know that other contributors will be providing the flesh, blood, and breath of a tale with vivid characters and an intricate plot. Having been a student in the College in the early 1950s, and having taught in the College from 1960 to the present, it is my flesh and my tale as well.

2

Requiem for the Hutchins College

F. Champion Ward

As Hitler rose to power in Germany while England slept, Great Britain's undersecretary for foreign affairs, Lord Vansittart, joined Eden and Churchill in sounding the alarm. After a long period of public indifference to the nation's peril, Vansittart noted that the cause was looking up at last. At social gatherings, people were now coming up to him and saying, "Of course, I wouldn't go as far as you would, but I am beginning to share your concern." On a somewhat less cosmic scale, I have been reminded in recent months of Lord Vansittart's experience by a flurry of worried reports deploring the "incoherence" of undergraduate studies and urging that "integrity" be restored to the Bachelor of Arts degree.[1]

This recurrence of concern for the state of the collegiate function has made it more than a historical exercise to look back on what is now called the "Hutchins College" of the University of Chicago as a uniquely thoroughgoing attempt to give coherence and integrity to the undergraduate course of study of a major research university. What Daniel Bell, himself a member of the Hutchins College faculty, wrote in 1966 remains true today: "The Chicago plan . . . was the most comprehensive experiment in general education in the history of American academic life. Its successes and failures, both intellectual and institutional, are worth careful study in the evaluation of general education today."[2]

Like nations that refuse to have a second revolution (one thinks of Mexico, France, and the United States), "most colleges . . . have at most one novel feature, the product of some extraordinary effort by an

A shorter version of this chapter appeared in the July/August 1989 issue of *Change*.

1. Three of these reports are of particular interest: "Integrity in the College Curriculum," Association of American Colleges, February 1985; Report of the New School's Commission on Undergraduate Education (Robert Heilbroner, chairman), June 1983; E. L. Boyer, *College*, Carnegie Foundation for the Advancement of Teaching, 1987.

2. Daniel Bell, *The Reforming of General Education* (New York: Columbia University Press, 1966), 38.

individual or minority who once drove quickly into a momentary opening in the wall of academic convention. These venerable novelties survive through their very uniqueness as one-time experiments. They perform a double service. They prove that the college which conceived them is a forward-looking place. They thus make further innovations unnecessary."[3] They also enable a given college to point for recruitment purposes to its special feature—winter term, senior thesis, nearby skiing—without threatening the major conventions which it observes in common with other colleges.

In contrast, the Hutchins College (henceforth, usually, "the College") was explicitly designed as a standing critique of liberal arts education as organized and conducted elsewhere in the nation. This memoir will attempt to identify the sources of the College's distinctiveness and the causes of its early demise. To that end, two chief sources will be used: my recollections and reflections thirty-eight years after the College was dismantled and a number of my previous writings and talks about the College, supplemented by internal records and correspondence with other administrators of the time.

Toward the end of my first year of teaching (1945–46), I was asked by Clarence Faust, the dean who had invited me to come to Chicago, to serve as associate dean with curricular and staffing responsibilities in the humanities. At the same time, Eugene Northrop became associate dean for mathematics and the natural sciences, and Meredith Wilson associate dean for the social sciences. For another year, I served with these three close friends. Then Clarence Faust announced his resignation and I was appointed to succeed him, in February 1947.

Serving as dean of the Hutchins College was an experience so satisfying and intense that it spoiled me for other posts in academic administration. To have full administrative responsibility both for faculty appointments and for the undergraduate course of study, to serve a talented faculty whose interests and duties extended well beyond the usual loyalties to department and guild, and to be part of a sweeping challenge to many of the unquestioned pieties in higher education, was a privilege of a high order.

To privilege was added the ardor of youth. Most members of the College faculty were still in their thirties, as I was, and like young reformers everywhere, we saw our enterprise as a unique outpost and, at the same time, a beckoning model for general change in the nation. Alas, the parade never formed behind our banner. The College remained unique, and its brief career is now shrouded in the mists of time. Some remem-

3. Clarence Faust and F. C. Ward, "Aspen College," *Journal of General Education*, State University Press, Summer 1978: 69.

ber it as a golden age; others dismiss it as a deplorable aberration or, at best, an "interesting failure."

I need hardly add that the views of the College which follow are ineradicably personal. They will tell the reader not so much what the Hutchins College meant *überhaupt* as what it meant, both at the time and when "recollected in tranquility," to one member of its faculty who served as its dean during the years of its brief flowering and its fall.[4]

Before the Fall: 1947–53

As a foil to my own views I will examine briefly an earlier attempt, by a distinguished social scientist, Robert Nisbet, to "explain" the Hutchins College. Nisbet's essay was published in 1964 but came to my attention only recently. In the course of reviewing a festschrift for Hutchins on the occasion of his sixty-fifth birthday, Nisbet had this to say about what he called "the celebrated College of the University of Chicago": "Rarely have those who would gladly teach been surrounded by so many who would rapturously learn. . . . No other enterprise in any university in this country has ever aroused support so passionate, memory so devoted, from its students."[5]

Nisbet tries briefly to account for the special strength he attributes to the College, first eliminating as possible sources all of the College's distinctive characteristics. He finds my festschrift chapter on the subject[6] "disappointing" and "unsatisfactory" because "no souls are saved by distribution requirements" (which I had been at pains to distinguish from the courses taught in the College); because "general education" is a "hateful idea"; and because any apparent relationship between the use of original works and the quality of teaching and learning in the College is "*purely* incidental." He thus leaves himself with no explanation other than the exposure of the College's students to "vigorous teaching minds that were concerned with the great themes and problems of Western society," and he is even forced to speculate that neither Hutchins nor I ever understood "the distinctive nature of . . . the College."

4. The incompleteness of this memoir has another source. It has been composed at a distance from Chicago such that research in the College and University files has not been possible. I can only hope that some future scholar may undertake a less subjective accounting, and for that reason I have prepared for the University's archives a set of questions that such a study might address.

5. Robert Nisbet, "Hutchins at Chicago," *Commentary*, July 1964: 53.

6. Champion Ward, "Principles and Particulars in Liberal Education," in *Humanistic Education and Western Civilization,* ed. A. Cohen (New York: Holt, Rinehart, and Winston, 1964), 120–37.

Nisbet does well to cite good teaching as one source of the College's educative power, and my essay may have erred in taking such teaching for granted. But his dismissal of other factors that shaped both teaching and learning in the College ignores the influence of the log on Mark Hopkins. In my judgment, the peculiar intensity of the Hutchins College derived in large part from the combined action upon its students and their teachers of a number of departures from the accepted norms of undergraduate education. In what follows, I will try to describe those distinctive features and their individual contributions to the totality of the College.

In the 1940s, as now, the programs of most liberal arts colleges were largely interchangeable, typically consisting of two principal components: specialized education organized in single-subject departments, and a mixture of electives and "distribution requirements" provided through fragile treaties of cooperation unevenly honored by the departments. The bachelor's degree was uniformly awarded at the end of the student's sixteenth year of faithful attendance at school and college.

Far from accepting this prevailing model, the program of the College rested on the following dissenting assumptions:

—that the ideal time for "general higher education" is the period between the middle of the present high school years and the middle of the present college years;

—that it is possible and necessary to decide what kinds of knowledge and competence all students, whatever their individual bents, ought to acquire before going their several ways, and to prescribe a common course of study to that end;

—that such knowledge and competence are best acquired through active examination and discussion of exemplary works, leading ideas, and central issues in the various fields of disciplined human enquiry;

—that because by the time they have had ten or more years of schooling, students are far from equal in skills and knowledge, they should be tested on entry to college and the results used to place them appropriately in the prescribed curriculum;

—that acquisition of the required knowledge and competence should be demonstrated through performance on comprehensive examinations and should be recognized by the award of the Bachelor of Arts degree;

—that even college and university presidents should be permitted to have and express views concerning the ends and the means of education.

The Best Time for College

In the aftermath of the bicentennial of the Constitution, one is struck again by the intellectual sophistication and almost ponderous maturity of the Constitution's young authors and by the weighty "adult" responsibilities many of them had borne in their twenties and thirties. But that was before America discovered adolescence and began that extension of the period of schooling which has brought the age of college entrance to approximately eighteen.

For the College, "early entrance" was essential to the success of a four-year program of general studies. This, for two reasons. The first was the obvious need to find time for such a program before the time at which specialized study normally begins. The second reason is less obvious but equally important: in their mid- and upper teens, young people display a generosity toward ideas and a readiness to explore and take to heart serious questions concerning the human condition, a readiness not yet smothered by anxiety over choosing a "major" and planning a career.

Although the capacity of some younger students to do college work and to hold their own socially in college has been demonstrated by the performance of "early entrants" to a number of demanding colleges,[7] it may still be argued, by hovering parents as well as professional educators, that many sixteen-year olds are not mature enough to tackle college-level work or to find their way socially in a college setting. Several considerations should allay such fears. One is the fact that not all of the early entrants to the College were "whiz kids" of unique aptitude for college work. In an article in the *University of Chicago Alumni Magazine* I described the younger students entering in 1949 as "intelligent, but not uniquely brilliant," and the same could be said of the groups of students who took part in the eleven-college Early Admission project of the Fund for the Advancement of Education.

In an article in *Education Week* I cited two other grounds for reassurance. One was the higher levels of physical and intellectual development now being reached by young Americans. In 1970 Kenneth Keniston described these changes: "The average 16 year old of today, compared with the 16 year old of 1920, would probably have reached puberty one year earlier, have received . . . more education, and be

---

7. See Fund for the Advancement of Education, *They Went to College Early* (1957).

performing intellectually at the same level as a 17 year old or an 18 year old in 1920."

The third reason for moving to a lower age of college entrance is a condition that had been important for Hutchins' advocacy of the "6–4–4" plan: "To date, high schools have struggled, with mixed results at best, to challenge or at least contain these more mature and demanding young people without questioning the prevailing twelve-year norm. As yet, no cure for 'senioritis' and related ills is even in sight."[8]

The high school of today still faces a daunting array of obstacles: the heterogeneity of its students, low pay and staff shortages in the sciences and mathematics, the absence of a scholarly ambience. In addition, not content to provide what might be called the "grammar" of precollegiate study, the high school, with its unfocused assortment of "electives" and "requirements" in the last two years, tends to imitate the next level of education, the college (just as many colleges, no longer sure of their specific mission, now seek to become "miniuniversities," while the graduate schools aspire to the condition of research institutes).

As for the perils of social immaturity, if the normal age of entrance to college were to be lowered to sixteen, the colleges would be free to provide appropriate rules and conditions for their younger students. The Hutchins College required attendance at classes in the first two years; it housed resident students in dormitories whose life it regulated; and above all it held to the view that "quite apart from regulations, intelligent young Americans in their middle teens are more apt to learn to conduct themselves profitably and with responsibility in the atmosphere of a college than in that of the high school."[9]

In the first instance, then, the College was distinctive in its assumption that the best time in a student's life to acquire a "general, higher education" is during the four years between ages sixteen and twenty.

Common Learning

Hutchins was wont to say that the College curriculum should be prescribed, since if students were capable of selecting the subjects they were to study, "they would already have had the general education we have prepared for them." Until the notion of a "common core" was revived in the present decade, prescribing undergraduate studies (other than those required of their "majors" by departments) was resented as arbitrary and oppressive, a denial of "diversity" and "the right to

8. Ward, "Should Schooling Begin and End Sooner?" *Education Week,* 16 March 1983: 24, 19.

9. Ward, "Is It True What They Say about the College?" *University of Chicago Alumni Magazine,* December 1949.

choose." Indeed, when requirements are combined with electives and major concentrations in a single degree course, resentment is almost unavoidable.

Strangely, I can recall no occasion on which students in the College complained that the work they were doing was required of them. How to explain this unnatural docility? There were three principal reasons. First, the faculty of the College gave to its students every appearance of knowing *why* the curriculum was the same for all. They thereby conveyed to the students a sense (familiar enough among faculty and students in professional schools) of taking part in a shared intellectual enterprise. Secondly, there was the belief—delightful to the young—that faculty and students, by defying the prevailing "cafeteria" model of undergraduate study, were engaged together in an important heretical movement. In its heyday, the "elective system" (an oxymoron if ever there was one) had itself been heretical, a break with the orthodoxy of classical studies, but by the forties, it had become novel to be "rigid" and normal to be "flexible." Thirdly, the students liked their courses.

Ten years after resigning as dean of the College, as my contribution to the Hutchins festschrift previously cited, I wrote at some length about the College. In what follows, I quote from that essay in outlining the curriculum of the College, its rationale, and its differences from the model that prevailed elsewhere in the forties and remains dominant today.[10]

> The College offered a balanced and prescribed program of studies in the humanities, social sciences, and natural sciences [three three-year sequences], mathematics, writing, and foreign language [three one-year courses], with culminating efforts to employ history and philosophy as means of integration [two one-year courses]. . . .
>
> The overall end of this education was to teach students "how to think." In a free and increasingly complex society, men and women are confronted constantly by diverse statements purporting to be true, by alternative courses of action claiming their adherence, and by individual works of art inviting their admiration. The College sought to give students the knowledge and intellectual competence to choose wisely and live well in such a society. . . .
>
> The course of study . . . embodied the notion that a liberal education should constitute a single whole, whereas most colleges in America will be seen to have two foci or principles of unity, variously called "general" and "specialized" education,

10. Ward, "Principles and Particulars in Liberal Education," 120ff.

"distribution" and "concentration," "lower" and "upper," "introductory" and "advanced," etc. These two foci coexist plausibly
enough in college catalogues, but in the actual education of students they are clumsily and uneasily conjoined.

The bifocal curriculum is subject to characteristic lapses and
strains that do not appear to have gone away in recent years. Because the program usually culminates in "majors" in single subjects for which academic departments are made responsible,
these departments become the principal points of attachment
for both students and faculty. As a result, when thus placed in a
single degree program with specialized education, general education contracts to fill the time available. Theoretically, there may
be an even division of the four-year course into two halves, but
close examination of the half devoted to general education reveals that the two years of work of which it is composed (a period,
in any case, too short to accomplish its purpose) becomes a pas-
tiche of survey courses for "non-majors," prerequisites required
or suggested by departments and professional associations, and
introductions to single subjects. It is almost inevitable that members of a faculty appointed and advanced by departments will
give pride of place to departmental interests and expectations. It
is predictable, also, that as between general and departmental requirements for a single degree, students will slight the former.

When attempted at all within the bifocal curriculum, interdisciplinary courses are commonly designed and maintained by
virtue of complex and precarious treaties among departments
which are natural rivals for student time. Thus, a distinguished
professor in one leading university once told me, "I have only
one injunction from my department as their representative in
this survey—'Maximize the segment devoted to sociology. . . .'"

The lack of a shared intellectual life in most American colleges
is not surprising when it is recalled that only American undergraduates and their teachers attempt to realize two primary purposes within a single degree course. Students of law, medicine,
and engineering pursue coherent courses of study which their
faculties do not hesitate to prescribe. The professional students
of a university, pursuing courses of study together, form with
their teachers educational communities that are often the envy
of the undergraduate division of the same university. The success of the College at Chicago in achieving an unusual degree
of shared intellectual life suggests that such an achievement
does not depend upon the age and vocational interests of stu-

dents, but upon a common curriculum realizing a single educational end.

In *The Idea of a University*, Newman cites two benefits to be expected of what he calls "liberal" or "university" education. For all the difference of idiom and context, these goods are so much like those that were sought by the College as to be worth citing here. The first value contrasts what the College called "general, higher education" with what Newman calls "confinement to a single study." Newman explains this contrast by quoting approvingly from a contemporary, John Davison, as follows:

> The elements of general reason are not to be found in any one kind of study; and he who would wish to know her idiom, must read it in many books. If many studies are useful for aiding, they are still more useful for correcting each other. . . . History, for example, shows things as they are, that is, the morals and interests of men disfigured and perverted by all their imperfections of passion, folly, and ambition; philosophy strips the picture too much; poetry adorns it too much; the concentrated lights of the three correct the false peculiar coloring of each, and show us the truth.

The second benefit of liberal education expresses what the rhetoric of the College sometimes called, inadequately, "education for citizenship." Here, Newman himself speaks:

> If then a practical end must be assigned to a university course, I say it is that of training good members of society. . . . It aims at raising the intellectual tone of society, at cultivating the public mind, at purifying the national taste, at supplying true principles to popular enthusiasm and fixed aims to popular aspiration, at giving enlargement and sobriety to the ideas of the age, at facilitating the exercise of political power, and refining the intercourse of private life.[11]

Learning How to Think

In a preface to *The People Shall Judge*, a volume of readings used in the first course of the College's three-year sequence in the social sciences, I

---

11. John Henry Newman, *The Idea of the University* (London: Longman, Green, and Co., 1912), 176.

wrote as follows concerning the central purpose of that course and, more broadly, of the College:

> This book expresses the faith of one American college in the usefulness of liberal education to American democracy. If the United States is to be a democracy, its citizens must be free. If citizens are to be free, they must be their own judges. If they are to judge well, they must be wise. Citizens may be born free; they are not born wise. Therefore, the business of liberal education in a democracy is to make free men wise. Democracy declares that "the people shall judge." Liberal education must help the people to judge well."[12]

How can liberal education help people to judge well? How can future citizens become good judges in general? The most compact answer is that they should learn how to think, and that if students are to learn how to think, they should be taught to be agents, not patients, in respect of the subject matters of their course of study. In the College, this aim entailed the subordination of the lecture in favor of critical discussion. In half of the College's courses, there were no lectures at all, and in the others lectures were secondary and, when given, were not talking textbooks devoted to laying out the subject. Instead, teaching and learning occurred in discussion classes of approximately twenty-five students, usually meeting three times weekly. In those discussions, students were expected to attempt to answer questions raised in the first instance by their teachers and, as the discussion proceeded, by other students and themselves. Frequently, the initiating question would ask, à la Plato's Socrates, about an apparent contradiction or other puzzlement in the text under examination.

I refer to a text, not a textbook, for in contrast to many colleges of the time, the materials brought under critical examination in the College were major, original works which had contributed to our rational understanding of a given subject matter. The use of such difficult, seminal works was, I believe, inseparable from the use of discussion as the principal means of teaching and learning in the College. One can be quizzed about a textbook (or an expository lecture), but it is next to impossible to discuss it, whereas, like the music of Mozart, an original text will reward repeated attempts to grasp its full meaning. Two anecdotes are pertinent here. I once asked Richard McKeon how he was faring as a visiting professor at the University of Arkansas. He replied that everything was going splendidly, in part because "the students don't know that they

12. Staff, Social Sciences 1 *The People Shall Judge* (Chicago: University of Chicago Press, 1949), vol. 1.

can't understand me." So it was with difficult texts confronted by the College's students. They often made very good sense of passages from works usually reserved for majors in other colleges. Above all, since they were constantly required to examine contrasting uses of such organizing concepts as the organism, causality, or culture, they learned to resist simplistic viewpoints and easy answers to hard questions. Those students who responded to the College's pedagogy in the manner intended did become "good judges in general," carrying into their later lives and studies an attitude of critical questioning which, while brash and unwelcome to their more didactic teachers, stood them in good stead in their own endeavors.

An incident in my own experience as a teacher brought out sharply the contrast between the College's pedagogy and that to which students from other colleges enrolled in the University's "divisions" were accustomed. I was teaching a divisional course in the philosophy of Whitehead and, for each of the first several meetings, assigned for discussion perhaps a dozen pages from one of Whitehead's early works, *The Principles of Natural Knowledge*. In the class sessions, I asked and invited questions about the assigned passages, questions which I refrained from answering myself. After a week or so of this, I was waited upon by a delegation of students, appropriately led by a Chinese student, who complained that so far they had nothing in their notebooks and would I please expound Whitehead's thought in a series of lectures so that they might take notes and know what would be required "on the final examination."

How distinctive was the College in teaching students how to think? Can't all liberal arts colleges make the same claim? Yes, and no. Most strong liberal arts colleges tend to give pride of place to the preparation of future scholars and scientists, whereas the College was more mindful of the importance to American society of men and women who would bring to a wide range of vocations and many areas of American life a capacity to deal discriminatingly with statements and issues characteristic of "fields" other than their own.

But something more than versatility of judgment seems to have been acquired by the College's students. Clarence Faust once told me that when he and Lawrence Kimpton were administrators at Stanford University, they brought together the former College students who were engaged in advanced study at Stanford and were struck by their unique and recognizable intellectual style. This showed itself most typically as a habit of phrasing and then revising questions and attempted answers, a habit that sometimes extended to offering, helpfully if not always endearingly, to rephrase the questions and statements of their elders.

Placing and Pacing Individual Students

Given a single curriculum, completion of which leads to a single degree, it is possible to place students within that program at points appropriate to their skills and knowledge upon entry. This was done by means of placement tests correlated to the College's various courses and year-end examinations. In the essay on the College that I wrote for the *University of Chicago Alumni Magazine*[13] I described the College's use of placement examinations:

> Only those portions of the work of the College which the student is found to need upon entry are required of him. Placement tests which measure his [already achieved] competence in various subjects determine the level and pace at which each student begins his work and the amount of time he will probably require to finish the College. Thus, first-year students are not defined, as are "Freshmen" at other colleges, as "those who just got here." In the College, "first-year students" are those whose abilities as measured when they enter have placed them in first-year courses.
>
> An advisor, looking over the results of these placements tests, may advise a student to begin with the second course in the humanities and the first course in the natural sciences, and to consider English as already disposed of. Another student may need remedial English, Humanities 1, and Natural Sciences 2, and may not need any more mathematics. Theoretically, someone who was extremely well prepared could be waived through the entire College curriculum upon the basis of placement tests alone. However, it will take a very blue moon to bring this about.

At this point, I was forced to add the following footnote:

> There must have been a blue moon. As this article goes to press, the Examiner's office reports that Mr. Joseph E. Nelson, son of an Oxford graduate and a student, before entering the College this fall, of a scientific lyceum in Rome and the Bronx High School of Science, has passed the entire set of 14 placement examinations and is therefore excused from registration in the College. Mr. Nelson is now registered for advanced work in mathematics.

Mr. Nelson's "success" in leapfrogging over the entire College program proved to be something of a Pyhrric victory and led to a limitation in the College's reliance on the placement tests. A press conference

13. December 1949.

was held on that occasion at which the dean of the College wished Mr. Nelson well in his advanced studies. Books read in the College were piled on a table as I handed our transient student a piece of paper in lieu of an undergraduate degree, good for immediate entry into the Department of Mathematics. When the reporters had left, Nelson looked back ruefully at the stack on the table and said, "I'd have liked to have read those books."

Chastened, indeed shaken, I recommended at the next meeting of the Committee on Policy and Personnel that all students entering the College henceforth be required to study there for a minimum of one year, however impressive might be their scores on the placement examinations. However, once their limitations as full surrogates for the College's actual work were recognized, the placement tests remained a valuable means of ensuring that students would be started off at levels appropriate to their demonstrated competence on admission.

In most colleges, the length of a student's residence is not determined by his or her competence and knowledge on entering. If a student is waived through one or more first-year courses, he or she simply takes more advanced work sooner than other first-year students, but in most cases, both will be in residence for four years, since four years of residence is the only common "meaning" of the bachelor's degree. In the College, whose single curriculum itself defined the bachelor's degree and which allowed students to present themselves for the comprehensive examinations whenever they believed that they were ready to take them, students proceeded to the degree at paces determined by their competence on entering and the rate at which they prepared for and passed the comprehensive examinations.

Comprehensive Examinations

In what has preceded, I may have given the impression that what was prescribed by the College was a set of courses, whereas, in fact, the only unavoidable College requirement was successful performance on comprehensive examinations given to students whenever they thought they were ready to pass them. Except for students in the first two years, registration in courses and attendance at classes were optional, one means only of preparing for the year-end examinations. The construction and conduct of these examinations were the responsibility of an independent Office of the College Examiner to which part of the time of individual faculty members was released to enable them to help the examiner's office staff construct the examinations in a given year.

In theory, the "comps" were to be more than year-end course examinations, and indeed they did include questions requiring the exercise

89

of skills sought to be developed in College courses but addressed to materials that had not been discussed in class during the year. However, the examinations remained tied to the year courses, and the knowledge and competence which each examination sought to measure were defined circularly as those that "may be expected of a student who has completed a year's work" in the subject in question.

In spite of the limited independence of the comprehensive examinations, their substitution for the usual course grading had a number of advantages: (1) taking courses was seen as only one way of preparing for the examinations; (2) it was no good studying or cultivating one's teachers, who were seen not as final arbiters but, like Oxford tutors, as aids in acquiring skills needed to survive the examinations; (3) preparing the examinations helped the teachers of a given course to define more clearly than would otherwise have been the case the knowledge and competence which the course sought to instill.

The Bachelor of Arts Degree

Of all the College's *differentiae,* none offended academic convention more than the award of the University's "counterfeit" Bachelor of Arts degree upon completion of the College's program of general studies. In 1964, I wrote that I believed, as I do now, that the College "was able to show that a collegiate program of general, liberal education must have a degree of substance, coherence, and rigor not attainable in [fewer] than three years of serious study; that such a program should be the responsibility of a single faculty of scholarly teachers, individually expert but not insulated from each other in conventional departments; and that the intellectual attainment of the graduates of such a program is worthy of the award of the Bachelor of Arts degree."[14]

The foregoing assertion rested in part upon two sets of data: (1) the strong comparative performance of a representative third of the College's students vis-à-vis national norms for the Graduate Record Examinations' Tests of General Education and Advanced Tests for college "majors" in five subjects which were pervasively encountered in the College curriculum; (2) results of a study of the records of three thousand of the College's graduates who had gone on to further study in the University's graduate divisions and professional schools, vis-à-vis other students placed at the same level who had gone to college elsewhere.[15]

It hardly need be added that, given the prevailing indifference to evi-

14. Ward, "Principles and Particulars in Liberal Education."
15. Details of these two studies were reported in the December 1952 issue of the *Journal of Higher Education* in an article entitled "The University of Chicago Bachelor of Arts Degree after Ten Years," by B. S. Bloom, then College Examiner, and the present author.

dence in education, these results had no effect at all, either in other universities or within the University of Chicago.

An Autonomous Teaching Faculty

If the University's Bachelor of Arts degree offended faculties elsewhere, the autonomy given the College faculty was equally offensive to some (but not all) of the University's other faculties. As dean of the College, I was not confined, as in most universities, to the role of broker-cum-mendicant, annually coaxing from the departments enough teaching time to staff the "lower division" courses for another year. Although some members of the College faculty held joint appointments in one of the divisions, most did not, and those who did taught in the College only with the approval of the College's dean and the appropriate College staff.

The achievement of autonomy by the College coincided with the opening of a large number of faculty positions. These resulted from two factors: the dropping, in 1946/47, of the Ph.B. degree with its elective options for two of the required courses and with it the departure of a number of divisional faculty members who taught those elective courses; and, secondly, growth in the College's student body as World War II drew to its close. As a consequence, a substantial number of new faculty members came into the University through the College door, not always with the approval of the graduate departments in their fields. Thus, there were philosophers, scientists, and historians who taught in the College and philosophers, scientists, and historians who taught in the divisions, and in most cases only the latter belonged to a department.

In an indirect way, the second door for appointments which the College provided sometimes proved beneficial to the University's research faculties. I can recall, but will not name, several enfeebled departments that initially opposed College appointees in their fields but which later were restored to good health in part through the contributions of those same persons. This degree of serendipity would not have been achieved if the College had sought "generalists" for its faculty. We preferred, instead, to appoint persons having the usual credentials in a single field, plus a readiness to teach and collaborate with other specialists in cognate fields. However, some forms of cooperation with the research departments had to be resisted, as when the chairman of the Department of Physics proposed to me that all of the members of his department (with the exception, I gathered, of himself) be transferred to the College faculty upon reaching the unproductive age of thirty-five, after which they might as well teach. Or when the Department of English sought to confine College teaching appointments of their doctoral candidates to those not able enough to be given fellowships.

Clearly, this duality was a source of tension, latent and actual, particularly in the physical sciences, where discontinuity between College and divisional courses and pedagogy was glaring. And yet, it was also an important source of the College's strength. It enabled the College to appoint three kinds of faculty members whom it would not have been permitted to appoint if departmental approval had been required. The first group consisted of persons who were more active and valuable in teaching and course development than in research. A second group included persons who were active scholars but who either did not comport with the predilections prevailing in their departments at the time of their appointments by the College, or who preferred the ambience of the College and were willing, as David Riesman used to put it, to "tear up their union cards." In later years, members of this group have become research professors, divisional deans and chairmen of research departments while retaining their interest in the work of the College. The third group consisted of practitioners of the arts. At one time, there were three painters and as many as five poets in the small College faculty. Although practitioners occasionally served the Division of the Humanities as visitors on short tethers, only the College gave them long-term appointments. Had these three groups not been available, the College faculty in any given year would have consisted of members of other faculties persuaded or assigned to teach the freshmen and sophomores. In that case, the continuous collective attention to the College program which marked the College faculty would not have been possible.

To the groups just cited should be added the names of a few senior divisional scholars who helped to shape some of the College's courses. Perhaps most influential was Richard McKeon, whose mark was most clearly imprinted on Humanities 2 and the last-year course in philosophical integration. Several literary scholars and critics—Ronald Crane, Clarence Faust, Norman Maclean, Elder Olson—helped to develop Humanities 3, and Faust also had a hand in shaping Social Sciences 1. Edward Shils helped to design Social Sciences 3 and the last-year course in Western Civilization. The other College courses were the handiwork of "regular" members of the College faculty who had the time and interest, as well as the knowledge, to devise general courses of unusual sophistication and interest to students.

Those courses were in the charge of faculty "staffs" which met weekly to discuss the text, problem, or other matter to be taken up in the next class meetings. At their best, these staff meetings took the form of interdisciplinary seminars in which one found one's own subject brought under perspectives rarely encountered in the course of doctoral study or intradepartmental teaching. A number of former teachers in the College have cited these staff meetings as important in their subsequent scholarly careers. In 1982, I was witness to a vivid case in point at a celebration of the fiftieth birthday of Social Sciences 2. It was attended by a number of former teachers of social science in the College, now widely dispersed in the nation, who quickly reverted, as if still teaching in the College, to the liveliest kind of substantive and pedagogical disputation.[16]

Leadership

And then there was Robert Maynard Hutchins, without whom the college recalled in these pages would never have come to be. From time to time since leaving the University, I have had occasion to say something about Hutchins and his relation to the College to which, many years after its demise, his name has been informally attached. What follows is excerpted from "Remarks" delivered November 2, 1984, at the University, on the occasion of a "Hutchins Legacy Dinner."

Not long after Mr. Hutchins left the University, in the midst of the melee occasioned by the normalization of the College, he returned to Chicago briefly and was quoted by the *Maroon* as saying to one of its reporters: "The question is whether to have a program or just let it go." Ten years later, on the occasion of Mr. Hutchins' sixty-fifth birthday, I tried to draw this distinction at greater length. I deplored what I called "the peculiar mixture of shallowness and volatility that marks the discussion and practice of education in America" and complained that "in mid-century, conformity is still preferred to agreement; tasks are undertaken before they are defined; ideas are forgotten before they are tested; and battles are lost that never were joined." In contrast, I continued, "Mr. Hutchins' dissent from this tradition made the University of Chicago uniquely interesting, and strenuous. Declining the accepted presidential role of gregarious referee, he retained to the end of his tenure a quixotic interest in education. He insisted upon the importance of education to the achievement of such national goals as the proper exercise of citizenship and the right uses of leisure and freedom. He had a tenacious belief that educational ideas should be stated sharply and pursued

16. I further described and discussed the organization of the College faculty in a volume entitled *Organization and Administration of General Education,* ed. H. Stickler (Dubuque: Wm. C. Brown, n.d.).

doggedly until their powers and limitations were plain for all to see. And he seemed to feel guilty when swimming downstream.

Mr. Hutchins' insistence on not just "letting it go" was felt in many parts of the University, but my own recollections center in the University's attempt during the Hutchins era to give sharp and clear definition to the collegiate function as distinct from the purposes of the many departments, schools, and institutes that surround a university college. Looking back now on the Hutchins College, I believe that what gave that college its special intensity for both students and faculty was its unitary character, its derivation from a single ruling idea of what a general, higher education ought to be.

Not that a general idea strictly entails one and only one curricular expression. Indeed, beyond the steadfast belief that the College should have a distinctive program to be developed autonomously by a single faculty and shared by all of the University's undergraduates, I was never sure of what Mr. Hutchins' view of the College's course of study was. I found him a most abstemious administrator. In my years as dean of the College, I recall only one occasion on which he ventured to raise a question about the College program. He then asked me if three years of general studies might perhaps be enough. But when I pointed out that without the fourth year our students would be largely ignorant of history, he subsided, murmuring, "I guess there's enough history." Had he persisted, or had I been less quick to defend the status quo, the subsequent history of the College might have been very different from what it has been.

For the College's students, Hutchins' voice (he was seldom physically present and once addressed the undergraduates in person "to dispel the illusion that I do not exist") was heard as a continuous call to arms against the intrusion of impurities into their general education. When the Bachelor of Arts degree was "relocated" in 1953, my wife heard one weeping student explain the impending debacle to her mother: "They're trying to stick in specialization," she sobbed. The sense among the students and their teachers that they were part of a movement of reform that was of national importance owed much to the remote charisma of the University's chancellor.

To charisma, unusual clarity of purpose, and intellectual power, one other, self-assigned characteristic should be added. As a member of the committee which chose his successor, I was detailed to solicit Hutchins' view of what his office required of its incumbent by way of personal traits. After citing the usual virtues, Hutchins paused, smiled almost sheepishly, and added: "And then he [the chancellor] has to have a willful streak. He's got to say, 'It's going to be this way because I want it to be this way.'"

It should now be apparent that those distinctive characteristics of the College that Robert Nisbet dismissed or did not notice were real causes of the total effect of "the celebrated College of the University of Chicago" on its students and their teachers. Two personal experiences may illustrate and perhaps reinforce this conclusion. In 1956/57, I returned from a two-year leave in India and taught Humanities 2, one of the Hutchins College's courses which had survived the relocation of the Bachelor's degree. Although the course and its teacher were unchanged, the attitude of the students in my classes seemed to me to be very different from that which I remembered. Humanities 2 had become a requirement to be gotten out of the way en route to a "major." A second experience came years later when, as a member of the College visiting committee, I asked a humanities major about the pedagogy she was encountering in her courses. "Is there any discussion?" I asked, "and if there is, what form does it take?" The reply was strikingly different from what would have come from a student of the Hutchins College: "Yes, Doctor X has said that we shouldn't hesitate to interrupt him whenever we have a question, but of course the science and social science students hesitate to ask questions."

I have belabored Professor Nisbet's obiter dicta concerning the College because they exemplify the common assumption in academe that rigorous general higher education of interest to critical and demanding students can be achieved without altering the institutional setting within which it is carried on or the career lines of those who are expected to provide it.

"Return to 'Normalcy'": 1953/54

In a letter to me, dated February 19, 1964, Hutchins wrote: "My mistake was that I thought I was a successful evangelist, when I actually was the stopper in the bathtub. I thought I had convinced everybody, when all I had done was block a return to 'normalcy.' I shall never cease to regret the pain that this mistake of mine caused you."

When Hutchins left the University in 1951, the "Chicago Plan" was left without its stoutest advocate and shield. As a member of the committee which chose his successor, I found the hunger for normality very strong within the committee. With a few wistful exceptions, the members, trustees, and faculty alike were like pupils released from the regime of a demanding school teacher. Hutchins had seen to it that the trustees read and discussed the "Great Books," and in bad times as well as good he had expected them to defend the University's freedom as "a center of independent thought." In words of Whitman which Hutchins was fond of quoting, the University, "Solitary, singing in the West," was to "strike up for a new world." The trustees found this duty honorable and often exhilarating, but also somewhat strenuous and lonely. There was too much that was hard to explain at one's club.

In their turn, many members of the research faculties had never wanted to be different and for some years before Hutchins' departure had plied his successor, Lawrence Kimpton, then dean of faculties, with their discontents. The two chancellors could hardly have differed more from each other. Hutchins was wont to put first things first but nothing second (for example, the need to restore the neighborhood), while Kimpton put second things first for lack of clear priorities of his own. "Don't make me chancellor," he was rumored to have said while the search was on, "I don't have any convictions."[17]

The contrast between Kimpton and Hutchins was sharply evident when, following Hutchins' departure, they addressed the question of the College's future. Hutchins, in conversation with me as the dismantlement of the College loomed, said that "If what the College is doing now is right, it should be continued for a hundred years, whatever the obstacles," and later in that fateful year, he wrote that "What is required—and all, I believe, that is required—is a strong declaration by all those in authority that the college as it is should be maintained."[18] Alas, strong declarations were not Kimpton's forte. In a conversation with me, first professing his own neutrality in the matter, Kimpton said that "a hard look" should be taken at what he called "the present location" of the University's Bachelor of Arts degree.

Not that "objective conditions" were lacking to provide the occasion for a review of the College's future. Most prominent of these was a sharp decline in undergraduate enrollment (always a problem at the University) as the G.I. Bill faded out. In 1952, I estimated that enrollment in the College would not exceed fourteen hundred in 1954/55, with predictable negative resonance in the divisions, themselves already hungry for students. In addition to this prospective drop in total enrollment, two structural characteristics of the student body darkened

17. The choice of Kimpton was a prime example of a process within search committees that may be called the "reverse high jump." Early on, in what Sir Christopher Cox, education advisor to the British Colonial Office, used to call the "Father, Son, and Holy Ghost" phase of its deliberations, with the bar set at seven feet, candidates of considerable distinction are found to be barely wanting. Months later, a tired and torn committee resignedly unites in support of a much less distinguished aspirant who barely clears five feet.

18. Letter to me of January 8, 1953. It should be noted that it was I who initiated both conversation and correspondence.

the prospect still further. One was the continued shortage of students entering the College before having completed high school. Such students never constituted more than half of the student body, and yet the four-year curriculum was designed for just such sixteen-year-olds. Compounding this difficulty was the increasing evidence, as experience with the placement examinations had accumulated, that for the average high school graduate, completion of the College's program required not two but three years of work. To the new chancellor's neutrality and the enrollment problems just cited should be added the continuing resentment of the College's autonomy on the part of some departments, entailing as it did reduced teaching opportunities for graduate students and appointments to the College faculty not initiated or always approved by the departments.

In a letter to Hutchins dated December 17, 1952, I summarized the situation, as I saw it, as follows:

> At its best the [situation] may be looked upon as a case of the lemon and the lemonade. The lemon:
>
> 1. A further decline in enrollment in the College and in the divisions which has exacerbated the tendency to blame the College for general ills;
> 2. Wide revival of divisional talk about reviving their own bachelor's degrees and demanding the exemption of College students from College requirements in their "special subjects";
> 3. The prospect that enrollment in the College will go down again before it goes up, in view of a prospective loss of scholarship funds, both from the Ford [early entrance] Program and from "free" University funds which are under heavy scrutiny and pressure within the University;
> 4. A suggestion by the chancellor that the College take a "hard look" at the present "location" of the B.A. degree as possibly an obstacle to recruitment and accreditation of students and to influence on colleges elsewhere.
>
> Given (1) to (4) above, how can the College survive with a minimal loss of its integrity? The method presently under exploration consists essentially of extending the normal length of the College curriculum for "terminal" students to four years for high school graduates and probably five years for nongraduates, and exempting "on-going" high school graduates from one to one-and-a-half years of this wholly liberal curriculum by permitting them to substitute for the exempted portion one to one-and-a-half years of work in a division or school. The nearest analogue

would be the student who spends three years at Reed, transfers to Chicago, and sends back to Reed for his B.A. after completing a year at Chicago.

The lemonade:

1. In the case of terminal students, I think that some very interesting possibilities exist for improving the present curriculum along the lines of the preceptorials which yielded the student essays I sent you last year;
2. "On-going" students and transfer students without bachelor's degrees would receive a more extensive general education than it has been possible to require of them in the past. This is even true of candidates for a joint B.S. degree combining general studies in the College and divisional work for both College candidates and transfers, which has been proposed to the College faculty by the Division of the Physical Sciences;
3. Discussion of this matter has begun to squeeze the water out of some of the master's programs for College students.

Put briefly, if I made an accurate estimate of the situation this autumn (it seems like a hundred year ago), the present year was the last in which the College could expect to be agent rather than patient in the determination of its future. If control of the initiative can be maintained through the next few weeks, the College may be stabilized at a higher level in the University than ever before and its resulting influence within the University and perhaps upon liberal education elsewhere may be increased.

On the other hand, the lemon may be dry. At least, we're going to find out before we are all much older. The big vote should come in February. Make what you can of this. This is what I am trying to do.

The lemon proved to be dry. At one point, I had the chancellor's assurance that he would oppose a formula which reduced the College's scope to two years, but someone else got to him after I did, and the chance to make lemonade was lost. My subsequent resignation was refused, and once the die was cast, a face-saving form of words was worked out. In fact, it was no contest. The College was outgunned from the first, despite the sympathy of many individual colleagues in the other faculties and the positive help of the Social Sciences and Biological Sciences divisions.

In 1984, Donald Levine, dean of the College, listed the series of steps in the dismantlement of the Hutchins College which followed the 1953 vote in the Council of the Senate:

One by one, most of the great staff-taught general education courses . . . were dissolved. The independent Board of Examiners was disbanded. The comprehensive examinations as a substitute for course credits disappeared. The custom of carefully constructed course syllabi disappeared. The notion of sequential work in the disciplines faded away. And the linch-pin of the Faust-Ward College, . . . the awarding of the B.A. after a program of general education . . . was pulled out."[19]

George Santayana once said of Hegel that Hegel "could be sure that the good would win out in the end, since whatever won out in the end was the good." It follows that all losers deserve their fate. In that spirit, as he leaves the subject of the Hutchins College in the essay previously cited, Robert Nisbet, puzzled that so fair a thing should have proved so frail, offers the consoling thought that had it survived, the College, like other educational "experiments," would have lost its élan and indeed may already have done so. I can say only that whatever the future might have held, at the time when "normalcy" was restored, rigor mortis had not begun to set in. Unlike ancient Rome, the College fell without first having declined.

A "Tingling in the Memory"

It would not be useful to recount the details of the long twilight struggle that led to the final Council vote to "normalize" the College, but even at this late date tribute must be paid to the solidarity and dedication that the College faculty and the College students displayed as the Hutchins College "faded into the light of common day." From the faculty there was no cry of *sauve qui peut,* and the students "demonstrated" peacefully—the only time I can recall when students demonstrated in favor of an existing and prescribed course of study. I have never forgotten them as they stood in silent remonstrance as the members of the Council filed into the meeting that would decide their college's fate. Their sense of helplessness and impending loss had been expressed in January in a statement that some 150 students had placed in the *Maroon:*

At this time when the very foundations on which the College has been established are being tested we ask you, the faculty of the college, not only to remember your faith which brought this

19. Remarks at the "Hutchins Legacy Dinner," University of Chicago, November 2, 1984.

great experiment into being but ours which it has created. As we are part of the college, it is part of us. We ask consideration of our feelings and views concerning the proposed change; for to deny them is to deny both a need and a right.

Later, in the second year of "normalcy" the editor of the *Maroon* tried to describe the difference in atmosphere between the "new," bifocal college and the college which it had replaced:

> Of college students today, there is an almost complete lack of unifying spirit. Students feel no tie binding, or even connecting themselves to their university or to each other. . . . A college which was once diverse has been atomized. . . . The old college spirit was, by and large, a quiet thing. One did not raise beer mugs to it. One did not sing songs about it. . . . There was a common faith in the values and prejudices of the intellectual life, the common antipathy toward conventional social life, the common attitudes toward athletics in general and football in particular, and the common love of argumentation and dispute. Still, there was something far deeper, binding us closely. One heard, as it were, a quiet echo of Shakespeare's Henry V crying to his army, "We few, we happy few, we band of brothers."[20]

When Hutchins died, in 1977, one of the happy few, David Broder, wrote as follows about the College:

> Those of us who went to Chicago in those years . . . knew that in that great research-oriented center of graduate studies . . . Hutchins had created an undergraduate college with a single shared liberal arts curriculum and a faculty dedicated to teaching over everything else. It was an unconventional college, which disdained the rituals of course credits, attendance taking, and academic bureaucracy. It took students without high school diplomas and granted them degrees with no pretense of preparing them for a profession. But there was an excitement of intellectual discovery, a sense of shared adventure there, that even now, thirty years later, remains tingling in the memory.[21]

20. Issue of January 28, 1955.
21. *Los Angeles Times,* May 18, 1977.

Part II

Soc 2 in the College

3

Classics and Conversations

Donald N. Levine

When, as dean of the College in 1982, I convened the symposium inaugurating our explorations of the history of Soc 2, I invited the participants to engage in a little thought experiment. I now repeat my invitation for readers of this volume. Imagine a dark and chilly night on a prairie somewhere in Nebraska. Five figures sit huddled around a fire. Having exhausted their repertoire of campfire songs, they turn to conversation. We see them only dimly, but can hear what they are saying. Their talk turns to comments on the years of violence in Ethiopia—the longstanding Eritrean rebellion, its escalation due to interventions by foreign powers, heightened hostilities among various ethnic groups, the political killings under the old Mengistu regime. As they talk, the conversation shifts to a more general question: the issue of violence and conflict in human relations. One of them comments: "I am not really surprised by all this violence. You see, the conduct of all human animals is energized by powerful instinctual forces, including a strong component of aggressive drives. Since modern civilization inhibits the casual expression of those drives, we must expect that they will become bottled up and intensified to the point that they seek discharge in occasionally explosive forms like war."

"My friend, you are mistaken," comes a voice from the other side of the fire. "Observe the enormous variability of human conduct that appears when one compares different societies. Human beings are basically amorphous, until they are shaped in a particular way by those ideas and values that their culture has selected from the great spectrum of human potentialities. Warlike cultures make people aggressive, pacific cultures make them peaceable."

At this point a figure somewhat off to the side breaks in. "If I may say so," he remarks, "this notion of complete cultural variability overlooks those fundamental patterns of human social life that are inherent in all social interaction. There are fundamental forms that recur whenever people associate, however different their purposes in coming together

103

may be. And I believe that patterns like conflict are just as essential in human interaction as patterns like cooperation and stratification. Indeed, conflict sometimes is a means by which the cohesiveness of groups actually becomes strengthened."

Suddenly a figure to his left breaks in. "Such naive and obfuscating gibberish! If you could just bring yourself to be realistic, you would acknowledge that conflict is not a necessary component of social relations. It is produced only when societies are divided into social classes unequal in their command of resources. Conflict comes about because of the recurrent struggle among those classes for control of resources, and if there is violence among different nations, that is because their ruling classes are competing for scarce resources. To eliminate conflict, all you need to do is eliminate unequal social classes."

"Well, well," says the fifth figure, who has been taking in everything most attentively, "I must say that that seems to me very simplistic. Human reality is much more complex than your formulas admit. Human actors are moved by a great variety of intentions and organized in countless ways. Different groups compete with one another for different things at different times: now for economic resources, now for political power, now for prestige, now on behalf of those great ideals enunciated by prophets. And because it is impossible to secure harmonious agreement in these diverse areas, there will always be conflict among social strata."

"Aha!" chimes the first speaker. "Have you not just given us what amounts to an elaborate rationalization, one that by intellectualizing the manifestations of human conflict obscures their ultimate origin in largely unconscious aggressive strivings?"

Just then, a large cloud moves westward and uncovers a bright full moon. The faces of our speakers are illuminated and we recognize them—of course—as Sigmund Freud, Ruth Benedict, Georg Simmel, Karl Marx, and Max Weber.

As I did to participants in the 1982 symposium, I ask you now to pause, to take out paper and pencil, and to write a short essay on the following question: how would the recent conflicts in Ethiopia be interpreted by Freud, Benedict, Simmel, Marx, and Weber, and with what arguments would they support those interpretations?

Questions of the sort just posed have provoked, delighted, frustrated, and enlightened many generations of students in the College. In celebrating the organized course of study known as Social Sciences 2 that spawned and today still spawns such questions, we seek no orgy of nostalgia or self-congratulation, but discussions devoted to critical reflection about this pedagogical tradition. This attitude, the only truly respectful one, is particularly necessary in the context of celebrating the University's centennial.

Whether Soc 2 has a single or multiple birthdates is more a matter of interpretation than is the nativity of the University and of the College as a whole. In chapter 4, David Orlinsky argues that the year 1931, when the grandparent general education course on the institutions of modern society was created by Louis Wirth, Jerome Kerwin, and Harry Gideonse, should be viewed as the true date of origin for the course. Others would suggest that it was 1947, when the staff substantially reoriented the course around the theme of "personality and culture," that the Soc 2 course we know and love really originated. Still others—including those who initially publicized the 1982 symposium as the fortieth anniversary—make the case for 1942, on grounds that it was then that Dean Clarence Faust and the College faculty established an integrated four-year curriculum of general education courses, in which the course became defined as the second-year course in a three-year sequence of social science courses and thereby acquired its generic name of Social Sciences 2.

Given the extent of plausible controversy about the true age of the course, we must conclude that it was less the historian's sense of an identifiable past even that prompted the the 1982 assembly and this centennial volume, than the anthropologist's sense of some significant social function deserving symbolic representation in scenes of collective effervescence. While I would hesitate to hang such an interpretation on one particular reading of the matter, I think it fair to suggest that the contrast between what is happening in American higher education today and the experience in the College of the University of Chicago is a further, major source for these inspirations and efforts. For it is the case that social science programs in American colleges today face a triple threat to their vitality: a growing sense of the poverty of prevailing patterns of curricular organization; a sense of crisis affecting the whole social science enterprise owing both to the reduction of public financial and moral support and a rash of internal identity crises; and a sense that the legitimate educational needs of students have been given short shift. In feverish response thereto, social science educators have been grasping for curricular novelties with which to express a renewed sense of purpose—and to capture headlines and students.

In stunning contrast, the Soc 2 sequence represents an educational program that has proved powerfully effective over a very long time—indeed, for sixty-one (or forty-five, or fifty) years! And so the thought arises that the community of social science educators might find something of interest in a series of reflections about a course and about more general problems regarding collegiate education in the social sciences by faculty members and former students associated with the course at different points in its history.

To say that some cultural creation has continuing significance as an exemplary work over many generations is in effect to call it a classic. If I am not mistaken, the intellectual mood registered in the essays in this volume is not unlike that we experience when we revisit a literary classic. And just as one of the hallmarks of a classic is its potential for eliciting divergent interpretations from different readers, so the special meaning of the Soc 2 course continues to be formulated in quite different ways. Let me add to the discussion some of my own idiosyncratic views about this curricular classic.

Much of what constitutes the claim of Soc 2 to status as a classic derives from its being part of a classic system of general education initiated by members of our faculty in the mid-1920s and perfected in the mid-1940s. The spirit of that enterprise was aptly conveyed by Louis Wirth, not long after Soc 2's grandparent course was launched in 1931. "It has been agreed," he wrote, "that the object of our college is to provide what we are pleased to call 'a general education.' But if this aim is to emerge out of the vaporizing state and is to be more than a stereotyped shibboleth we shall soon have to devote some thought to its meaning."[1] It is hard to imagine a place where more serious thought was devoted to the meaning of general education than in this College in the 1930s. And in the essay by Wirth from which I have quoted he goes on to express some of the core ideas which animated the general-education program of what is often called the Hutchins College.

In the first place, he says, "General education should not deal with each separate phase of the curriculum as if the student were going to specialize in it. It should, however, clearly exhibit the nature and peculiarities of the subject matter and methods of procedure, and the relation of each subject to all the rest."[2]

In doing this, he adds, it should avoid "the type of course known as the 'survey course,' that offers excursions into every imaginable field and penetrates beneath the surface of scarcely any."[3] This can be accomplished by choosing "one major theme for selective exploitation." College education, Wirth observes, will be "effective only in the measure that it is creative, for we cannot transmit knowledge without in some measure altering what we started to transmit. A culture will, in the

---

1. Louis Wirth, in *General Education: Its Nature, Scope and Essential Elements,* ed. William S. Gray, Proceedings of the Institute for Administrative Officers of Higher Institutions (Chicago: University of Chicago Press, 1934), 6: 25–35.
2. Ibid., 28.
3. Ibid., 31.

course of time, degenerate into a body of sterile ritual and rigid dogma unless it is refreshed by constant commentary and criticism and by new discovery."[4]

Wirth goes on to comment on the advantages to the faculty of participating in a program of general education.

> Each of us who has participated in the general education courses in the four major fields and in English, through which for the time being we are attempting to set up the groundwork of a general education, has acquired an acquaintance with a number of other disciplines which have extended his range of vision, of interest, and of knowledge. Each of us has at least begun to see interrelationships of which hitherto he was more or less oblivious.[5]

For the students of such a program, finally, he wrote,

> It is largely in the process of acquiring a general acquaintance with our culture that we can hope to discover our special aptitudes and interests and to develop them to the utmost. The purpose of general education is to give to the students who will go on living if not studying after they are graduated a sense of the whole of modern thought which shall be sufficiently ordered and impressive that it will succeed in penetrating into whatever realms of life or thought or science with which they may become preoccupied.[6]

These observations by Wirth may be taken as early expressions of ideas that have long been shared by the members of our College faculty and that were imaginatively realized in those outstanding courses created here in the 1930s and 1940s, of which Soc 2 remains an excellent exemplar. Schematically formulated, these are the notions that: (1) general education should be an *enabling* experience for students, giving them both access to the major fields of human culture and opportunities to discover and cultivate their special aptitudes and interests; (2) general education courses should not be introductions to specialized subject matters, but should provide acquaintance with the basic ideas and methods of different fields and how these related to one another; (3) general education courses should resist the temptation to be comprehensive survey courses, but should afford students depth of understanding by intensive treatment of selected themes or problems; (4) the materials covered in these courses should be presented critically, not

4. Ibid., 28.
5. Ibid., 29.
6. Ibid., 31.

dogmatically, and be related to current frontiers of scholarly inquiry; and (5) the faculty teaching these courses should themselves be stimulated and educated through continuous interaction with colleagues from other disciplines.

My own judgment is that these ideas remain no less valid today than in the past and that those aspiring to be innovators in collegiate education in our time would be well served by considering their relevance to the curricular needs of the 1990s.

Having asserted that what distinguished Soc 2 was its embodiment of notions that informed the College curriculum as a whole, let me relax my former dean's perspective a bit and confess that there was something special about this particular course after all—many things, in fact, of which I shall name only two. Here again, a passage from Louis Wirth's notable essay of 1934 is instructive.

> In the field of the social sciences one of the chief problems we face consists of the fact that students are likely to come to us with the belief that they already have the right answers to all of the important questions with which we deal. . . . This is more true in our field that it is in the physical and biological sciences, and probably in the humanities. The person who has undergone a general education in social science, therefore, probably begins such training with more convictions and ends with fewer convictions about what ought to be done about things than the ignoramus possesses. . . . A major part of our effort consists in making the students aware of their biases and of the presuppositions derived from their cultural heritage with which they come to us.[7]

It is surely the case that the challenge of having to reexamine one's taken-for-granted beliefs about human conduct and the social world has been a central, powerful, and continuous experience both for the students and for the faculty of Soc 2.

No curriculum, however good, teaches itself well. There can be no doubt that the quality of the faculty associated with the course in its formative years was phenomenal. In the late 1940s, when the current orientation of its curriculum was defined, the faculty included an array of truly powerful and creative minds, including Daniel Bell, Reinhard Bendix, Lewis Coser, Joseph Gusfield, Barrington Moore, Benjamin Nelson, Robert Redfield, Philip Rieff, David Riesman, Milton Singer, and Sylvia Thrupp. David Orlinsky, in the following pages, conjectures that "the intellectual force of such a group is overwhelming, and the

7. Ibid., 33.

course they created must have had an unforgettable impact on all who participated in it." I was there—and I can confirm that he is right.

This last observation recalls one other feature of a classic I would like to mention. Classics are not only exemplary and enduring, and evocative of diverse interpretations; they are also *memorable*. They have an impact on our lives at the time we encounter them, and we return intermittently the rest of our lives to recall them and reflect on them. There is no easy way to know just how memorable the experience of the Soc 2 course has been for its tens of thousands of alumni. We do know that dozens, if not hundreds, of the country's leading social scientists have produced work that clearly bears the imprint of their experience here. We also have pretty suggestive indicators in the fact that some 150 alumni of the course from the Chicago area joined us at the 1982 conference, and another two score who could not be here on that occasion phoned or wrote their good wishes. The *University of Chicago Magazine* received some eighty communications in response to its article on the symposium, and Soc 2 faculty members traveling to alumni meetings around the country reported great enthusiasm. One of the letters received in 1982 read as follows.

> Dear Dean Levine:
>   When I received your letter regarding Social Sciences 2, I thought back to the late forties when I took the course and would briefly like to share my thoughts. Unfortunately I will be out of town at that time so I will be unable to attend but will look forward to the written report.
>   When I took the course in 1948–49 I wondered what possible benefit it would have for me as a future Finance man and Lawyer. While I enjoyed the reading I couldn't see the reasons. Now some thirty years later it is quite plain to me. It was the courses like Soc 2 which prepared me for finance and law and more importantly made me a better citizen, person, father and husband. I salute the effort to "revisit Social Science 2."
>   My best wishes for a successful celebration.

Such simple and straightforward expressions offer the weightiest possible testimony to the general education values of courses like Soc 2.

We expect to receive more such communications in response to this centennial volume, but again we do not wish simply to bask in reminiscence and eulogy. Although it is impossible to remove all revivalistic overtones from this book, it will have to be deemed a failure if it does not serve the larger purpose of spurring some genuine inquiry into the constant and varying features of the course and their relationship to the challenge faced by collegiate social science education in our time. The publication of these essays is intended to expand the conversation beyond Chicago alumni, encouraging ongoing dialogue among social science educators elsewhere.

To that end, I shall pose three questions that may serve to organize such conversations. First, what have been the essential virtues of this course, and what its characteristic shortcomings? Second, what is the contemporary relevance of a course such as Soc 2 both for us locally as we periodically review the College curriculum and for other colleges elsewhere in the world? And finally, how might the participation of faculty from diverse disciplines in a course of this sort stimulate social scientists to undertake more meaningful kinds of inquiries?

The chapters that follow address these questions in varying ways. In concluding this one, I propose to join the debate by taking up an issue that cuts across all three questions: What is the value of classic social science texts in common core curricula?

One of the enduring features of the Soc 2 course has been its extensive reliance on texts that have been glossed as social science classics: works by authors such as Freud, Benedict, Simmel, Marx, and Weber, to whom I referred in the thought experiment with which this chapter opened. Such writings are indeed durable, exemplary, ambiguously stimulating, and memorable—the qualities I listed above when describing the Soc 2 course itself as a curricular classic. Nevertheless, one may rightly ask if these qualities provide sufficient reason to justify including such works in a college course required of all students as an introduction to the types of thinking and research found in the social sciences. Two types of consideration argue against such inclusion.

The first reason is suggested by some very contemporary controversies over the suitability of canonical works in common core curricula. Since, the argument goes (and I fear I know no other way to present it than in what may appear to some readers as a caricature), to say "classics" is to say Great Books of the Western world, and inasmuch as this canon was written exclusively by white males, either it should be supplemented by a proportionate representation of works by nonwhites and females or it should be scrapped as a general requirement.

If the point of such a requirement is to introduce students to insightful formulations regarding human customs and motivations, then of course one could readily find a range of authors outside the universe of white Western males to draw on. If, however, the rationale for the requirement is to introduce students to the intellectual foundations of the social sciences, then one is restricted willy-nilly to the circumscribed universe of chiefly West European white males who created the intellectual capital used to launch the enterprise of the modern social science disciplines. When confronted with the racial/gender makeup of their classic authors, social science educators may be entitled to a modicum of petulance when they ask: Are the physical and biological scientists being asked to produce a comparable accounting?

The moment they do so, however, they run into further trouble. If social scientists identify biological and physical scientists as their standard, then they become vulnerable to the reproach that the latter in fact pay no attention to their classics in general education courses, let alone in research. At which point, of course, the social scientists will exclaim that, well, they really are closer to the humanistic disciplines than to the hard sciences—which in turn makes them vulnerable to the earlier reproach regarding multicultural distortion.

I see no way out of this vicious circle other than to do what one must always do when reaching an impasse on curricular choices, namely, to raise the fundamental question: what is the *educational purpose* at hand for which the texts being debated are to be selected? No text justifies itself, just as no text teaches itself. The need for ultimate justifying principles proves inescapable. Resolving that question will equip us to know not only whether classic texts should be read but, more vexing yet if the answer is positive, *which* classics should be read and *how* they should be read.

One possible principle could be that of cultural *diversity*, on grounds that exposing students to the widest possible range of human voices both stretches their humanity and equips them to live in an increasingly multicultural world. To this I believe the consensus response at Chicago would be that that is a plausible educational objective, but not one suited to ground a particular curricular sequence. Diverse human voices should be and are encountered in a variety of our generally required courses—through poetry, drama, and fiction, and through art and music (in our Humanities requirements); through acquaintance with another medium of verbal expression (in our language requirement); through encounters with documents of a world-historical culture area (in our Civilizations requirement—and our unwillingness to specify a particular civilization presumes inter alia that the voices of a Solon or a St. Augustine may be no less exotic for our students than those of an Asoka or a Lao-tse); and—in the way customarily achieved in the Soc 2 course—through anthropological accounts of exotic cultures.

Instead of diversity, one might appeal to the principle of *quality*, on grounds that a great way to educate students is to expose them to something like "the best that humans have thought and said." This was a major rationale behind the idea of constructing a curriculum around a set of Great Books, and there is much to be said for it. Such a curricular principle was seriously considered at Chicago in 1937—and then rejected, forcing its proponents to move to St. John's College in Annapolis in order to set up a consistent Great Books curriculum.

The Chicago faculty instead deepened their commitment to a curriculum based on acquainting students with the major forms of reasoning and expression produced within the intellectual disciplines. Quality, or excellence, remained a pervasive concern, to be sure; but *types of discipline* rather than instantiations of excellence constituted the central working principle of curricular construction. Consequently, although classics played an essential role in all the social science core sequences, they never played an exclusive role. Indeed, at times a mediocre piece of work might be deliberately inserted to make some educational point. More important, the classics were frequently accompanied by readings that represented specimens of contemporary social research: ethnographic reports, clinical interviews, lab experiments, structural analyses, and the like. This remains the dominant practice in social science core courses at Chicago today.

Affirming the principle of constructing general education curricula so as to acquaint students with generic forms of intellectual discipline yields not only a partial rationale for including the social science classics, but also suggests certain ways in which those texts should *not* be taught in these courses. For example, one should not read Durkheim's *Suicide* as a document expressing the culture of France during the Third Republic, although that may be a perfectly legitimate if not indispensable way to read it for other purposes. Nor should one read a particular work mainly with an eye to its role in the historical development of a particular research tradition, either as a source of concepts or techniques that have later been exploited in novel ways or as a source of propositions or data not yet incorporated in the mainstream literature. Instead, one should examine it as an exemplar of a generic way of raising the solving problems about society and human behavior.

At this point it is perhaps time to make the case, more forcefully than was hinted at above, that if our objective is to represent the disciplines of the social sciences then we should not waste time on the classic texts today. Proponents of this position would hold that, as in the natural sciences, whatever is valid in the classic texts has been incorporated into the current stock of knowledge in the disciplines; whatever has not been incorporated has been omitted because it is not valid; and spending time on archaic formulations detracts us from attending to the most up-to-date methods and analyses. The spirit of this position found expression in the intimidating epigraph by Alfred North Whitehead which Robert Merton affixed to successive editions of his widely influential collection of essays, *Social Theory and Social Structure,* "A science which hesitates to forget its founders is lost," and in the notable memorandum which W. F. Ogburn circulated at the University of Chicago in the early 1950s, urging his colleagues to abstain from scholarship on earlier texts and likening the use of such texts in instruction to teaching about alchemy in chemistry courses.[8]

Against such a position, I would argue that the social science classics remain essential today both for educational and collegial functions. To convey a sense of the way social scientists think today necessarily requires us to represent a wide variety of contending doctrines, such as—to take a random example—divergent interpretations of the nature and significance of conflict in human relations. There is no better way to gain access to the substance of these contending positions than to examine each in its locus classicus, the point where it was freshly elaborated with keen awareness of its necessary premises. What is more, examination of divergent classic formulations immunizes us against a false sense of closure when complacency reigns. M. H. Abrams has celebrated the classics of literary criticism in terms well suited for arguing that the mission of the social sciences is in good part to sustain a rich variety of speculative instruments for addressing the human condition: "A humane study that forgets its founders is impoverished," writes Abrams; "a great critic is subject to correction and supplementation, but is never entirely outmoded; and progress in fact depends on our maintaining the perspectives and the insights of the past as live options, lest we fall into contemporary narrowness of view, or be doomed to repeat old errors and laboriously to rediscover ancient insights."[9]

It is even possible to argue that in spite of indisputable advances in techniques of observation and analysis, contemporary work in the social sciences has never surpassed—in some respects, has never equaled—the disciplined intellectual work of the major classics. While this may not be true for most of economics, demography, and experimental psychology, it is arguably the case in anthropology, political science, psychoanalytic psychology, and sociology. Speaking of the sociological tradition, for example, Edward Shils has long argued that although present-day work in sociology exhibits strikingly superior scientific qualities compared to that of earlier generations, the classics possess "permanent relevance" for contemporary sociologists. This is so because they afford access to certain primal realities of social life that cannot be represented by abstract formulas but can only be appre-

8. The Ogburn memorandum was sent on August 12, 1952, to Dean Ralph W. Tyler, and can be located in the Philip M. Hauser Papers and Addenda, box 14, folder 11, Department of Special Collections, Joseph Regenstein Library, University of Chicago. See also Stephen Turner, "Salvaging Sociology's Past," *ASA Footnotes* 19 (5 May 1991): 6.

9. M. H. Abrams, "What's the Use of Theorizing about the Arts?" in *In Search of Literary Theory*, ed. M. W. Bloomfield (Ithaca: Cornell University Press, 1972), 52.

hended through the revelation of deeply personal experiences by persons of exceptional sensibility and intellect.[10]

Beyond their function as exemplars of divergent viewpoints and disciplined intuition, moreover, the social science classics figure as role models for supradisciplinary and transgenerational conversation. The fact is, Rousseau *was* addressing Hobbes; Marx *did* debate Adam Smith, and Weber, Marx; Durkheim *was* engaged in dialogue with Comte and with Spencer; and Malinowski *did* debate Freud. I have argued elsewhere that the social science community has been become so specialized and fragmented that its morale as a professional intellectual community has become jeopardized, and that heightened awareness of our classical heritage "may help us to overcome the parochial isolation of our divided specialities and to temper the exorbitant and sterile polemics of many of our scholarly exchanges."[11] However that may be, the demonstration of such conversations among the classics, and the elicitation of comparable discourse among their readers by competent teachers, remains, I am convinced, one of the most enduring accomplishments of the Soc 2 experiment and one of the grounds for its continuing relevance for social scientists both as teachers and as participants in a collaborative investigative enterprise.

10. "The Calling of Sociology," in *Theories of Society*, ed. T. Parsons, E. Shils, K. Naegele, and J. Pitts (New York: Free Press, 1961). For other arguments regarding the continuing relevance of the sociological classics, see Bryan S. R. Green, "On the Evaluation of Sociological Theory," in *Philosophy of the Social Sciences*, 7 (1977):33–50; Dirk Käsler, *Klassiker des soziologischen Denkens* (Munich: C. H. Beck, 1976), 1:7–17; Robert K. Merton, *Social Theory and Social Structure* (New York: Free Press, 1968), chap. 1; Robert A. Nisbet, *The Sociological Tradition* (New York: Basic Books, 1966); Edward A. Shils, *Tradition* (Chicago: University of Chicago Press, 1981); Arthur L. Stinchcombe, "Should Sociologists Forget Their Mothers and Fathers?" *American Sociologist* 17 (February 1982).

11. Donald N. Levine, "On the Heritage of Sociology," in *The Challenge of Social Control: Citizenship and Institution Building in Modern Society, Essays in Honor of Morris Janowitz*, ed. Gerald Suttles and Mayer Zald (Norwood, N.J.: Ablex, 1985), 19.

4

Chicago General Education in Social Sciences, 1931–92: The Case of Soc 2

David E. Orlinsky

I

The systematic development of general education in social sciences started at the University of Chicago with the inauguration of the New College Plan in 1931.[1] The plan required all undergraduates to pass comprehensive examinations in each of four year-long introductory general courses, and in addition to pass examinations covering a second year of general study in two of those fields. The general areas to be examined were humanities, biological sciences, physical sciences, and social sciences, following the administrative reorganization that had just been made of the University's departments into four graduate divisions. (Students were also required to take one year of English composition, and could elect three one-quarter courses.) This curriculum covered grades 13 and 14, normally the freshman and sophomore years of college. After their two years of general education, students were expected to take two more years of specialized work in one of the divisions in order to earn an A.B. or S.B. degree.

The Introductory General Course in the Social Sciences, listed simply as "Social Sciences I" in the 1931–32 *Announcements,* was designed by Harry D. Gideonse (Economics), Jerome Kerwin (Political Science), and Louis Wirth (Sociology). The course sought to give students an integrated understanding of the problems of contemporary society by tracing the parallel evolution of economic, social, and political institutions, from the folk society of the medieval manor, through the vicissitudes of the Industrial Revolution, to the urban industrial societies of the twentieth century.

This course has continued through various transformations for six decades. As part of a major curricular change in 1942, Social Sciences I became the second in a required three-year social science course se-

1. C. S. Boucher and A. J. Brumbaugh, *The Chicago College Plan,* 2d ed. (Chicago: University of Chicago Press, 1935).

quence, at which point it was relisted as Social Sciences 2 (known familiarly as "Soc 2"). Then in 1960, it was renumbered Social Sciences 121–122–123 during another major change in the College curriculum. Yet despite continual evolution in both form and content for sixty years, much of the original conception is recognizable in the course today.

From the first, for example, the course avoided reliance on textbooks. Rather, course readings were drawn directly from classic and contemporary primary sources, supplemented by a course syllabus. The first year's reading list included selections by Kant, Malthus, Adam Smith, Marx and Engels, as well as W. G. Sumner, Franz Boas, John Dewey, C. H. Cooley, Robert and Helen Lynd, and other notables. Works by Adam Smith and Marx and Engels continue today to be pivotal in the autumn quarter studies.

Instruction was offered initially in thrice-weekly lectures, mainly by Gideonse, Kerwin, and Wirth. Lectures were supplemented by once-weekly discussion sections and individual conferences with members of the staff of course instructors. Gideonse lectured in the autumn on economic history and institutions, Wirth in the winter on the character and transformations of social institutions, and Kerwin in the spring on political institutions. Despite this initial disciplinary division of labor, their intention from the beginning was to emphasize the "altogetherness" or unity of social phenomena, as against the separations of departmentalized social science. Over the years the approach to course materials has become thoroughly interdisciplinary, and the instructional emphasis has shifted from lectures (now once weekly) to small-group discussion sections (three hours weekly).

The optional second-year General Course in Social Sciences, listed originally as Social Sciences II, was inaugurated in 1932–33 by Gideonse, Kerwin, Wirth, and Eugene Staley. At first this course dealt in a more advanced and detailed fashion with a number of the topics covered in Social Sciences I. However, by 1936–37 the character of the course had changed distinctively by taking the theme Freedom and Order as its organizing principle. This concern with freedom emerged first as the specter of totalitarian dictatorships in Europe cast a foreboding shadow across the continuing economic crisis of the thirties, yet the concern with freedom remained characteristic of the course for many years thereafter.

II

Alongside its main curricular plan, the College in 1937–38 constructed a small experimental four-year program by integrating its two-year curriculum with the last two years of work in the University High School (one of the University's laboratory schools founded by John Dewey). This experimental curriculum spanned grades 11 through 14 (the normal junior year of high school through the sophomore year of college). After completing this, students finished their undergraduate studies by transferring either to a departmental program at the University or to another college. This experiment was the forerunner of changes in the College that were put into effect six years later.

One part of the experimental curriculum was a three-year sequence of general education courses in the social sciences. The first year of the new sequence originated as a year-long high school course in American history, and was transformed into a historically oriented analysis of American political institutions by Robert Keohane of the University High School faculty. The second and third years were built out of the materials previously covered in Social Sciences I: economic institutions of modern society through the Industrial Revolution, as the new second year; social institutions, up to and including urban society, as the new third year.

In 1942, at the instigation of President Robert Hutchins and Dean Clarence Faust, the faculty of the College merged the two-year New College program established in 1931 with the experimental four-year curriculum. The College was converted into a single four-year program consisting entirely of general education courses, beginning with grade 11 (normally the junior year of high school) and ending with grade 14 (normally the sophomore year of college). Students could now be admitted to the College after two, three, or four years of study at any high school, and were given placement examinations upon entrance. They were required to take only those courses from which they were not excused by satisfactory performance on those exams.

The most radical aspect of this new scheme was the awarding of the bachelor's degree by the College upon successful completion of the general education requirements, either by placement or by course examination. This was normally expected to be at the end of the student's fourteenth year in school. As the conventional location of the bachelor's degree, then as now, was at the end of the sixteenth year, many educators and College alumni opposed the new program as a "cheapening" of the baccalaureate. Moreover, since baccalaureate degrees under the New College Plan had been awarded not by the College but by the University's departments and professional schools, the new plan was viewed by many faculty as an incursion on their prerogatives. The change was justified by Hutchins on the grounds that the national emergency following Pearl Harbor would require young men bound for military service to compress their education.

The curriculum of the radical new program was to include four separate three-year course sequences (in humanities, natural sciences, reading and writing, and social sciences) plus a year-long course dealing with interrelationships among the various fields of knowledge (Observation, Interpretation, and Integration, or "O.I.I."). Eventually, after about five years of trial and reform, the curriculum was revised to include three-year sequences in humanities, natural sciences, and social sciences, and five more one-year courses. These were English, mathematics, a foreign language, and two "integrative" courses—Organizations, Methods, and Principles of Knowledge (formerly "O.I.I.," now "O.M.P.") and History of Western Civilization.

The new independence of the College from the graduate departments and the organization of course staffs gave rise to another change which had extremely important consequences. As it depended less and less on departmental faculty, the College found that it needed to make its own faculty appointments, and was given that power. Thus, in contrast to earlier and later times, the College faculty came to be predominantly one that was devoted exclusively to developing and teaching general education courses. Soon, the end of the war brought a fresh supply of new faculty eager to make their mark, just as it also brought a mass of students eager to challenge and learn from them. These full-time College faculty members devoted themselves to implementing and refining the experiment in general education that Hutchins and Faust had set in motion.

In the social sciences area, Keohane's course American Political Institutions became the first course in the new three-year social science sequence and was listed as Social Sciences 1 (known familiarly as "Soc 1"). The original Introductory General Course that had been known since 1931 as Social Sciences 1 became the second-year course ("Soc 2"). The elective second-year course dealing with freedom and order, which had been known as Social Sciences 2, was renumbered Social Sciences 3 ("Soc 3").

At first all three of these courses were taught pretty much as they had been previously. There was a shift from three weekly lectures and one discussion session to two weekly lectures and two discussion sessions. Otherwise the changes in these courses were no greater than those stemming from normal year-to-year fluctuation in content. Gradually, however, more significant revisions were undertaken as the College social sciences faculty worked to make the three-year sequences into an intellectually coherent program.

Social Sciences 1 was the first course to be extensively revised. Starting in 1944, a faculty committee that included Keohane, George Probst, Malcolm Sharp, Alan Simpson, and Milton Singer, began to experiment with a new approach to the historical study of American political institutions. Emphasis was placed on exploring a series of crucial debates on public policy in American history through the examination of documentary sources. After four years the results of this experiment were codified and published in 1949 as the renowned two-volume work, *The People Shall Judge*.

The second-year course, Soc 2, kept generally to the themes and format that had been established by Gideonse, Kerwin, and Wirth in 1931 (with cumulative yearly modifications by subsequent course staffs) for the first four years of the new regime. Then in 1946–47, under the direction of David Riesman and the general guidance of Robert Redfield and Milton Singer, the staff substantially reoriented the course around the theme Personality and Culture. Continuity with the work of Soc 1 was achieved by focusing on contemporary American social problems (opening, for example, with Gunnar Myrdal's *An American Dilemma*), and devoted half its length to the study of culture and personality in the context of urban industrial society. There was, nevertheless, a significant difference in design and intent from what the course had been for the preceding fifteen years. The course now derived its central thrust from the conceptual tension between the individual and the collectivity, subsuming the earlier emphasis on interrelations between the various aspects of collectivity.

Social Sciences 3, whose name was Freedom and Order, seems to have remained much the same course throughout the 1940s, the curricular reorganization of 1942 notwithstanding. This was probably due to the fact that it had undergone an ambitious program of revision and refinement by a new staff in 1939 and 1940, the work of the sociologist Edward Shils (formerly an assistant to Louis Wirth) together with Gerhard Meyer, Maynard Krueger, Earl Johnson, and staff chairman Walter Laves.

By 1947 the new three-year Social Sciences 1, 2, 3 sequence was essentially complete, and its rationale was stated by Milton Singer,[2] who succeeded Robert Redfield as chairman of the College Social Sciences faculty. Each course was designed to introduce the student to a different type of social scientific data and a different mode of social scientific inquiry. Social Sciences 1 utilized American documentary materials to demonstrate historical methods of inquiry. Social Sciences 2 used comparative psychological and cross-cultural data to illustrate the new "empirical" social sciences. Social Sciences 3 brought philosophical analysis to bear on major issues of social policy related to freedom in economic,

---

2. M. B. Singer, "The Social Sciences," in *The Idea and Practice of General Education: An Account of the College of the University of Chicago,* by Present and Former Members of the Faculty (Chicago: University of Chicago Press, 1950).

political, and international relations. The staff of each course presupposed this division of labor in planning their lectures and reading assignments. Taken as a unit, the three courses were intended to develop the student into an informed citizen of a modern democracy, capable of critical judgment in the use of social science concepts and literature, both in public and in professional contexts.

To many, this was the classic era of social science general education at Chicago, and the most brilliant era of Soc 2 as well. Probably its most dazzling feature was its staff, whose roster reads like a veritable Who's Who of American social science. A partial list of lecturers for 1947–48 includes, in order of appearance: Morton Grodzins (course chairman), Robert Redfield, Bruno Bettelheim, Everett C. Hughes, Allison Davis, Daniel Bell, Joseph Schwab, David Riesman, Malcolm Sharp, Sol Tax, Barrington Moore, Milton Singer, Robert Havighurst, Fred Eggan, Livio Stecchini, Sylvia Thrupp, Christian Mackauer, Benjamin Nelson, Reuel Denney, and Philip Rieff. The list at other times would have included Reinhard Bendix, Bert Hoselitz, Joseph Gusfield, John Seeley, Edward Shils, Martin Meyerson, Sebastian de Grazia, Philip Hauser, and Robert Winch.

The intellectual force of such a group is overwhelming, and the course they created must have had an unforgettable impact on all who participated in it. Yet there must have been something vital in the course itself, too, that attracted such people and excited their energies. That vital element was, I think, the way in which the staff always reached beyond the materials it taught, elaborating conceptual frameworks in which to present them to the students, transcending the limitations of particular authors and their works by creating dialectical contrasts. There was a sense, indeed, in which the course served as a vehicle for the development of a unified, multidimensional theory of human behavior and its sociocultural context. That was a quest of heroic proportions, yet also one very much in tune with the general intellectual climate of the College, and it elicited the best efforts of many of the most thoughtful and original people of their generation.

III

In 1953 the four-year general education curriculum of the College was abolished as the sole requirement for the bachelor's degree, and the mission of the College, which since 1931 had been "to do the University's work in general higher education," was modified. Divisional specialization was combined with general education in proportions that varied from one division to another, and often from department to department within the same division. Each graduate department negotiated its own degree program with the College faculty, although the latter continued as the "proprietor" of the general education component of the curriculum.

In some divisions, students were able to take only eight or even six of the fourteen year-long courses that had made up the comprehensive general education curriculum. However, most of the degree programs that were negotiated with departments in the Social Sciences Division permitted students to take nearly all of the previously required courses in general education; and, in these, the old curriculum for a time was maintained virtually intact. Thus even under these changed circumstances, Social Sciences 1, 2, and 3 were all continued, though it was no longer required of all students to pass either the placement examination or the comprehensive examination for each course.

After several years of frustrating experience with this piecemeal curriculum, an Executive Committee on Undergraduate Education was appointed by President Lawrence Kimpton. The committee's report proposed a standard curricular format for the College that was adopted in 1958: two years of general education for all students, plus one year of specialized concentration in a department and one year of "free" and "guided" elective courses. Under this new dispensation, the three-year course sequences in the humanities, natural sciences, and social sciences were each required to contract into two-year programs. The actual changes were wrought in different ways during the 1959–60 academic year. The Humanities faculty chose to eliminate its first-year course ("Hum 1," an introduction to literature, music, and art) and to retain its second- and third-year courses on literary analysis ("Hum 2") and the principles of criticism ("Hum 3"). The Natural Science faculty, on the other hand, eliminated the third course of its three-year sequence, and retained basic courses on physical science ("Nat Sci 1") and biological science ("Nat Sci 2"). The Social Science faculty chose a different path. As the school year consisted of three academic quarters, each of the year-long courses was reduced from three to two quarters. Then, one quarter of Social Sciences 3 course material was attached to the remaining two quarters of Social Sciences 1, and a second quarter of the former Social Sciences 3 was appended to the remaining two quarters of Social Sciences 2.

The first course in the new two-year sequence (two-thirds of Soc 1 plus one-third of Soc 3) was relisted as Social Sciences 111–112–113, under the title American Democracy: Its Development and Present Policy Problems. The second course in the new two-year sequence (two-thirds of Soc 2 plus one-third of Soc 3) became Social Sciences 121–122–123, its disparate materials only nominally integrated under the heading Culture and Freedom. Some members of the Soc 3 staff (e.g.,

Maynard Krueger) joined Social Sciences 111–112–113, while others (e.g., Donald Meiklejohn and Gerhard Meyer) joined the staff of Social Sciences 121–122–123. For many, it was not only a forced but an unhappy marriage.

In Social Sciences 121–122–123 (still Soc 2 in the vernacular), the curricular effect of the merger under the rubric Culture and Freedom was to combine empirical-scientific and social-philosophic concerns within a single course. Plato, Kant, and John Stuart Mill had to find an intellectual home in the company of Freud and Marx, Durkheim and Weber, Malinowski, and Mead. The initial tension within the staff between the proponents of these diverse perspectives was very harsh and often quite personal. Yet, with some defections along the way, harmony was gradually achieved thanks in large part to the learned, devoted, and unobtrusive guidance of Gerhard Meyer. Conflict in the course material and in the staff gave way to creative effort, and a complex dialectical synthesis of themes was achieved.

IV

After six years of gradual adjustment and refinement in the two-year Social Sciences sequence, yet another reorganization of the College curriculum was introduced that required further change in the social science general education. In order to achieve a better integration between the College and the graduate departments, Edward Levi (then provost and acting dean of the College) proposed in 1965 that the College be divided into collegiate divisions which would parallel the graduate divisions. Thus were created the Biological Sciences, Humanities, Physical Sciences, and Social Sciences Collegiate Divisions—plus a fifth small unit, an undefined space for experimentation, called the New Collegiate Division. A pattern of joint faculty appointment between the departments and the College was initiated in order to support the intended reintegration of the College into the University as a whole. To offset the centrifugal effect of this design upon students, and to allow them some time in which to choose a field of concentration, the Levi plan mandated that one of the two years of general education in the College be a common year of studies intended mainly for first-year students. The content of this common year, and of the second year of general education, was left unspecified in the Levi memorandum.

The curricular problem of the common year (since renamed the common core) was resolved by an interdivisional committee under the chairmanship of Norton Ginsburg, associate dean of the College, in a mechanically "democratic" fashion. Much as in the New College Plan of 1931, all students in the College were required to take one year-long general course in each of the four main collegiate divisions. (The New Collegiate Division, which as yet had no content or faculty, was excluded from this division of the spoils.) In the same spirit of delegation to experts, the content of these core courses was left to be determined by the faculty of each collegiate division. The Levi plan mandated a "second tier" of general education in the form of four additional year-long courses, and the content of these too were left to be determined by each of the several collegiate divisions for its own students.

The immediate consequence of this change for general education in the social sciences was to compress further the two-year general education sequence into a single year-long course. To accomplish this, the first- and second-year courses were declared to be alternative means for satisfying the student's common core requirement, without regard to their differences in content, aim, or method. This was, of course, a far cry from the integrated program of general education in social science that flourished from the mid-1940s through the mid-1950s. The desire for a more coherent plan led the social sciences faculty in 1966–67 and 1967–68 to experiment with a common core format in which students would choose the first two quarters of one or the other sequence (Social Sciences 111–112 or 121–122), followed by a common third-quarter course for all students (Social Sciences 125).

Social Sciences 111–112 took the old name of Soc 3 (Freedom and Order) and devoted itself "to the study of man in his political and economic order, principally in the context of the American experience." Social Sciences 121–122, which was renamed Character and Society (recalling the old title of Soc 2), stressed "the disciplines of empirical observation, comparative study, and theoretical analysis of regularities and variations in human behavior." The common spring quarter, Social Sciences 125, took a title similar to that formerly used by Social Sciences 111–112–113, Democracy in America, and set itself to consider "the convergence of traditions and concerns represented by Social Sciences 121–122 and 111–112, namely, the scientific study of society and design and justification of civil institutions. . . . Following an analysis of various conceptions of equality, the nature and consequences of stratification in urban-industrial society, and the organization of politics in the United States, the course proceed[ed] to examine the situation of the American Negro in these perspectives and to explore alternative bases for public policy."

This reorganization of the social sciences common core was maintained for two years. By 1968 the faculty decided to revert to the principle of student choice and extended the available options to four alternative year-long courses: Social Sciences 111–112–113, Freedom and Order; Social Sciences 121–122–123, renamed Self, Culture, and Society; Social Sciences 131–132–133, Conflict and Stability in Modern Society; and Social Sciences 141–142–143, Modernization in Old and New States.

The policy of joint appointment to departments and the College was only partially successful. While full-time College appointments ceased, departmental faculty were often reluctant to become very involved in teaching the general education courses. Gradually more and more of the faculty members who did teach general education found themselves also dividing their time between the undergraduate concentrations and graduate teaching, to say nothing of the research which was crucial to their academic advancement. The design and teaching of fully common courses came to demand more time than a "part-time" faculty could devote to it. Finally, ease from the problems of staff recruitment and curricular planning was sought through a scheme in which each of the four parallel courses would have only the autumn and winter quarters' work in common. In the spring quarter, instructors were allowed to offer specialized course variants of their own design, and students were allowed to choose among them.

The common theme for Social Sciences 121, for example, was The Individual and the Collectivity, concentrating intensively on the writings of Freud, Durkheim, G. H. Mead and Edward Sapir. The common theme of Social Sciences 122 was The Life Cycle: Sociocultural Systems and Individual Development, in which students read topically organized selections from Max Weber, Talcott Parsons, Erik Erikson, Jean Piaget, Arnold Van Gennep, Gregory Bateson, David Schneider, Daniel Bell, Robert White, and Bernice Neugarten. In Social Sciences 123, each section was in effect a different course that in some way exemplified the general course theme of Self, Culture and Society, e.g.: Self and Group Processes; The Northern Ghetto; The Phenomenology of Self; The Student, the University, and Social Change; Socialization and Achievement; Social Psychology of International Relations; Law, Deviance, and Compliance; and Adult Socialization—Psychology of the Professions.

Although the search for commonality in the social sciences common core offering was brief, it effected an important redistribution of curricular content and themes among the general education courses, especially Social Sciences 111–112–113 and 121–122–123, which remained the largest course sequences. Social Sciences 111–112–113 had become much more like the old Soc 3 than the old Soc 1. Social Sciences 121–122–123, on the other hand, lost those elements of the old Soc 3 that had been injected into it in 1960, and become much more like the old Soc 2.

V

By 1974 or 1975 at the latest, Self, Culture and Society returned to a fully common three-quarter format. Gradually, the thematic structure of the course came to be that of the present day. The autumn quarter was devoted primarily to the study of social institutions, especially the comparative economic and political institutions of preindustrial and industrial societies, with the reading material typically centered on selections from Marx, Smith, and Weber. The winter quarter was devoted primarily to the analysis of collective and personal symbols and symbolic systems, in such forms as religious rituals and civic ceremonies, dreams and beliefs, with reading selections typically drawn from Freud, Durkheim, Lévi-Strauss, and Foucault. Finally, the spring has characteristically been devoted primarily to the comparative study of psychological development, with the main theorists being Freud, Piaget, Luria, and Vigotskii, and the field of application being gender, race, and ethnopsychology. When reading lists were reviewed by the staff each year, selections from the classic authors were modified in light of recent teaching experience, and the best current writings on these topics were chosen for trial inclusion.

From the 1930s through the 1970s, general education in the social sciences at Chicago has spanned the Great Depression, the rise of dictatorships, the devastation of World War II, the cold war and its domestic threat to civil liberties, the struggle for civil rights, and the campus-led movement to stop the Vietnam war. Under the dedicated leadership of Bert Cohler and John MacAloon, it has valiantly struggled to maintain its vitality through the 1980s. At each stage in its development, it has reflected the intellectual, the social and (in a very broad sense) the political concerns of its faculty and students, while anchoring itself in the paradigmatic works of modern empirical-analytic social science. Thus despite constant change and experimentation, there has been an impressive continuity of purpose.

As Social Science I from 1931 to 1942, as Social Sciences 2 from 1942 to 1960, and as Social Sciences 121–122–123 since then, this course and its companion courses have aimed to use the social sciences to test and develop their ability to help us—as students and faculty, scientists and citizens—to observe, reason, and act rightly in the complex social reality in which we live. The greatness of the course as an intellectual venture is that it has never been content merely to teach what the diverse social sciences are, but has been persistently committed to being a means of creating what a unified social science ought to become.

5

A Ruminating Retrospect on the Liberal Arts, the Social Sciences, and Soc 2

Michael Schudson

Faculty who came to Soc 2 did not all arrive in the same way. Some did not "arrive" at all; they grew up in the College and came to Soc 2 as a natural progression in their lives. Some of the most loyal and distinguished faculty in the course took the class as undergraduates themselves. Reinhard Bendix took Soc 2 when Harry Gideonse, Louis Wirth, and Jerome Kerwin were each teaching separate quarters. David Orlinsky, Bert Cohler, and Mark Galanter, though they tested out of Soc 2, had been students in the College; Joseph Gusfield had taken a special intensive social science course with Milton Singer for students going into the military service. Donald Levine, Sharon Stephens, Robert Foster, and Charles Nuckolls took the course and like Philip Rieff, James Redfield, Melinda Moore, and others, received both their undergraduate and their graduate degrees at Chicago before going on to teach in Soc 2. These faculty members have played a special role in carrying on the traditions of the course and urging on themselves and their colleagues that it live up to their best recollections of what it once was. Gilbert White grew up in the University neighborhood, attended the Lab School, received his A.B., A.M., and Ph.D. from Chicago, and then turned down a teaching job at the University to become president of Haverford College. But he returned in 1956 and taught in Soc 2 "because I enjoyed that style of teaching, knew I would learn much from it, and wanted to demonstrate my support for the approach taken by the College."

Others, especially in the 1940s and 1950s, before Chicago became part of a more tightly integrated national system of universities, were recruited on a very personal, unbureaucratic basis. David Bakan, at the University of Missouri, heard David Riesman lecture there and talked with him. A year later, Reuel Denney came to neighboring Stephens College for a semester, and he and Bakan became good friends. Later, in the 1960s, Denney brought Bakan to the College. Denney himself had come to the College on the urging of David Riesman who had known him when Riesman was at the University of Buffalo Law School and Denney was teaching high school in Buffalo. Denney had been "scouted" by an assistant to Robert Hutchins earlier when he was in Chicago writing a piece on Marshall Field III for *Fortune*. Elsewhere in this volume Lewis Coser recounts the story of his own unorthodox recruitment. Martin Meyerson got to know David Riesman while working in urban renewal on Chicago's South Side. He left Chicago for a research fellowship at Harvard, but returned when Riesman, Morton Grodzins, and Champion Ward asked him to teach in Soc 2. "I said I wasn't qualified," he recalls. "And they told me, 'That's why we want you.'"

Perhaps it was. Many of the key figures in Soc 2 did not have conventional academic credentials. Riesman had a law degree. Denney had no advanced degree. Lewis Coser was a free-lance writer. Daniel Bell was a political journalist, also without an advanced degree. He was introduced to the College through Maynard Krueger. They knew each other through the socialist movement, especially the National Educational Committee for a New Party. Mark Benney had been a professional thief but had no other academic credentials.

As for Riesman, he was brought to the College by Edward Shils and, with very little social science training, used Soc 2 to educate himself in social science while he taught it. "I had four children, I could not go get a Ph.D., this was a unique heaven-sent opportunity to learn on the job." In the 1940s, Shils took a special, proprietary interest in the College and was personally responsible for recruiting many of the faculty who figured in Soc 2. During the war, Shils worked for the Office of Facts and Figures, where he came to know Sebastian de Grazia, Morris Janowitz, Barrington Moore, and Sylvia Thrupp. He was instrumental in bringing all of them to Chicago—and de Grazia, Moore, and Thrupp joined the staff of Soc 2.

From the vantage of the 1990s, this pattern of recruitment is unique. There was no set procedure, no bureaucracy to run through, no advertisements to post. Moreover, there was no "department" to hire into. People were hired not to be productive scholars, they were hired to teach undergraduates in a course with a curriculum already set (though annually renegotiated) and a pattern of pedagogy already established. There was little or no concern with tenure, long-term academic careers, and so forth. The College, as Lewis Coser remembers it, was "the most unbureaucratic institution in higher education ever."

This was not to last. But some of the strength of this early pattern was sustained by a kind of elective affinity. Not a few of the people who came to the course in the later years came already socialized into the peculiarity of interdisciplinary undergraduate teaching. Cesar Grana, who came to the College in the mid-1950s, found nothing surprising in Soc 2. It was "comfortable" for him, as well it might have been. He had a B.A. in art history, an M.A. in history, and Ph.D. in sociology at Berkeley where he studied under Leo Lowenthal and under former Soc 2 instructor Reinhard Bendix. Susanne Rudolph, when she moved to Chicago in 1964, was already familiar with the course and its ethos from her experience in teaching with David Riesman at Harvard. I myself was led to the course by David Riesman and Daniel Bell when I came in 1976; indeed, Daniel Bell was the person who urged me to think about Chicago in the first place—and precisely because he believed I would be well suited for the free-wheeling interdisciplinary air of the College. I was further presocialized as an undergraduate at Swarthmore College in a newly established Department of Sociology and Anthropology, founded by Leon Bramson, a student in the College and in Soc 2 who instituted at Swarthmore a program marked with visible signs of his Soc 2 roots. In the introductory sociology-anthropology course, I read Marx, Weber, Durkheim, Freud, and urban ethnography, including *Street Corner Society*. Soc 2, to me, seemed natural.

Increasingly, however, recruitment to Soc 2 occurred after a faculty member had been committed to a department, not before. In part, this came through recruiting Chicago graduate students in sociology or anthropology who had not themselves been students in the College—such as McKim Marriott, Ralph Nicholas, Paule Verdet, and Rosalie Wax. In part, it came through persuading junior faculty recruited by the graduate departments to devote teaching time to the College. Richard Flacks, for instance, came to the Department of Sociology in 1964 from Michigan. Don Levine urged him to teach in Soc 2. He tried it out and eventually the course came to be his primary allegiance at the University. Levine, and before him Elihu Katz, acted as a kind of College representative in the Department of Sociology and encouraged colleagues there to teach in the College.

What was the experience of these and other faculty members in Soc 2? Why does the course continue to mean so much to the faculty who stay at Chicago and to many of those who have moved to other institutions? I offer some of my own thoughts here, aided by interviews and correspondence with a number of people involved in the course through the years. This essay has less the weight of "oral history" than of reflections, guided by and responding to the recollections of many others.

When Richard Flacks told his department chairman, Philip Hauser, that he was teaching in Soc 2, Hauser replied that "there have never been any sociologists who have taught Soc 2" and so he thought that Flacks would be a good addition to the course. His remark made it clear to Flacks that there was tension between the department and the College, something that, as a newcomer to Chicago, he had not understood. Oldtimers did not necessarily understand it either. Howard Becker, who taught in both the College and the Department of Sociology between 1951 and 1953, recalls that he was oblivious to the wars raging between the two groups. As a student of Everett Hughes, he was more aware of the links between them, recalling that David Riesman used to sit in regularly in Hughes' classes.

But the extent of the gulf between the departments and graduate divisions, on the one hand, and the College, on the other, is difficult to exaggerate. Gilbert White recalls that some of his colleagues in the graduate division told him he was wasting his time teaching in the College. The president of the University told him the same thing when he won the Quantrell Award for excellence in undergraduate teaching. White found the inclination of some of the graduate faculty to treat the College faculty as second-class citizens "a continuing source of irritation"—despite the fact, as he recalls, that the sections in Soc 2 were generally more exciting than graduate seminars.

Most universities in this country experience tension between the demands of graduate teaching and research and the demands of undergraduate instruction. But nowhere do these conflicts possess the drama they do at Chicago, and nowhere, with the possible exception of Columbia, do the partisans of undergraduate teaching have so weighty and even arrogant a posture in the conflict. In most institutions, people who emphasize undergraduate teaching see themselves as failures at "real" scholarship or as embattled populists, defending the rights of the downtrodden undergraduates against the imperialism of self-seeking graduate departments. Sentiments of the latter sort can be found at Chicago, certainly. But there is a stronger tradition at Chicago. The College faculty, especially in the 1950s, felt themselves the elite, more learned and original than their counterparts in the departments. In the later forties, the Soc 2 staff was surprised that David Riesman deigned to sit in on classes in the Department of Sociology. The departments seemed beneath the serious intellectual interests of College faculty. Joe Gusfield recalls that the end product of the departments was a correct answer, the end product of the College was "good talk," and the College faculty saw "good talk" as the greater achievement. Elihu Katz, in David Orlinsky's recollection, said that he came to teach in Soc 2 as well as the Sociology Department so that he "could have opinions." For some, the College came to be seen as the home of true scholarship as against narrow professional research.

The College arrogance did not necessarily serve the College well and, according to David Riesman, its self-righteous rejection of the graduate divisions was neither wise nor prudent. Riesman took issue with those he called the "College patriots." He recalls, "I thought they were alienating the divisions. I thought it was a mistake when they succeeded in making the College self-sealed by institutionalizing O.M.P. and history. Don't close off electives, I advised, so the divisions can have a stake in undergraduates." (Organizations, Methods, and Principles of Knowledge and the History of Western Civilization were courses designed to extend general education through the senior year, although Western Civilization began as a reaction against O.M.P. and an alternative to it.) It seemed to me in the late 1970s that the Soc 2 staff spent inordinate amounts of time complaining that the administration or the departments did not treat the College right. There was a lot of bitching combined with a certain arrogant "Who needs the departments anyway?" defiance, a sense that Soc 2 was (and would have to be) its own majority.

The meetings of the Soc 2 staff have been the heart of the course and they have often been, as Joe Gusfield recalls, "brilliant conversations." They are in many respects the most vital product of the course, the test of the quality of education itself. Daniel Bell wrote of Chicago in his study of general education at Columbia: "The courses, as I can testify from personal experience, were extraordinary intellectual adventures for the teaching staff; and perhaps this was its prize, if unintended virtue, for what a teacher finds exciting he can communicate best to his students. Whether in the end the courses had the intellectual unity or theoretical clarity claimed for them is moot." Reinhard Bendix agreed that staff meetings were scintillating during his experience in the mid-1940s, but he found them "scintillating to the point of exhaustion, and this finally drove me out, scintillating for the sake of scintillating." This was particularly true, he believes, not in the regular staff meetings but in the time devoted to making up questions for the general exams. The staff worked all year long on the questions, and they would only accept questions (these were of a multiple-choice sort) that the staff members themselves would all answer in the same way. This was difficult in itself; in addition, people were constantly trying to "be brilliant." For Bendix, the enormous pressure of this peer-group situation contributed to his leaving the University. For Joe Gusfield, the situation prompted him to move from the Soc 2 staff to the more nurturing environment of Soc 3. David Riesman remembers the "intense intellectuality" of the College as both "its glory and its nemesis," a sentiment echoed by many others I talked to.

The staff meetings that are remembered with such fondness, and such pain, from the 1950s continued to be intellectual cauldrons in the 1960s and, to some extent, have continued so ever since. In the 1960s,

David Orlinsky remembers, the staff often met over lunch at the Quadrangle Club and sometimes the discussion was so intense and engaging that no one wanted to leave the table. In the very early sixties, however, the staff meetings had been scenes of bitter fighting as the effort was made to meld Soc 3 with Soc 2, and Orlinsky remembers leaving those meetings with a splitting headache and recalls seeing Gerhard Meyer sometimes in tears, though it was in part his saintliness and his erudition that helped hold the enterprise together.

Later, I think, while the staff meetings have continued to be intellectually stimulating and convivial, they lack the intensity that, from all accounts, they once had. Less has been at stake during the past decade, when almost the entire staff has been rooted in graduate departments, even if their more heartfelt loyalty is to the College. Reinhard Bendix remembered what Gerhard Meyer said to him when he left Chicago: "You can leave, I cannot. I have become a specialist in general education." Soc 2 now has no such specialists—at least, none who are not also fully accredited as research scholars. The link to the past is through the Levines, Orlinskys, and Cohlers who remember, learned from, and taught with the Meyers and Kruegers and Mackauers. But more and more of the staff now are not born with general education in their hearts, though they may achieve an attachment to it—or even have it thrust upon them.

Moreover, there has been less at stake in the social sciences than there once was. The energy and passion of the 1970s and early 1980s, it seems, lay far from the concerns of Soc 2 in aspects of cognitive science—perhaps more with mathematical modeling in economics and sociology, and with other areas where more and more sophisticated work speaks elegantly to fewer and fewer people. In the 1950s with culture and personality, the 1960s with questions about modernization and new nations, there was an energy in the social sciences that fed into Soc 2 rather than skirting it. The work in the 1970s and 1980s concerned with the great questions of social theory that Soc 2 focuses on tended to be skeptical and critical, an anthropology that pokes holes in generalization and historical work that makes one suspicious of social theory altogether, revisions of Marx and revivals of Weber that blur all lines between them. Excitement in psychoanalytic circles about the work of Heinz Kohut in the late 1970s, it seems to me, never reached a level where it could be translated to the classroom, let alone to staff members who were not "adepts" themselves in psychoanalytic theory.

Today, however, much of the old drama has returned to the staff meetings, according to John MacAloon, spurred by the course's encounter with the new "cultural studies" approach in its various aspects. Critical theorists like Moishe Postone and David Laitin, younger anthropologists interested in transnational cultural flows, like Sharon Stephens, Andrew Apter, and Robert Foster, and feminist scholars like Lisa Disch, Melinda Moore, and Pauline Strong, among others, have revitalized debates about how the course today should realize its abiding commitment to the encounter of Euro-American modernity with varieties of "otherness." In the 1980s, these new energies in large part resulted from the influx of Harper and Mellon instructors, three-year postdoctoral teaching appointments initiated and controlled entirely by the College. While these appointments were in part a response to a growing unwillingness (or inability) of departmental faculty to teach in the general-education core courses and to the university-wide decreases in the number of assistant professors, Soc 2 was able to refresh itself with fine young scholars committed to cross-disciplinary research and general-education teaching. Because of the term nature of these appointments, however, they hardly represent a return to College hiring independence of the forties and fifties. But they have helped make Soc 2 once again a center of social science debate for accomplished teacher-scholars who in some cases are too unconventional for the graduate departments.

If the staff meeting has been one center of the course, the classroom has been another. But what kind of classroom? In private higher education there is what might be called a cult of the seminar. The Carman Committee at Columbia University embodied it well: "For many years we have given in Columbia College no required courses of the pontifical type, in part because the students know the defects of the type, but principally because the man-to-man effectiveness of a proved instructor, young or old, with a small group—usually twenty or twenty-five—has had much to do with active undergraduate interest in the introductory work, and with the easy and steady improvement of the courses themselves." At Chicago, discussion sections of this sort met twice a week, but these were combined with two general lectures a week for all the students. The lectures in the early 1950s were central elements in the course, particularly for the faculty. They provided an arena for the faculty to show their stuff to one another. But by the 1970s, the role of the lecture had declined sharply. Lectures were once a week, not twice a week. By the late seventies, they were presented only during the first six or seven weeks of the quarter, since student attendance declined precipitously thereafter. Instead of seeing the lecture as a great opportunity to impress one's colleagues, it came to be seen as a chore. The chairman of the course often found it difficult to recruit staff members to deliver the lectures. As often as not, the key lectures were offered by other University faculty, specialists in some field, rather than members of the Soc 2 staff. (This was to some extent true in the early years, too.

132

Bruno Bettelheim, who never taught in the course, is well remembered as a lecturer in it.) For students, the lectures came to be regarded as a kind of "extra credit" rather than central orienting materials for the course. Without a common exam, abandoned in the sixties, each section is very autonomous despite a common reading list. In recent years, the lectures seem to be making a comeback in both faculty and student involvement, but they are not the showcase they once were. Parts of *The Lonely Crowd* and Philip Rieff's *Freud: The Mind of a Moralist* were presented as Soc 2 lectures. Students in the forties and early fifties were, in a sense, students of the whole staff; lectures were important and students attended a variety of sections, moving around at will if they so desired.

Despite the importance of lectures, the focus on the classroom was intense in the early years; indeed, Donald Meiklejohn, among others, tried unsuccessfully to do away with the lectures and institute a plan of four sections a week. The classroom was taken seriously. Leon Bramson, a distinguished sociologist who founded the Department of Sociology and Anthropology at Swarthmore College, recalls being a student at Chicago in the late 1940s: "The lectures were not where the action was; they were not a waste of time but I didn't get very much out of them. What Dan Bell did with us in the classroom, grasping the essentials of the reading, that was where the course really happened. And it was difficult, reading Freud, reading Marx, reading Mannheim. It was my introduction to the social sciences; it was also an introduction to how to be a great teacher."

From the teacher's side, it was also an introduction. "My education began at Chicago," Bell told me. "I'd be up till two, three, four in the morning trying to stay ahead of the students." He had read some Weber in graduate school, but no Freud, and little in economics besides Marx.

Howard Becker was assigned to the "midyear" class for high school students entering the College after a January high school graduation. It was a big class by College standards, thirty-five or forty students. The contrast, Becker recalls, with his experience teaching graduate students in sociology at the same time, was extraordinary. In the Department of Sociology, Becker substituted for Everett Hughes in a class on fieldwork. "Here I was, an instructor, nobody, and all the students wrote down everything I said. But in the midyear Soc 2 class, you couldn't say what time it was without starting an argument." Milton Singer, master of the social sciences, came to sit in on one class. Becker recalls that, even then, Milton Singer had an air about him; his distinction and his wisdom were almost palpable. Still, when Singer entered the class discussion after fifteen or twenty minutes, he was not met with much

133

deference. He raised his hand, made a comment, asked a question, probing, trying to push the discussion along. But the position he took was one that the class had gone over and found holes in during the previous session. "Someone started to criticize him," Becker remembers, "and then others joined in and before long the students were jumping all over him. He just sat back grinning."

Becker also remembers learning a great lesson about classroom teaching by sitting in on David Riesman's sections—it was common practice to sit in on the sections of colleagues. "I sat in on Riesman's classes frequently. He taught me an incredible lesson—there wasn't anything too dumb a student could say—everything he treated with respect and treated seriously," a style Bert Cohler embodies in the course today. Soc 2, Becker says, "was and still is a model of how to do undergraduate teaching. I still hate giving lecture courses. . . . I picked up a lot of tricks about how to do that kind of discussion-section teaching, not only from Riesman but from others too."

Others have similar recollections. During Riesman's years at the College from 1948 to 1958, he was for many a model of teaching excellence. Paule Verdet recalls Riesman's warning his colleagues against being too aggressive with the more naive students, even warning them against dislodging the students from their simple views. "He was very sensitive to what held a person together. Intelligence is not all." Not that Riesman was a self-assured teacher himself. He recalls how competitive section leaders were for students, and remembers that Dan Bell's and Phil Rieff's sections always had enviably high enrollments. Some section leaders were more spellbinding than others, and Riesman remembers that he could "hear the raucousness of Dan Bell's section through the thin walls of Cobb Hall."

Reuel Denney remembers, "I was never any good at popular Socratic methods sometimes used in the College," and it is clear from his tone, and that of others, that the pressure to use a lively discussion format was severe. Denney recalls:

> One of my sharpest memories is of an early year in my work with Soc 2 when I had a class just after lunch on the top floor of Cobb Hall. In this class I maintained a low-pressure conversational approach, and at the end of the fifth week I had only three students left. (In another section I had an over-registration overflow.) Each day when I climbed up I wondered when I would run out of students entirely and have to report my bankruptcy to Chairman Milton Singer. But *one* student, a World War II veteran who was majoring in chemistry, must have seen how desperate I was and he kept on coming. So for the rest of the term we had the

discussion to ourselves and after that I avoided after-lunch classes on the fourth floor of Cobb.

(Robert Ginsberg, a student in Denney's section in 1953–54, who has contributed a memoir to this volume, remembers Denney as "an engaging teacher, gifted with sparkling expressiveness," and as a teacher who, as a poet himself, was a gentle reader of students' own hesitant efforts.)

Paule Verdet remembers the competition between sections, too, in her first year of teaching Soc 2 in 1956. She taught three sections. Her 9:30 section, sparked by one marvelous student, was wonderful. Her 11:30 section was good, though not so sparkling. And her 1:30 class (there may be a pattern here) was terrible. In that section, one young woman urged her to sit in on Sally Cassidy's sections to see someone who really knew how to teach. Verdet, a close friend of Cassidy's and her colleague today at Boston University, said to the student, "Sally Cassidy thinks and talks very fast. I think and talk very slow. I have to find my style." Whether that was important to the student or not, Verdet says today, she does not know, but it was important for her to articulate that point for herself. "There was," she recalls, "this heightening of the personality of each of us. It came in no small part from sitting in on people's lectures. And their sitting in on yours. It had to be the very best you could do."

Riesman's style, which Becker and others so admired, was a personal style he brought with him when he arrived at Chicago. He was an ethnographer of the classroom, intent on knowing who his students were and what aspirations and abilities they brought to their education experience. In 1936, when he and others from the Harvard Law School took over the University of Buffalo Law School, he stood apart from his colleagues in his teaching inclinations. The others, including Mark DeWolfe Howe, were all ardent New Dealers, eager to teach constitutional law and administrative law, the subjects of greatest national political and intellectual interest. Riesman chose to teach property law and criminal law and started a new course on Ordinances of the City of Buffalo. "I taught them," Riesman recalls, "how to attach a refrigerator in New York State." He recognized that the students at Buffalo were headed for local law practice as solo practitioners or in small firms and would not, except in the rarest instance, want or have the opportunity for a cosmopolitan legal career. But he did not see his focus on local ordinances and unglamorous statutes as a descent to a lesser intellectual level. He was genuinely interested in the nitty-gritty of the law and in the realities of the lives of his students; he saw, and wrote about, and taught to the larger issues concerned in both, but there, as later at Chicago, through the medium of the thoroughly empirical.

135

So when Riesman came to the University, he was ready to question the Chicago ethos of Great Books. "Great Books had 'mana' for students and staff," he found. He rebelled at this and took up as his mission the introduction of more contemporary social research, especially fieldwork, and the use of "raw materials" in the course (as Jonathan Smith does today). If one axis of pedagogical choice was finding the right balance between lecture and section, another concerned the balance between Great Books and empirical social research. This is one of the continuing tensions in the course. While in the recent past there has been an understanding that both kinds of material deserve a place in the course, the battle in the earlier years was less accommodating. One side felt that a classical *explication de texte* approach, focusing on the great social theorists and playing down, or leaving out, works of contemporary social science, should be the style of the course. Others felt that the classics should not be treated as a sacred canon but as sources of ideas to which contemporary research in the social sciences gave substance. Lew Coser left Soc 2 over this issue. Riesman's influence was especially strong. "I did not know," Coser recalls, "that junior members of the staff were not supposed to object." He objected, argued for a focus on the great theorists, but his viewpoint did not prevail. He left Chicago to finish his doctorate at Columbia, and went on to teach at Brandeis thereafter. (Not that Coser was without empirical inclinations himself: Don Levine, a student in the course in 1948–49, recalls that Lew and Rose Coser led students on tours of the Gary steel mills.)

Howard Becker says he remembers having worked to include a piece of contemporary industrial sociology, by Donald Roy, on the reading list, and that he thought that was going against David Riesman's wishes—though, in retrospect, he is not certain that that was so. There was tension in the course centering on Riesman. Riesman held strong ideas about how the course should proceed, but he also held a commitment to being democratic. When things were not going his way, some colleagues recall, he would visibly sulk and this would make people anxious.

Some years later, after Riesman had left for Harvard, Elihu Katz came to Chicago from Columbia, interested in Soc 2, but skeptical of what to him was still too great an emphasis on sacred texts. One of his memos from the early sixties indicates his skepticism about the sacred cows of the course: "I now agree that Veblen is a serious candidate for omission. There is a certain delight, still, in reading Veblen, but I think we can do more for him by reading some of his successors. We need not always honor these men by reading them in the original. By the way, it seems to me that the lecture on Veblen ought to draw on materials from consumer research. The whole field of 'motivation research' is a direct outgrowth of Veblen plus psychoanalysis plus survey research." Even more heretically, he wrote: "Weber, too, is very difficult going for the students. Again, I am not sure whether some alternative reading might not be more desirable. For example, there is Blau's little book called *Bureaucracy in Modern Society.*" That degree of heresy did not find a sympathetic response, though Blau's work was later read in combination with Weber.

By the 1970s, the battle between classic texts and contemporary social research was settled. The core of the course would be the classic texts but there was to be (if possible) the reading of a full ethnography of a simple society and there was to be a sampling of contemporary social research illustrative of issues raised by the great theorists. The difficulty, however, was to get people to agree on what current social research was both exemplary and available in paperback. Agreement on Freud, Marx, Weber, and Durkheim was easy—though *which* Freud or which Marx or which Weber was a matter of dispute. On Durkheim, in the past decade, with the strong influence of the anthropologists on the staff, there was no question but that *The Elementary Forms* was the text of choice. Other theorists have not had the same lasting power, though Veblen, and later Erik Erikson, George Herbert Mead, and Jean Piaget appear in different eras with some frequency. Of ethnographic works, favorites have been William Whyte's *Street Corner Society,* Evans-Pritchards's *The Nuer,* Victor Turner on the Ndembu *Forest of Symbols,* and Janice Boddy's *Wombs and Alien Spirits.* In the 1970s, detailed studies of industrialization in America or England gained favor as a kind of ethnographic work themselves, especially E. P. Thompson's *Making of the English Working Class* and A. F. C. Wallace's *Rockdale.* Today, debate centers on inclusion of books like Foucault's *Discipline and Punish,* Todorov's *The Conquest of America,* and Sahlins' *Stone Age Economics* as mixed theoretical and historical texts.

In a memo to the staff in 1966, Richard Flacks stated the concept of the reading list well: "The overall design . . . has been to take certain central 'classic' works as a starting point, then to develop a series of topics and readings which illustrate how a scientific tradition has emerged from the issues embodied in the classical work. Interwoven with this perspective is an attempt to illustrate the variety of research methods available in sociology, psychology, anthropology, and social psychology. Finally many of the readings have been selected because they seem likely to illuminate aspects of social life with which students have had direct experience."

The search for a reading list was a recurrent concern of the staff, not always one regarded with enthusiasm. Cesar Grana recalled from the 1950s that it was "a chimerical enterprise, the search for the ideal reading list." He recalled the staff's "alchemical notion" that texts or a group of texts would embody the idea of the whole course. "Every year we went on the search."

Some things taken for granted in the search were not necessarily accepted in the rest of the academic world. For instance, the idea that the social sciences could and should be integrated was assumed. Howard Becker remembers, "I always regarded sociology and anthropology as the same thing. I knew there were people in the two fields who didn't know that, but they were simply wrong." Becker came to Soc 2 with this emphasis, having studied with W. Lloyd Warner and Robert Redfield, but Soc 2 embodied this same spirit, not so much as a program to champion but as an intellectual starting point.

The assumption of the unity of the social sciences could take on extreme or heroic proportions. If Riesman's approach, emphasizing the variety of human experiences, doggedly returning to the empirical, was at one end of the Soc 2 mode, Benjamin Nelson is recalled by many as standing at the other end. Riesman remembers Nelson's message to be that " 'all these writers are saying the same thing': there was a great push at Chicago for the unity of knowledge, and Nelson did it with great erudition and panache." Nelson would walk into Mandel Hall for lectures with several assistants carrying huge piles of books, and before the lecture was done, he would have quoted from each one of them.

The quest for unity in thought and a pantheon of great authors was sometimes matched by a drive for coherent curricular structure. I have read sheafs of memos trying to articulate the deep structure of the course, the reasons why readings would be presented in a certain order, the intricate dialectical connections between the three quarters of the sequence. When I taught in the course in the late seventies, David Orlinsky regularly employed his own variant of the course, sacrificing the principle of a common curriculum for all staff and students in favor of what seemed to him the more vital principle of structural coherence. He felt, I think, that the reading list each year was becoming too much of a compromise and too much a list of the staff's favorite books, regardless of the sense the books made as a curricular unit. He was right, but it is only now that I understand his faith in the enterprise of creating purer conceptual coherence in a reading list.

Soc 2 came to have a classic structure with considerable continuity through close textual analysis of Smith, Freud, Marx, Weber, and Durkheim. At the same time, the College was losing its classical structure during the 1950s and 1960s in a process that David Orlinsky and Champion Ward describe in their essays. While local Chicago lore sees the weakening of general education requirements and the overarching ideal of general education as a posthumous attack by the divisions on Robert Hutchins, the pressures that led to changes at Chicago were pressures of national scope. When Chicago abolished a four-year general education curriculum as the sole requirement for the bachelor's degree in 1953, Columbia in the same year confined general education to the first two years, to be combined with a "major" system. To fulfill major requirements, Columbia students often took introductory disciplinary courses first and postponed their general education courses till later, further weakening the unity of the system.

For Hutchins, the College had been a terminal educational experience for most students, not an interim step on the way to professional schools. But with growing numbers of students moving on to graduate school after World War II, the context in which general education had been conceived was changing. As David Orlinsky recounts in this volume, Soc 2 was originally the second year-long sequence of three courses in the social sciences. In 1960, Soc 3 was disbanded and its subject matter distributed to Soc 1 and Soc 2. By 1965 Soc 1 and Soc 2 became alternative, rather than successive, common-year courses. Students were obliged to take only one, and several other alternatives sprang up as well. In 1968 the third quarter of Soc 2 became whatever the individual instructor chose, so that the "common" curriculum in the social sciences was reduced to two quarters. With Ralph Nicholas as course chairman, there was a "restoration" as Nicholas, Donald Levine, and McKim Marriott tried also to bring back the common, multiple-choice exam, but gave up the project in the face of tremendous student resistance. Restoration was very incomplete, though a full-year common Soc 2 was restored in 1974 and continues to this day. But the general education sequences, by the 1970s, were closely linked to the respective graduate divisions. Unitary general education, divorced from graduate education and the divisions, no longer exists. As a grand vision, the Hutchins College is long gone.

The decline of general education as a full, four-year lock-step curriculum came about for a number of reasons, and former Soc 2 faculty member Daniel Bell has discussed this better than anyone. Some of the reasons for the decline of general education were intellectually salutary. At both Columbia and Chicago, the rise of interest in Eastern civilizations forced the question of why the colleges offered such a Western-centered curriculum. Graduate schools grew in power and once again the prestige attached to research rather than teaching was on the increase. This was not simply the triumph of vocationalism. In the social sciences in the 1950s and 1960s, there was a sense of great promise and intellectual enthusiasm, from culture and personality studies to cognitive psychology to systems theory and cybernetics to new developments in economics, and there was a sense that it might just all break open and come together. At Chicago and Columbia, at least, in Bell's view, the changes in general education were prompted more by genuine intellectual considerations than by crass vocationalism.

The question of non-Western civilization has probably been the most intellectually perplexing challenge for Soc 2. Even at the fiftieth-anniversary celebration in 1982, Kim Marriott's renewed plea for a less ethnocentric course proved very controversial. When Susanne Rudolph made the apparently even more modest remark that Marx and Weber do not apply to India and China, I saw several of my former colleagues in the course wince as if physically struck. Susanne Rudolph had begun Social Science 141–42–43 in 1968 as a new core course that would focus on non-Western civilizations. The comparative emphasis she and others stressed emerged under the influence of Robert Redfield and Milton Singer. Redfield had pioneered work on general education courses in Indian, Chinese, and Islamic civilizations, and Singer carried on his project while at the same time creating the country's leading program in Indian studies. Singer, one of the key figures in the course for many years finally left Soc 2 because he felt it too ethnocentric. "I've had second thoughts since then," he said, "but contact with other cultures shows me our ethnocentrism is not so easy to slough off." Soc 141–42–43 did not work. It was shaped too much by the professional interests of the faculty, Rudolph believes, and not enough by concern with general education. By the early 1970s, most of its pioneers had returned to Soc 2.

But not, I think, without significantly changing the course. Despite Riesman's insistence on culture and personality as a focus of the course, this still meant, for most of the 1950s and 1960s, striving for a unitary view of human psyche and society. An anthropological concern for the special qualities of different cultures made more of a dent in the course after the 141–42–43 interregnum, it seems to me. This has been represented in the staffing of the course—with anthropologists Raymond Fogelson, Kim Marriott, Ralph Nicholas, and John MacAloon as key figures. Can one even speak of *personality* or *self* in non-Western societies? Are not our very concepts culturally specific? Questions of this sort entered the curriculum more centrally in the 1970s. When, in the late seventies and eighties, the course was filled out with Harper and Mellon Fellows and was serving (haphazardly at first) as a training ground in teaching for postdoctoral scholars, the staff regularly found anthropology Ph.D.'s the most attractive candidates for Soc 2. The orientation of the course fit better with graduate training in anthropology than graduate training in any other field. This was not entirely coincidental. When Ralph Nicholas taught the first-year graduate anthropology seminar, he essentially adapted the Soc 2 reading list for more advanced students. The orientation of anthropology to the study of whole societies is consistent with the Soc 2 emphasis. On the other hand, Soc 2 emphasizes the rise of *industrial* society or, alternatively, of modernity. But it may be that the the course's interest in Weber is more on the concept of authority than the modern forms of bureaucracy, and the interest in Durkheim as much in understanding principles that govern the "world we have lost" as in discussing his diagnosis of the problems of organically solidary societies.

The apparent continuity of the reading list may mask changes in the meanings attributed to the readings. One theme in the course which has probably been represented by different figures at different times is pessimism. Freud, at one time, embodied this theme, although, as the chosen reading shifted from *Civilization and Its Discontents* to *Interpretation of Dreams* and *General Introduction to Psychoanalysis*, I think the lesson of Freud may have changed from the idea of human limits (as exemplified by the notion of the "economics of libido") to the idea of scientific possibility (as shown by the capacity to interpret the apparently uninterpretable and by the model of human connection and communication exemplified in the analytic relationship). Marx, meanwhile, has become less an embodiment of hope—socialist convictions did not run strong in the Soc 2 staff in the 1970s—than an exemplar of passion. I suspect it is the energy of his prose rather than the convictions of his analysis that sustains staff interest in Marx today. But I am guessing here, and it may not be possible to characterize the staff as a whole for any era. There has always been more agreement on what the great texts are than on what the key messages of the texts might be.

The substance of Soc 2 became less political between 1972 and 1982, it seems to me, in subtle but important ways. From early on, Soc 2 focused not only on society but on *democratic* society. An introduction to Soc 2 from 1947–48 makes it clear that the course concentrates on questions of inequality in American society because they are urgent matters to "believers in democratic ideals." Readings not only dealt directly with contemporary "social problems" but compared the Soviet political system to the American. This emphasis was somewhat muted in the "culture and personality" heyday of the mid-fifties but came back strongly with the efforts in the early sixties to merge Soc 2 and Soc 3 into a course called Culture and Freedom. When Soc 2 became an independent three-quarter sequence again, the "freedom" dropped out and by 1967–68 the course was known as Character and Society, later Self, Culture, and Society. The course in the 1970s was a far cry from the 1962–63 version, for instance, with a winter quarter devoted to questions of social class in Chicago, delinquent gangs, the structure of social services, and urban housing and educational policy, and a spring quarter on the Soviet system and readings from John Dewey to C. Wright Mills to Talcott Parsons on the "mass democratic model" of politics in the United States.

The student movement, the civil rights struggle, and the antiwar movement of the 1960s did not by any means leave Soc 2 untouched, but the continuity of the course in the face of the turbulence of the sixties may underline what Daniel Bell recalls as a strain of pessimism in Soc 2 in the 1950s—and in the fifties in general. Bell was part of a study group initiated by Rabbi Maurice Pokarsky at the Hillel Foundation, which included another Soc 2 instructor, Ben Nelson. The group examined theology and theologically inclined writings, including Reinhold Niebuhr, Kierkegaard, and Kafka, and talked of the sources of evil in the world, of the quest for power, of idolatry, of egoism as a will to power. This tempered Bell's enthusiasm for conventional social science and interested him in alternative models of sociology, like Dilthey's. Bell's direction was not typical of Soc 2 faculty in general, but it seems right to me to identify a skepticism in the Soc 2 curriculum, at the least, and perhaps a pessimism. Freud, despite his own staunch belief in the possibility of a true science, offers continuing support in Soc 2 for the conviction that people cannot have all they want, indeed, cannot even control the expression of their desires. What optimism exists in the course has been more for the achievements of close reading and critical analysis as a method of approaching the world than for any substantial change that analysis—or political action, for that matter— might bring about.

Most recently, American economic and political decline, the end of the cold war, renewed public attention to homelessness, racism, and underclass poverty, the greater numbers of children of the new immigration, on the one hand, and of middle-class divorce, on the other, currently populating Soc 2 classrooms, as well as the Persian Gulf war, are altering the public context of the course for instructors and students alike. Considerable staff efforts have been made of late to distribute readings centered on gender politics across the curriculum, replacing, for example, *Rockdale* with Nancy Cott's *The Bonds of Womanhood*, Goffman with Arlie Hochschild's *The Managed Heart,* and Geertz's writings on Bali with Lila Abu-Lughod's *Veiled Sentiments.* The presence in and around Soc 2 of intellectual historians like Steve Lestition and American studies specialists like Howard Brick and Martin Burke, together with the Ford Foundation–sponsored Core Course Workshop and visiting-lecturer series, have helped regularize and expand staff debate on curricular politics and public politics. Selections from Foucault and, less frequently, Bourdieu, on schooling as political discipline and status acquisition have been deployed, with mixed results, to engage

student interest in curricular politics. Whether these current developments will alter the strand of critical pessimism I detect in the Soc 2 tradition remains to be seen.

As the overall structure of general education at Chicago became less
overbearing or comprehensive, the examination structure of the course
also changed. In 1963–64 Soc 2 began to give quarterly rather than
yearly grades. As late as summer 1962, the course had been graded on
the basis of a single comprehensive exam. From 1963–64 on, grades
were based on term papers as well as final exams. The exams had been a
centerpiece of the course. "The big trauma associated with that class
were the examination questions," Howard Becker says. He remembers
his best solution to the problem of making up "those damn multiple-
choice questions." He and Rosalie Wax went to work on the questions
over a pitcher of martinis. "When you're stoned enough you can make
them up by the bushel basket." They sorted out the salvageable ones a
day or two later.

Paule Verdet, who became College examiner for a time, does not remember the comprehensive examinations fondly. "What it gave me was
a sense of how arbitrary those multiple-choice questions are. My colleagues couldn't answer each other's questions. They knew too much.
How could we know our students knew just enough?" Still, the abandonment of the common exam meant also that staff members had less
stake in one another's teaching and could more easily tolerate a diversity of viewpoints rather than seeing diversity and disagreement as a
challenge to greater clarity and a call to fierce discussional battle.

When I began teaching in Soc 2 myself, in 1976, I felt very lucky to
be a part of the course. I remember my first staff meetings, and my
awed recognition that a number of the people around the table—
Kim Marriott, Don Levine, Bert Cohler, David Orlinsky—had won the
Quantrell teaching award. (Ralph Nicholas, another figure at that table,
won the award that year and John MacAloon, yet another colleague that
quarter, won it two years later.) These were master teachers, and I felt
something of an imposter in their midst.

But how to learn to teach from them? I did not quickly learn what
Paule Verdet had discovered twenty years earlier—that one has to find
one's own strengths to teach from. Yet the evidence should have been all
around me that there were a variety of paths to fine teaching. Ralph
Nicholas, himself a most caring and humane teacher, characterized the
styles of some of his colleagues. John MacAloon, he said, "is probably
the greatest Soc 2 teacher I've ever seen," and noted his intuitive grasp
of how students are approaching a problem. Bert Cohler, in a wholly
different style, has an uncanny knack for stimulating students: "He asks
questions which you and I might think are sophomoric—but it's fine for

freshmen! When Bert is on, he may be the finest discussion leader around." David Orlinsky is unequaled in "pursuing a line consistently; he pursues a line of discourse through a class with unparalleled accuracy." And Kim Marriott, as many of his colleagues observe, has an almost superhuman capacity for tolerating silences. He can wait and wait for student response: "He uses the Socratic method without being Socrates."

Little of this came up for discussion, however. With all the emphasis on teaching, teaching remained intimate, personal, rarely a topic for staff meetings. The practice of sitting in on one another's sections had passed. People willingly took over one another's sections when professional meetings or other business called a staff member out of town (a far cry from David Riesman's recollection that he never missed a day of teaching except because of illness). I longed for something more, since I had been part of a staff-taught course at Harvard that David Riesman headed. Ritually every Wednesday night, the staff met at Riesman's home for dinner. A pre-dinner sherry was occasion for informal discussion, dinner was the time to talk about how the past week's sections had gone, and after dinner one teaching fellow each week would lead discussion on the materials for the next week's sections. The discussion leader was not expected to make a brilliant exegesis of the texts but to outline a pedagogical approach, looking for the questions most likely to open students to the reading.

In Soc 2 staff meetings, in contrast, people plunged headfirst into the text and, as I imagine Talmudic scholars doing, nodded in agreement, spoke in disagreement or correction, or winked at puns, jokes, and obscure references to let others know that they knew, too. It was a sharing and resharing of a common, perhaps overworked, culture, and I was not always sure, much as I admired and liked my colleagues individually, that the staff meetings were not pretty self-indulgent. The discussions were not tutorial enough for my taste. If we were reading new material, discussion could be a pleasure. But with old material, though it might be new to some of the newer members of the staff, the veterans spoke in code of settled interpretations—or settled disputes—and the novices participated as if in a conversation in a foreign language where they could catch the drift but not really contribute.

There were rarely discussions of teaching method. I share in the Soc 2 consensus that understanding the texts is the best method and the best preparation, but it seems to me there was less interest than there should have been in Don Levine's experiments with simulation games in the classroom, Carl Pletsch's somewhat ill-fated idea of trying out different styles of authority in the classroom as a living case study of the problem of authority, and Bert Cohler's and John MacAloon's assignment to students of interpreting one of their own dreams after reading Freud. Through the years, pedagogical discussion came in through the interstices, and was invariably preempted in staff meetings by attention to the texts.

Still, the Soc 2 staff meetings were the center of my life during four years at Chicago, the place which I felt belonged to me most—and yet, it did *not* belong to me. I was warmly welcomed and appreciated in Soc 2, as if a person of my apparent intelligence and sensibility and Daniel Bell/David Riesman pedigree obviously was a member of the home team. But, in retrospect, I was not entirely at home—perhaps no one was. I remember feeling very good when the staff adopted for the reading list an article I had suggested—Nancy Chodorow's feminist revision of Freud on the development of sex-role identity. I felt I had made a mark on an important institution and contributed in a small way to the education of my colleagues. So, too, I made something of a mark with a lecture on the Industrial Revolution which, as those close to me realized, was merely forty-five minutes of social science worked up so that I could indulge my own desire to read aloud to a captive audience two minutes of Charles Dickens' *Hard Times*. I felt myself equal to or better than many of my colleagues in the lecture room, but I worried about my ability in the give-and-take of class discussion. If Dave Riesman worried about the liveliness of Dan Bell's classes next door, I worried about the liveliness of classes I did not hear but heard of, from my students.

When I left Chicago for U.C.–San Diego, and knew I would have as my colleagues some former teachers in Soc 2, and learned that the founders of that university had read and studied Goodspeed's history of the University of Chicago, I had some hopes that a Soc 2–like curriculum might exist or might be created. Soc 2 has set up colonies, in a way. Robert Keohane, Sr., who taught some years in Soc 2, as well as in Soc 1, helped transplant the College curriculum whole to Shimer College, but this was a special case. Sally Cassidy and Paule Verdet brought some of their Soc 2 experience to developing the experimental social science curriculum at Monteith College. Indeed, Paule Verdet recalls the intensity of interaction with students at Monteith as greater than at Chicago, practically a tutorial system. "We went wild with teaching as a calling at Monteith and everything became centered on our students." The Soc 2 course, for all its devotion to undergraduates, could never be thought of as student-centered, nor did it create, in most cases, a particularly sociable relationship between students and faculty. Reuel Denney carried Soc 2 to Hawaii, setting up a general social sciences sequence (with the help of a graduate of the College teaching at Hawaii), and David Bakan was active in educational reform in Toronto. In 1989 the provost of Third College, one of the five undergraduate colleges at San Diego,

responded to some memos I had written urging a common general education curriculum by asking me to head a committee to draft a new
core course. The three-quarter sequence we came up with, "Diversity,
Justice, and Imagination," has unmistakable echoes of Chicago and
Soc 2.

"Soc 2 is the hardest course to teach," Richard Taub remembers. "Either I've oversold Marx or Freud or I've been too smart-ass in criticizing
them." Just what gets across to students in Soc 2 is not easy to know.
Robert Ginsberg recalls that he "took little notice of the overall structure of the course" in 1953–54, and it seems doubtful that other students have noticed much more over the years. Ginsberg "rejected
Freud" and found Marx "heavy-handed" and was most touched by the
fiction that found its way into the course—Richard Wright's *Black Boy*
and Aldous Huxley's *Brave New World*. One of Bert Cohler's students
told him: "By the time we're done, no book is worth reading." This is
the other side of the "mana" Riesman criticized: it is not simply that the
books in Soc 2 have power for students (and staff) but that one absorbs
these powers and takes them inside, not by swallowing whole but by intellectual mastication. The attachment that results is not to the books
themselves only, but to the process of chewing.

To think of the realities of Soc 2, one is quickly confronted with both
the good and bad, the genius of the design of the course and the curriculum, but the disappointments as well as the pleasures of the staff meetings, the elements of community that still exist around the course
(I remember a staff picnic in Robert Dreeben's backyard as one of the
best social occasions of my years at Chicago) but also the sense of a community in tatters, the older staff members recalling nostalgically some
better time or some wonderful former staff member, the younger faculty wondering what tribe they have joined and when they are likely to
learn its language. To think of Soc 2 from the standpoint of teaching at
another institution, however, one is likely to feel like a man without a
country, an exile from some paradisiacal teaching situation. One faculty
member referred to his present institution as "such a waste of mind."

Soc 2 lives on, but not significantly through its influence on other
curricula. It has not been easily transplanted. But it does live in the
work of the faculty still at the College and of those who have left.
Reinhard Bendix saw his own work as greatly influenced by Soc 2 and
the emphasis on "modernization" as a problem that the course took seriously. Milton Singer, on reading a draft of Bendix's *Kings or People*
said, "It's astonishing what Social Science 2 did; I didn't think this book
could be written." Bendix's *Work and Authority* began in 1950 under the
influence of Soc 2.

How has Soc 2 survived sixty years? What keeps a tradition alive?

This is the kind of question Soc 2 staff might ask on their exams. They would expect students to draw on Marx in recognizing the ways in which self-conscious conflict between groups with different interests (College and divisions, in this case) helped establish a kind of oppositional spirit—though some instructors might argue that Simmel, rather than Marx, would be the better authority here. They would expect students to know by reflex that what is at issue is the establishment of solidarity, a sense of community, and a set of sacred symbols (and sacred texts) that embody that community—and students would not need to be reminded to cite Durkheim. They would be pleased when students discussed Weber's notion of the "routinization of charisma" and the problems and possibilities that bureaucratization brings with it. And they would look for students to recognize, with appropriate Freudian gloss, that the Soc 2 tradition has been sustained in part by the libidinal energy connected to it, unleashed often by experiences of present faculty with books or teachers in the course when they themselves were students, and still providing fire and light many years later.

It is astonishing what Soc 2 did and does. Its history is too singular, the institution that gave it birth and continues to nurture it too unusual, for the course to be much of a blueprint for education elsewhere. But if not a blueprint, it is still a beacon for higher education and for social science.

6

Through the Lens of a Career: A Student's Recollections and Assessments of Soc 2

Robert Ginsberg

It was in my second year of college, 1953–54, at the age of sixteen that I was introduced to the social sciences by "Soc 2." Class section DA met in 302B of Cobb Hall around the great oval table that obliged everyone, students and teacher, to be in the front row of discussion. Mr. Pehrson was my official instructor. I have no record of his full name or titles. It was the Chicago custom to address our instructors, no matter how distinguished they might be in the scholarly world, as Mr., Miss, or Mrs. In turn the students were given the same form of address. Thus, the handful of pages which are all that remain of my classnotes for Soc 2 record comments by Mr. A. and Miss Z., who were my fellow students.

Mr. Pehrson was of Scandinavian appearance if not origin. He was an anthropologist who had done fieldwork in Lapland. Anthropology thereby became keenly alive for me. We read Margaret Mead's *Coming of Age in Samoa* and *Sex and Temperament in Three Primitive Societies,* and Ruth Benedict's *Patterns of Culture.* The books which lie on the desk before me with yellowed pages are Mentor paperbacks each costing 35¢. They are classics now and may have been then. The College saw to it that we cut our teeth on the Great Books whatever the field we were studying. Yet we had no sense of awe before authoritative monuments. They were merely the texts for discussion and assessment.

Anthropology stimulated my imagination much as travel literature and novels of adventure were later to do. I was delighted by the exoticism of the cultures studied. But deep philosophical issues were also raised and continue to haunt me: questions involving pluralism and cultural relativism, cross-cultural values and universal human traits. The terms of the discussions were those sharp contrasts studied by Mead and Benedict in the gentle Arapesh, the casual Samoan, the treacherous Dobu, the tranquil Zuñi, and the theatrical Kwakiutl. It seemed that everyone in the College was prepared to enter into discussion of these extremes of human configuration, and this was because everyone had in common the same education, including Soc 2. Discussion therefore was not limited to the classroom, nor to those students currently taking the course. The great issues were open to consideration by everyone throughout the College experience. Even today old Chicagoans reveal themselves in writing or conversation by a reference to Dobuan duplicity or Kwakiutl ostentation.

My second instructor for Soc 2 was Mr. Denney. Since each College course was staff-designed and staff-taught, and since the student's grade was determined not by a single instructor's judgment but by a comprehensive exam read at the end of the year by the staff, we felt free to visit other sections of the course to see how well they were doing and whether we could learn more from them. This was one of the great intellectual pleasures of the college. We could continue the discussion of matters that were especially interesting by attending the next teacher's class. Over the lunch table or the ping-pong table students would report on the state of the question in their section of Soc 2. If all the students in the College at one time or another were working on the course, it was good to know that a faculty staff was also working on it.

Mr. Denney was Reuel Denney. I was attracted by his liveliness, subtlety, and agile communicativeness. Reuel Denney was also a poet. In due time I brought him a packet of my juvenilia which he dutifully perused. He made gentle suggestions concerning technical devices and to illustrate them handed me a tearsheet of one of his published poems. I was proud to become the owner of it. "Palpitant" was a word it used, and palpitant was the poetry.

Poet and sociologist, Mr. Denney had collaborated in David Riesman's *Lonely Crowd*. Everyone in college was capable of swinging the categories "other-directed" and "inner-directed" into any discussion of personality. Mr. Denney was an engaging teacher, gifted with a sparkling expressiveness. A few years later I clipped an illustrated article from *Newsweek* or *Time* reporting on his paper to a scholarly conference about the communicative significance of nonverbal gestures.

I sat in on Mr. Denney's section at mid-year. It was intended for students entering the College when the year-long courses were already underway. The mid-year section was intensive. It provided an excellent way for me to review the course still in progress. That we had already discussed certain topics in my official class did not mean that they had been finished off. Everything in Soc 2 remained open to further consideration.

In addition to its many discussion sections, the course featured a regular lecture period in which members of the staff and guest social scientists offered their best insights about some pertinent topic. The lectures helped to fill in the terrain out of which arose the peaks of the readings. The lectures also relieved the tension that goes with an education

149

founded on the discussion method: for a change we could sit back and let the teachers do all the work. Of the lecturers I especially recall three.

Mark Benney was a social psychologist who spoke from thoughtful experience with the English working class. "What is the effect of the observer on the observed?" Mr. Benney asked, gazing at us in the lecture hall. And my notes say that he was "concerned with analyzing the effect of his questions rather than being preoccupied with the answers." I often observed Mr. Benney, when I was in graduate school, sitting in the front window of one of the "intellectual" bars near the campus. He had his regular place, from which he would hold forth, as if in a British pub.

Kermit Eby was a labor organizer with a religious background. He was a compelling speaker who wove a spell over the audience, organizing us emotively by means of his verbal presence. "Every economic decision I have made," his voice boomed from the podium, "has had moral implications." The Burton-Judson dormitories hosted a Sunday tea to which faculty members were invited in order to meet students informally. Eagerly I went to the tea when Mr. Eby was the guest. Only three other students had made it. We sat in easy chairs in the lounge as the accomplished orator spoke in the gentlest tones of his experiences and values. He let us in on his secret of how to establish a bond with an audience: go to the meeting place early, size up the lecture room, see what is going on, chat with individuals, and get a feel for their humanity. I could tell that he had done just this here, caring enough to be well-prepared for the people he would be with. Since then I have made good use of the strategy he revealed.

The most formidable of our lecturers was the legendary Bruno Bettelheim. It was a painful experience to meet him, to see him, and to hear him. With bald head, thick glasses, and thick accent, Bettelheim provoked thick hostility. In an instant he awakened unconscious antipathies and threw his audience into psychic turmoil. Concentration-camp survivor, principal of the unique institution for "truants from life," the Sonia Shankman Orthogenic School, Bettelheim had dwelled amid the human abysses. He had an uncanny ability to draw upon these depths in an audience that had come to listen to him but instead found itself probed by his questions. Here was a Socrates of the unconscious life. Whenever Bettelheim gave a talk for some campus group I always attended. He professed displeasure with such interruptions of his serious work, and this made a good opener for hostility. Bettelheim did not lecture on theory and cases; instead, he made his audience experience, despite themselves, the substance that theory is concerned with. We became the cases. I was delighted by the methods Bettelheim used so forcefully in dialogue. He was able to effect substantial progress toward understanding just by getting everyone to be against him. Hostility did not curtail communication fruitlessly; it fueled it creatively. Bettelheim's performances may have given assurance to the conduct of dialogue amid conflict that has become the principal mode of my own teaching as a philosopher.

While some were scandalized by Bettelheim's conduct, which they attributed to nastiness, I detected a tender caring at the heart of his efforts, although if brought to his attention, any such traits would be dismissed as determined features of personality. In Soc 2 we read one of Bettelheim's cases, "Harry," involving a resident of the Orthogenic School, which was located just down the street from where I resided at Burton-Judson.

The University grew in meaning for me as we read its authors, heard its celebrities, and penetrated its institutions. Whatever the content of the Soc 2 lectures, I learned from the lecturers about the rhetoric of communication.

We read Freud: the lectures on the *Origin and Development of Psychoanalysis,* which I found eminently clear and distasteful, and *Civilization and Its Discontents,* which I found unnecessarily saddening. I rejected Freud. His reduction of life to sordid factors beyond our control seemed to deny noble ideals. Psychoanalysis offended my sense of poetry. It replaced the romantic vision of life with a grubby scientism. It impugned the motivation of my interest in the young women in the course. College is important for the opportunity it provides us of rejecting values and interpretations, as well as for the opportunity of adopting them.

My rejection of the psychoanalytical insights lasted a few years and then completely vanished. I read through the works of Freud, did a master's thesis involving psychoanalysis, and spent a year practicing analysis upon my dreams. Freud's vision became second nature to me when I found it could be made compatible with the highest ideals of life.

My edition of *Civilization and Its Discontents,* imported in hardcover from Great Britain ($1.50), bears a troubling passage on its final page underlined in electrographic pencil. (This pencil was required for the machine scoring of all our multiple-choice exams in the College; I also used its dark, bold lines for marking my textbooks.) Freud says,

> Men have brought their powers of subduing the forces of nature to such a pitch that by using them they could now very easily exterminate one another to the last man. They know this—hence arises a great part of their current unrest, their dejection, their mood of apprehension.

This was written in 1930, before the atomic age, but it puts its finger on the central problem of continued human existence. Most of my professional life has been dedicated to this problem.

Among the other classics assigned were Marx and Engels's *Communist Manifesto*, which I found heavy-handed—and still do. Thorstein Veblen's *Theory of the Leisure Class* was entertaining to read, especially because of its egregious style. The inside back cover of my paperback edition is scribbled with a vocabulary that must have raised my eyebrows then and in some cases does so still: *lusory, ferine, innutrition, agnatic, predaceous, sedulous, sublation, genuflexional, hieroduces, obloquy, deckel*. Frederick W. Taylor's *Principles of Scientific Management* proved fascinating. William F. Whyte's *Street Corner Society* was delightful, the more so because of its reportage of street dialogue and its sketches of characters than for its analysis of role playing. In Soc 2 we all became adept in applying role theory at a moment's notice. W. Lloyd Warner's *Democracy in Jonesville* was similarly a treat for its portrayal of small-town life. We read Max Weber on the Protestant ethic, Ruth Underhill on the Papago culture, Talcott Parsons on social structure.

Many of these readings were anthologized by the staff of Soc 2 and printed by the University in several volumes and supplements. Blue covers designated the social science readings. Selections were usually printed by photo-offset, so we had the chance to read the original texts. Each volume was preceded by an extensive outline of the topics for that part of the course or else by a general introduction. Thus we were frequently reminded of where in the world we were, yet I took little notice of the overall structure of the course. I did not matter to me what the outline was since we would get to the topics sooner or later. This indifference to organization may have been reinforced by the year-long extent of the course. What I experienced and recall are not the great units, but the great readings, discussions, and problems. Only now do I see the grand architecture of Soc 2 as outlined in the syllabi: (1) The Study of Culture, (2) The Process of Individual Development, (3) The Child in the Community, (4) The Individual in the Modern Industrial System, (5) Ideals and Experiments in the Formation of Personality. I had missed the forest for the trees. Or I had been working away in different corners of the forest without noticing the shifts in terrain. In my subsequent experience in teaching I have found that the syllabus for a course is the instructor's ideal vision of its identity, whereas to the students the course consists of its concrete assignments.

Every couple of years the readings for Soc 2, and all the other College courses, would be revised or reissued with new supplements. These volumes are impressive books. Given the resources of the University of Chicago Press, the talents and interests of the course staff, and a market consisting of the entire student body, outstanding results naturally followed. In comparison, recent efforts in academic publishing to produce a teacher's own book of readings for a course appear amateurish.

The two readings in this course in the social sciences that had greatest immediate impact upon me and that have retained permanent interest were works of literature. One of these, Aldous Huxley's *Brave New World,* is a superbly exciting novel, written in the early 1930s but which still seemed prophetic to us in the early 1950s. Today's reading of it is made poignant by recognition of the dire prophecies fulfilled. In Soc 2 we were all deviants obliged to face the world vision of Mustapha Mond.

A while back a questionnaire requested the ten books that have most influenced or moved me. I only managed to list six or seven, thereby leaving the door open to further education. On the list was a required reading in Soc 2, that other work of literature, Richard Wright's *Black Boy:* a book I could not put down, an experience I could not forget, a revelation I could not deny. Wright wrote with a ringing passion for truth. The story of the black boy raised in the South opened a new world to this white boy raised in Brooklyn. The harsh suffering and the vibrant sensibility of the young Wright went right to the heart. I felt that part of my heritage as an American was being made available to me. The shamefulness of American institutions was evident, but in the indefatigable soul of Wright I recognized my fellow American and the best of the American spirit.

This was my introduction to the black experience in America. I am grateful for this, for otherwise I might not have come to see the Other as myself. Among the sixty residents of my dormitory—Matthews House—there were no blacks. Chicago was then so ordered demographically and socially that intimacy between white and black was systematically precluded.

I was struck by the story's incident of attempted voyeurism under an outhouse which led to a disastrous slide into the cesspit, and I was moved by the conclusion of the southern experience with a trip north— to Chicago. *Black Boy* was a hardcover book, costing $1.25, in the Living Library. I did not mark any of the pages, a sign of respect in those days for books that had special value. This edition is effectively illustrated by the prints of Ashley Bryan, and its importance is signaled with a preface by Dorothy Canfield Fisher. Finally, it is wrapped in a quality dust jacket with an effective design in black and brown. This is a product of suffering that I felt invited to treasure as a work of the human spirit.

Black Boy is written with the immediacy of autobiography. By contrast I found Wright's novel *Native Son* contrived and theoretical. Wright took up exile in Paris where I found myself a student in the 1960s. He was a favorite subject for interviews on the injustices of American society. I was pleased to hear these, for as an expatriate I enjoyed the luxury of criticizing my country at long distance. Wright died disillusioned. I returned to America with hope in its humanity.

Of my written work for Soc 2, only two papers remain. One is "Mead's Data on the Arapesh and Freud's Views." The grade in Mr. Pehrson's hand is C−, but beneath the "−" is the trace of an erased "+", evidence of a second reading. Several times in college I found the grade on my papers lowered by such second thoughts. Mr. Pehrson's judgment: "Too much quotation. Not enough analysis."

I examine the two-and-a-half pages of typescript now gray with dust. There are five lengthy quotations from Freud, two from Mead. That leaves seven sentences by Ginsberg. No page references are given for the quotations. "Not enough analysis" is generous: there is no analysis. The paper keeps its author out of the conflict of views by obliging the assigned authors to confront each other. I am evidently stuck in the primacy of the texts and have not taken the leap of thinking. If I were to grade this effort now, having had occasion to correct ten thousand student papers since then, I would give it, at best, a C−.

The other paper is "An Other-Directed Anthropologist among the Dobu." Here there is more thinking on the part of the author, with only a single quotation (unreferenced). This gives Mr. Pehrson something to enter into discussion with. He keys my page and a half of text with five numerals and attached a typed page of his comments. To my severe warning, "the Dobuan dogma is that the closely associated person is a dangerous threat to your life," Pehrson perspicaciously counters: "provided this person does not belong to your *susu*." I earned a B.

The topics of these assignments were typical for Soc 2 and were most probably invented by the staff rather than the instructor. We were forever applying one mode of theory to a fresh body of observation, one set of distinctions to a quite different social domain, one kind of method to another area of experience. Hence, the course not only moved forward, it moved backward in important ways. We turned back to what we had "covered" in order to uncover it in the light of different kinds of consideration. Problems settled in the course of the year became unsettled. Great questions had a way of becoming enriched by moving on to other questions.

Soc 2 was perforce interdisciplinary, although I do not recall that term being used then. As a course in social sciences, we delved into anthropology, sociology, political science, social psychology, economic history, and psychoanalysis. But these were not studied in isolation as mere chapters in a grand survey. They were obliged to interact. We crossed disciplines daily as we probed fundamental problems. The result was both an occasional blending and a frequent sharpening of the disciplines of the social sciences. "Interdisciplinary" in recent discussions has often come to mean nondisciplinary eclecticism.

Soc 2, like the other courses in the College, was pluralistic in construction and outlook. Diverse and competing theories on what we are as social beings emerged from the readings. The staff of social scientists illustrated fundamental differences. The discussion method allowed us to work together for understanding and judgment amid differences of values and experience. The course was designed to get the student into the act, responsibly and articulately. We had to learn to make judgments, not receive them. The course was not primarily informative; it was formative.

As I try to remember and assess Soc 2, I cannot separate the content from the mechanics, the form from the material, or the methods from the goals. These things were integrated into the wholeness of the learning experience. Thus, the choice of topics is inseparable, it seems, from the reading required, and the publishing facilities made such requirements feasible. The lectures that supplemented the readings and discussions highlighted the diversity of disciplines involved, which were amply represented by the staff for the course. You were free to wander from the section taught by the anthropologist to the one offered by the sociologist or the social psychologist. The system of examinations was painstakingly designed to assess skills at the end of the course and to assist learning during it. Your teachers included all the social scientists at the University who might give talks to groups or come to tea. All these things were intrinsic to the learning.

So was my life, for I too was a social being. The College was a multicultural world for me, and my residence hall was a remarkable society. During my year of Soc 2, I began to play a leadership role in dormitory society. Or, put in other terms, Soc 2 terms, I was undergoing the transition from inner-directed shyness to other-directed gregariousness. The discussion method that we learned in class was our principal mode of social intercourse. College was an open-ended discussion during which we grew up into who we were. Those midnight pizza parties, those long walks to the Jackson Park lagoon, those forays to the movie palaces in the Loop were also part of Soc 2.

What was the true subject of the course? Myself, my classmates, the College, the University, Chicago, America, the world.

No course in the College existed in a vacuum. We did not have the now popular cafeteria style of electives, taking what we want when we want it, which also means not being educated in what we do not want. Soc 2 was an integral part of an ingenious plan for the whole of undergraduate education. On the blue covers of the readings for this course stands the legend: "A Second-Year Course in a Three-Year Sequence in the Social Sciences." Soc 2 had its significance within the context of this sequence. During orientation week I had placed out of Soc 1, that is, received credit for it by examination. It dealt with American history and government. I sometimes regret that I did not take the course, although later I was to be active in this area. So it came about that Soc 2 was my initial experience in the social sciences. Soc 3 exposed me to the dismal swamp of economics. I had a dreadful time getting through it.

If a course was part of a sequence, the sequence was but one simulta-neous dimension of College work involving other sequences. I had also placed out of Natural Sciences 2, and I was struggling with Nat Sci 3 (gray covers), on the limits of biology and physics, while taking Soc 2. And I was taking Humanities 2 (red covers). Here history, rhetoric, drama, fiction, and philosophy formed an impressive array, rivaling the disciplines and human interest of Soc 2. Herodotus and Gibbon, Plato and Bertrand Russell, Shakespeare and Dostoyevsky, Lincoln and Douglas took the field and blended into my consideration of the mate-rials in social science. A year later, while I was sinking in Soc 3, I flour-ished in Hum 3, signing up for the variant in art and auditing the sections in literature, French, and music. It was some time during this third and last year in college that I chose as graduate school the Hu-manities Division and applied for admission to the interdepartmental Committee on the Analysis of Ideas and Study of Methods.

The three sequences—social sciences, natural sciences, humanit-ies—each comprising three one-year courses, were supplemented by three nonsequential yearly courses in skills pertinent to several disci-plines: English, foreign language, and mathematics. All was topped off in the final year by two integrative courses: History of Western Civiliza-tion and the formidable O.M.P.: Organizations, Methods, and Princi-ples of Knowledge. The latter, in effect a course in philosophy, gave everyone a chance to rethink the place of the social sciences in the edi-fice of knowledge. The fourteen courses were equivalent to three-and-a-half years of college work, thus leaving room for at least two electives of advanced courses in the fourth year.

Having placed out of two courses, I was able to graduate after three years, at age eighteen. The Hutchins bachelor's degree in general, lib-eral education was universally regarded as worthless for further educa-tion in America, since its recipient had not majored in anything. The University of Chicago, however, did accept me for graduate work—five years of it. When I received my bachelor's degree in 1955 and was wel-comed into "the community of the learned," the College did away with its unique structure for teaching every student a core curriculum in which they developed their core humanity.

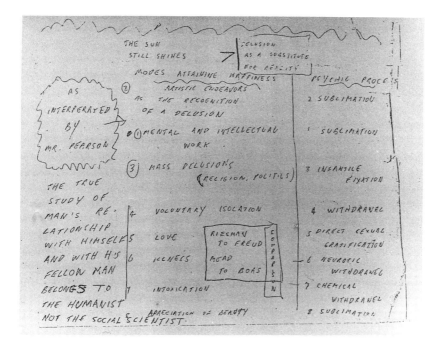

Classnotes of Robert Ginsberg, Soc. 2, 1953–54. Photograph by Mary Matus.

Among my notes for Soc 2, I find a half sheet with a fragment of po-etry, a definition of *delusion,* a set of comparisons of authors, a list of eight modes of attaining happiness as interpreted by Mr. Pehrson, with a corresponding list of psychic processes, and a most startling message written in large letters: "The true study of man's relationship with him-self and with his fellow man belongs to the humanist, not the social sci-entist." Had I recorded something said in discussion or something disclosed in reflection? Did I save this scrap of paper when long ago I disposed of college notes, because of the comprehensiveness of Mr. Pehrson's list or the shining light of this solitary insight?

Looking backward from a career spent in the humanities, I see what attracted me in Soc 2 was not the scientific status of social science en-deavors but their literary style, their communicative strategies, and their imaginative powers. What struck most deeply was not the theories and methodologies of the social sciences, which were clever intellectual constructions, but the human content colored with suffering and em-bedded with values. In subsequent training at Chicago I was to explore literary and aesthetic matters, while later in my education, upon my re-

157

turn from France, I was to face in the study of social philosophy the human issues raised by Wright and Benedict, Marx and Freud.

The educational measure of a course of study is not how much it has taught you, but what you become, thanks to its assistance. Thirty-eight years later I am still learning from Soc 2.

Part III

Intellectual Biographies and Institutional Settings

7

A College Remembered

Lewis A. Coser

Let the reader beware: what follows does not pretend to be an objective account of what Social Sciences 2 "really was" when I taught it between 1948 and 1950. This is rather a recollection, partly marked by nostalgia, of how I now view that experience more than four decades later. It is an account largely based on the flood of memories that came to crowd my mind at the 1982 meeting celebrating the fiftieth anniversary of Social Sciences 2. In addition, the contemporary reader must keep in mind that the course in those years, as indeed the whole of the College, was largely autonomous and only loosely linked to the graduate departments and divisions of the University.

Among the key characteristics that marked the course when I came to teach it was its remarkably unbureaucratic character. I have never again taught in as unbureaucratic an atmosphere. To illustrate, it might not be amiss briefly to describe the rather unconventional way in which I was recruited to teach in the course.

I had come to this country in 1941, shortly before Pearl Harbor, as a refugee from Nazi Germany who had spent the years between 1933 and 1941 in that most bureaucratic of all European countries, the France of the Third Republic. During the war years and immediately after, I had worked for various U.S. government agencies, mainly the Office of War Information. After the war's end, I briefly became an editor of the magazine *Modern Review* but soon resigned because those who controlled the magazine and called the shots wished to make it into an organ of what soon came to be known as the cold war. Trying to make a living as a freelancer proved difficult, and my career opportunities looked bleak. I therefore decided to resume graduate studies in sociology at Columbia—a subject I had studied at the Sorbonne before the war.

One morning, early in 1948, my then friend and then a young radical Nathan Glazer, phoned me and asked, "Do you know David Riesman?" When I answered in the negative he informed that Riesman was a brilliant young lawyer who had recently been hired by the University of Chicago to become a key member of the Social Sciences 2 course and to reinvigorate its offerings. Riesman was in New York in order to interview likely candidates for a teaching position in the social science courses of the College. Would I like to meet him? I certainly would, and indeed did soon afterward. Riesman loved long walks, and so we walked up and down Central Park, talking about everything under the sun, but not very much, as I recall, about college teaching. I must have made a favorable impression on Riesman, since he asked me at the end of the walk: "How would you like to teach at the College of the University of Chicago?" I was more than delighted, of course, but nevertheless managed to ask: "What do you expect me to teach?" The answer was: American History. My heart fell, and I replied: "I am sorry, Professor Riesman, but I don't think it's a good idea to import somebody from Berlin and Paris to teach American History in the Midwest. My knowledge of American history is, to put it charitably, exceedingly spotty. Thank you very much for the offer, but I must decline." There, so I thought, went a splendid opportunity to join the American academy.

Things turned out very differently, however. A week or two later, the telephone rang in my apartment: "This is Champion Ward, dean of the College," said the voice at the other end, "I wish to talk to you about the appointment to the College." "I'm sorry," I said, "but I have already explained to Professor Riesman that I do not feel qualified to teach American history and hence have to decline the offer." "Don't worry," was the answer, "we have moved someone from Social Sciences 2 into Social Sciences 1" (American history), "and so you can now teach in an area of your competence." I gladly accepted, and it was in this highly unbureaucratic manner that I received my first teaching job in America, a hiring procedure that was never to repeat itself as I subsequently moved up the academic ladder.

When I joined the staff of Social Sciences 2 in the fall of 1948 I soon discovered a key characteristic of the faculty: it was not a loose collection of individuals who happened to teach similar topics but a true community of scholars. The notion of a community of scholars plays, of course, a large role in the PR efforts of academic administrators. But, as I learned subsequently, this is mainly cant. At the College it bore some close approximation to reality. Not that several of my colleagues were not highly individualistic in their life styles or their approaches to the subject matter we taught. If Philip Rieff, to mention just one of them, had any communitarian urges he managed to repress them without undue difficulty. But, as a whole, the staff, partly of course because all of us taught the same subject matter, managed to develop a Gemeinschaft and shared a collective vision of the educational enterprise that was rare, if not unique, in the American academy. Interchange between colleagues, not only at the regular weekly meetings but practically at any hour of the working day, went on in a never-ending stream. The flow of uninhibited communication, of intellectual give-and-take, kept one constantly on the alert and sharpened the mind. In retrospect, the whole enterprise seems like a miniature version of Juergen Habermas's utopian vision of a world made truly human through the undistorted flow of communication between all human actors.

At the time I was working on my dissertation on the positive functions of social conflict. Hence I was especially sensitized to the fact that many of the distinct qualities of the College were created, or at least reinforced, by continuous conflicts and disagreements with the staff of the graduate departments. Graduate teaching, as we perceived it, was approached in a spirit of high seriousness. It was methodical, disciplined, infused by a spirit that was at least a close cousin to the Protestant ethic. Students were prepared for the academic "calling." Teaching and research were pursued with what the Germans call *tierischer Ernst*— animal earnestness. Animals, of course, cannot smile at all, and graduate teachers, so we came to think, smiled rarely. We handled things different in the College.

What most distinguished the College with its never-ceasing flow of intellectual interchange was the capacity to play with ideas. Huizinga would have been pleased with the spirit of Social Sciences 2. *Homo Ludens* found here a welcome refuge from the "Protestant" earnestness of the graduate school. Had Veblen come to the University of Chicago some fifty years after he in fact arrived there, he would have preferred to join the College faculty rather than the graduate division; he was after all among the relatively few American scholars who loved the play of the mind. The College not only played with ideas; it eroticized them in a manner that Herbert Marcuse with his heavy German earnestness never managed to do.

The graduate divisions were built on sharply delimited and institutionalized hierarchical layers and levels. Their norms were based on a rather rigid structure that governed most intercourse between its members. The College, by contrast, was built, to use Victor Turner's distinction, on the antistructure of *communitas*. "Vision becomes sect, then church, then in some cases dominant political system or prop for one," writes Victor Turner, "until *communitas* resurges once more against it from the liminal spaces and instants every structure is forced by its nature to provide. . . . These interstitial spaces provide homes for antistructural visions, thoughts, and ultimately behaviors."[1] Turner con-

1. Victor Turner, *Dramas, Fields, and Metaphors: Symbolic Action in Human Society* (Ithaca: Cornell University Press, 1974), 293.

163

ceives of *structure* and *communitas* as occurring in chronological succession; the college showed that they could exist side by side. This was an instant, to use Mannheim's term, of the contemporaneity of the noncontemporaneous.

The graduate departments jealously guarded the boundaries between disciplines, although there was a good deal of talk about "cross-fertilization." Those teaching in the College ignored such boundaries, and in fact were hardly aware of their existence.

Loneliness is the fate of most scholars. They usually hack a lonely path through the wilderness; it is rare that they are favored by a responsive echo. In the College, by contrast, one sometimes wished for a soundproof room since there were so many echoes to contend with all the time.

The divisions mainly produced "normal science" in Thomas Kuhn's sense. The College did not produce revolutionary breakthroughs either, but it produced creative discontent with merely normal science.

As we all remember, when Gertrude Stein lay on her deathbed she asked her companion Alice Toklas: "What is the answer?" When Toklas remained silent, Stein said, "Then what is the question?" The divisions tried to produce answers, the College specialized in questions. While the members of the divisions largely pursued their work within the established groves of scholarly inquiry, the College community, at least in its majority, used, and sometimes abused, its privilege to think otherwise.

I do not wish to denigrate the work of the scholars in the divisions; it was most of the time of considerable value and merit. In fact, the College could hardly have proceeded in the way it did had it not been for the constant awareness that the work carried on by the divisions was of enduring importance. In a sense, College and divisions operated in a way that Gestalt psychologists speak of when they point to necessary relations between figure and ground in the world of cognition. The characteristic figure of the College could only emerge in contrast to the ground of the divisions.

Individual as well as collective memory tend to embellish the past even as they attempt to preserve it. It is likely that I have painted too rosy a picture of the College in the preceding pages. The memoirs of others in this volume are likely to provide contrast and correction. It may well be that truly objective accounts can emerge only through reconciliation and synthesis of recollections that can never fully shed an element of subjectivity. If so, then the reader of these essays may attain a truer picture than any of their individual authors may possess. In what follows I shall attempt to draw some contemporary lessons from the image of the College that is anchored in my memory.

First of all, the general education approach that formed the mainstay of the College's teaching is needed today perhaps even more so than it was in the past. In an age of increasing specialization and its attendant compartimentalization of knowledge, it seems of the essence that there exist at least in some educational institutions a counterweight to the tendency of much current educational effort to teach more and more about less and less. The overall trend toward early professionalization and specialization can hardly be reversed in our postindustrial society. What is possible, however, is that here and there inquiring students may, for at least a few preparatory years, be offered an opportunity to expose their minds to the general ideas and overall intellectual trends from which more specialized types of knowledge have evolved. There is a real need to continue and strengthen general education even if realistically we can only expect it to enlighten a relatively small and restricted remnant. Young men and women who will have profited from exposure to general education courses will later inevitably require further specialized training, but their minds will be stretched and their outlooks enlarged through prior exposure to a course of studies that gives primacy to general ideas and their roots in our common cultural past.

In some European countries, but even there to a rapidly diminishing extent, the last year of the high school sequence provides some access to such general ideas, but, as we all know, the American high school hardly does so. The first- or second-year undergraduate curriculum in the majority of American colleges does not remedy this sad state of affairs. One becomes especially aware of this if one teaches, as I did until recently, in a large public institution. One drastic illustration will have to suffice. Just before taking my plane to Chicago for the 1982 College symposium, I taught a morning class in sociological theory on the intellectual and social roots of Karl Marx's thought. I mentioned in passing that Marx during his student days in Berlin belonged to a somewhat bohemian group of young Hegelians who spent as much time in Berlin coffee houses as in the lecture halls of the university. At this point a young woman raised her hand in astonishment. Said she: "My parents came from Bohemia, how come that there were so many Bohemians at Berlin at that time?" It is highly unlikely that this young woman would have taken a general education sequence even had it been available to her, but others might have. Such a course provides the most favorable setting for turning gaffes into learning experiences. This is why we must continue to struggle mightily for its continuance and growth even if, as I said earlier, only a relatively small number of students can be realistically expected to avail themselves of the opportunity to attend such courses.

165

The University of Chicago is, of course, not the only university that currently offers such courses. But somewhat similar courses such as those at the College of Columbia University seem too rigid and inflexible in their course requirements. On the other hand, Harvard, which has recently moved to a greater emphasis on required general courses, tends to staff these courses with teaching assistants, thus curtailing the chances for young minds to come into contract with senior scholars. In other places again, watered-down Great Books approaches tend to teach ideas in a kind of social and cultural vacuum, neglecting the social and intellectual context in which ideas developed roots and gathered strength. Following in large measure the Jesuit mode of pedagogy, they tend to treat ideas as if they had grown in a historical no-man's-land.

I have not made a systematic survey of general education such as Daniel Bell provided a few years ago, but from my limited knowledge it still would seem that, even though there is surely room for improvement, the Chicago approach remains, by and large, the most promising. But surely, the College must go back to two years of required social science coursework. Just one year is clearly insufficient to cover the wealth of materials the faculty wishes to deal with. But be that as it may, I do hope that Social Sciences 2 will thrive for another sixty years and that it may continue to be, as it has been in the past, an essential component of the coat of many colors that goes by the name of the American educational system.

8

The Scholarly Tension: Graduate Craft and Undergraduate Imagination

Joseph R. Gusfield

I entered the University of Chicago College as a freshman in September 1941. Two months later the United States was at war, and by April 1943 I was a soldier. Despite the intensity of existence in a nation deeply committed to the war effort, that year and a half of college life was marked by an intellectual excitement arising from study unrelated to the contemporary or the immediate. For me, the peak stimuli came from my work in Social Sciences I (later 2) and Social Sciences II (later 3). Soc 1 was then in the form of a survey course, emphasizing the "great transformation" from a traditional society to an industrialized one. It was an evolutionary framework whose sociological assumptions I later came to criticize.

I returned to campus in January 1946, completed my college requirements that quarter, and entered the University of Chicago Law School. That quarter I also began teaching Soc 3 as an extension course at the Downtown College and I continued this during my first year in Law School. In the fall of 1947 I became a teaching assistant (later instructor) in Soc 2. That experience, plus some work in the sociology of law and in jurisprudence, lead me to leave the Law School and enter the Department of Sociology as a graduate student. (I still have vivid recollections of Milton Singer and Ben Nelson arguing whether I should go into the Committee on Social Thought or the Department of Sociology.) My most definite experiences as a member of the Soc 2 staff came then while I was also a graduate student in sociology.

The Soc 2 staff of 1947–49 (while I was getting my master's in sociology) was one that would, if gathered today, more than gladden the heart of any university chancellor. Among its members were David Riesman, Dan Bell, Lewis Coser, Milton Singer, Philip Rieff, Ben Nelson, John Greene, Reuel Denney, Sylvia Thrupp, Martin Meyerson, the late Morton Grodzins, Rosalie Hankey (later Wax) and Murray Wax. C. Wright Mills joined it for one year. Except for Philip, they all seemed slightly older or more academically advanced that I. In its content, teaching the course was my introduction to Weber and to Durkheim. The intensive reading in the "great masters" (Freud, Marx, Durkheim, and Veblen) was my most nourishing introduction to the social sciences.

The staff itself and the weekly staff meetings, or seminars, were a feast of intellectual energy and joy that has remained for me an ideal of academic talk; one whose level I have never since been able to find or to recreate. The erudition, incisiveness, and originality were great and exciting spurs to my developing interests in academic work. That high flow of conversation was also a noisy battlefield of competing egos seeking an acclaim they had yet to receive elsewhere. It was intimidating to a young and unsure scholar, but it was also immensely fruitful as a period of learning.

That College that I revisit in memory is an amalgam of my recollected experience as a student and as a teacher, in Soc 2 and later in Soc 3. (I left the University in the fall of 1950 but returned and taught Soc 2 or 3 for several summers and one fall quarter.) My graduate-student experience took place against the background of my college teaching, mostly in simultaneous fashion. Comparing the two places—the College and the Department of Sociology—the graduate school seemed much the worse at the time. The Sociology Department and its courses, in contrast to the staff and content of the College social science courses, appeared provincially narrow, rigid in its specializations and naively unlearned, despite the scholarly reputations of the faculty. Disappointedly, I viewed it solely as an expedient needed to obtain the union card for academic membership. The College—that's where the action *really* was!

I was joined in that feeling by many other graduate students in other departments as well as Sociology and among both former students in the College and others. The graduate departments and the College coexisted in an atmosphere of intellectual tension. They not only had separate faculties, in the main, but they represented different approaches to social science—approaches best crystallized by the Social Sciences 2 course and its faculty. In the College, I found a scholarship where a premium was placed on breadth, originality, and significance. It gave the student theoretical systems that encompassed major areas of life and great flows of time. Its models, both for the student and for the staff, were found in the great writings of social scientists like Weber, Veblen, Durkheim, Freud, Marx, Schumpeter, Tocqueville, Piaget, and in books like *The Protestant Ethic and the Spirit of Capitalism* and *The Theory of the Leisure Class,* books which we examined closely. What they did was provide us with a means for interpreting both ourselves and the social order of our time. Such content provided the stuff by which an intellectual life could be lived on the model of what James Redfield calls "good talk." Its end product was the capacity to interpret the world, and its embodiment could be found in the conversation of the Soc 2 staff seminars as I saw them. The course content and the course teachers represented a form of creative thought: imaginative people of an intellectual cast reacting upon their observations and interpreting the world where their minds took them.

That vision of conversation and creative understanding made the graduate experience seem initially dull to me and to graduate-student friends, who envied my exposure to a richer intellectual diet. The College seemed like expensive chateaubriand, the department like hamburger. Its model of academic interchange was the research report, a presentation of methods and findings, whose final embodiment was the Ph.D. dissertation, that Holy Grail the production of which was the end point and the raison d'être of the entire graduate experience. At Chicago it was enshrined in the famed Chicago Sociology Series of urban ethnographies, which included Zorbaugh's *The Gold Coast and the Slum;* Wirth's *The Ghetto;* Anderson's *The Hobo;* and the then recently published *Street Corner Society,* by William F. Whyte. These were wonderful examples of observational and interactive research but hardly *Civilization and its Discontents.*

The mission of the College, and especially of Soc 2, was (or so I imagined) to develop interesting people by having them examine interesting ideas with the guidance of interesting teachers. The department's mission was profoundly different; it aimed at producing professional sociologists, members of a craft. Though the Chicago department was thought of as qualitative and hence unmethodical, the emphasis was nevertheless on how to know something about a specialized area. There was an association of people who possessed a discipline with a history, a set of standards and boundaries that clarified who belonged and what was necessary to claim membership. It gave the neophyte a sense of continuity with an older generation whose judgments counted and were worth respect. Your entry into that association of craftsmen was earned by demonstrating that you had mastered the craft and could discover something new and as yet unreported.

Tension between these two modes of doing scholarly work was hard to avoid. One mode, that of the professional sociologist, constrained and bound the scholar closely to the empirical world and his or her direct observation—to the tools and limits of craft. The other, that of the interpreting mind, was impatient with such limitations and with the very specialization inherent in the idea of craft itself. I don't want to push this (or any other) dichotomy too far, but there was in this tension something of what Max Weber has described as the tension in modern education between the "cultivated" man of liberal education and the "specialized" man of training.

As you may imagine, from the very rhetoric of this paper, I came to appreciate and internalize the codes of my craft, to value the integrity, constraint, and empirical humility which detailed observation and systematic analytical reflection represent. The tension between an interpretive and creative stance, which the College embodied, and an investigative, specialized stance, which the Department of Sociology embodied, became a more constant, less escapable one. The dialectic of these two appears now, to me, a source of profound significance for the educative process, for the so-called social sciences, and for the adventure of scholarship.

The substance of that tension in all these dimensions might be well expressed in the statement attributed to a Chicago sociologist at the time, but which I only learned of two months ago. This professor is reported to have said to a graduate student, who was a College alumnus, that he always liked to teach students from the College: they were ignorant and couldn't recognize an empirical problem—but they were so smart! In those days, the late 1940s and early 1950s, the University of Chicago Department of Sociology was often thought to be a humanistic center because it was associated with an emphasis on fieldwork, on ethnographic observation, on seeing the world from the standpoint and meanings of your subjects. But that perception hides the ethos, the underlying meanings and values which that graduate experience conveyed about the social sciences.

Of the three methodologies then most dominant in American sociology, the University of Chicago was, in my judgment, the most empirical and atheoretical. A small parable invented by one of us graduate students at the time may convey the limited and empirically constrained vision of the Chicago approach. We used to say that a thesis on drinking written by a Harvard student might well be entitled *Modes of Cultural Release in Western Social Systems;* by a Columbia student it would be entitled *Latent Functions of Alcohol Use in a National Sample;* and by a Chicago graduate student as, *Social Interaction at Jimmy's: A 55th Street Bar.* It was a methodology that held the student firmly to what he or she could see, hear, and experience at first hand. Your interpretations, your imagination were to be subordinated. Abstractions and concepts ungrounded by experience with concrete observations were suspect. I remember first hearing Talcott Parsons present his theoretical perspective at a lecture in Mandel Hall at which he was introduced by Professor Louis Wirth, who then sat in the front row and proceeded to read his mail during Professor Parsons' presentation!

For me, the conflict (on one hand) between a deep respect for the grounded character of events, along with recognition of the partiality and misleading quality of abstractions and generalizations, and (or the other hand) the quest for significance, understanding, and imaginative synthesis has been a constant and enriching factor in my life as time has led me into new work and new experiences. It is fallacious to suggest that such tensions between alternative modes of scholarly work did not also exist within the department and within the College, that craft and imagination were not at war in both places. Yet each place personified and embodied, each symbolized, one pole of the dialectic. Having completed a thesis about the Women's Christian Temperance Union and the "natural history" approach to social movements, I was left with an emptied feeling—a sense that I had not resolved the question that had impelled my initial interest in that organization: the salience of alcohol issues in American politics in contrast to economic concerns and interests, as might be expected. I had met the department's payroll but had not produced anything that someone in the College might respect. To answer those questions and to provide some understanding of American politics required an act of imagination, of interpretation, that reaches beyond data. It led me to study the American temperance movement in the ambit of American reform politics.

Looking back at my experiences in these two domains of intellectual and scholarly life, I realize that this tension between the graduate department and the undergraduate College was a crucial and exceptionally salutary part of becoming educated. Whether you wish to call it the clash of the general and the particular, of cultivation versus training, of nominalism versus realism, of theory versus empiricism, or humanism versus science, the tensions and conflicts are inherent in knowledge and in scholarship. They are not avoided by fiat. Knowing thoroughly some limited sector of human activity made the student aware of ambiguity, paradox, contradiction, and the complex and situated character of events. The craftsman's empirical and atheoretical mode in the department served this payroll well. The College's drummer had a different beat, exemplified so well in the Soc 2 course. It rewarded direction, significance, a pluralism of theories. That model of the endless dialogue that Soc 2 seminars created was itself a view of social science; a constant series of clashing and complementing perspectives. It was less a procedure through which to find truth than a conversation about possible truths. Social science was a means of enriching and clarifying that conversation. In the Department of Sociology it was assumed that the dialogue was a means to an end, which was finding the right answer. It was a closed system of serious work. In the College it was its own end, an open form of intellectual play.

The existence of these alternative and alternating methods of doing social science and their alternative methods of pedagogy—the Socratic dialogue and the didactic lecture—was itself a profound form of education. Whether or not individual students attended both College and department was not so essential to the influences on them. They knew that what was hallowed in Cobb Hall was often derided at "1126" (the Social Science Research Building) and vice versa. The influence lay in the interaction of students in their classes, in the speakers and in the events that made up many campus events.

I have only occasionally seen that rich and vivid part of education as it took place in the College occur elsewhere. Undergraduate education generally suffers from its absence, whatever version of "good work" is dominant. Today, I view American colleges and universities as over-developed in the graduate school model of education. Whether or not curricula encourage early specialization or emphasize breadth, the content of courses is that of preparation for induction into the craft. We begin to produce neophyte sociologists at the freshman year. It misleads students into believing that the world is divided into packages labeled according to university catalogs.

Taking the theme of personality and culture, the Soc 2 course brought the student—and the faculty as well—into an intellectual culture that provided concepts and perspectives which, in clashing and pluralistic form, induced a self-reflection and an open-ended critical posture. Endless arguments about the virtues and viciousness of the world according to Freud or Marx or Weber or Ruth Benedict were not steps in the process of becoming an anthropologist or a clinical psychologist. They had their significance as depictions of how to go about developing an interpretation of where you were—in history, in social structures, in your own self-development.

In many places and on many campuses today we talk about undergraduate and graduate education as a clash between teaching and research. What I am describing is not that trite, superficial conflict. The tension between graduate and undergraduate education seems more significantly a tension when it is about content and process. Here the College, and especially Soc 2, used the social sciences as a means of achieving an understanding, an interpretation, of self and society and one's culture which was often quite different from the socialization and empiricism of the graduate research atmospheres.

Thirty years of teaching, of studying, of gathering facts and interpreting them in writing have deepened for me the richness of that tension, led me to refocus it and to refine my sense of what the social sciences can be and, at their best, are. That sense owes much to my experiences in the College but also to several strands of my later experience. It is captured for me particularly in my adventures with other cultures—especially that of India, but also of Japan—with my own research, and with the intellectual ferment in the social sciences occasioned by the linguistic and epistemological concerns of scholarly and intellectual movements of the past twenty years in Europe and the United States.

One development within the dialectic about which I speak has been a growing disenchantment with theory and generalization. I first encountered non-Western cultures at close range in the early 1960s, while teaching and doing research in northern India. Armed with the conventional sociological schemes of industrial and preindustrial societies, of community and society, of tradition and modernity, I thought they gave me useful ways of understanding the world. It was not that the theory of modernization lacked credence which disturbed and startled me. It was rather that the dualistic and contrasting concepts on which so much of sociology had been predicated did not appear useful, at least in the Indian context. Tradition was far from being always, or even often, in opposition to modernity, equality to hierarchy, or the secular to the sacred. Neither culture nor social structure possessed those qualities of unity and consistency which the evolutionary schemes of Western social scientists like Durkheim or Marx had maintained.

Nor was the matter simply one of industrial versus nonindustrial societies. Subsequent periods of residence in India and research in Japan made me caustic about the sweetness of the metaphysical base of the traditional sociological concept of societal types or systems. The Japanese certainly had, and have, an industrial technology, but the convergence hypothesis according to which the sociologist assumes that all industrial societies come to resemble each other is enormously misleading. Both India and Japan have remarkable similarities and differences in relation to each other and to Western societies, which in turn are only superficially summed up as "Western." The craft boundaries that exclude history and cultural anthropology could not, I learned, be swept away for the convenience of theory.

There is much more to this than the standard recognition that the empirical world deviates from the theoretical models implied by general concepts. In using the natural sciences (or at least our view of them) as metaphors for the construction of knowledge, the social sciences have so often striven for generalizations conveying predictability and certainty. My skepticism about theory is more than that. It is closer to the apocryphal French saying that all generalizations are false, including this one. A scholarship that seeks to explain or to understand events in their historical here and now, their fullness, finds the abstract character of theories and models and ideal types insufficient to describe the ambiguous nature of the empirical world. As Weber recognized, specific, particular, and real events cannot be deduced from laws or factors or even ideal types.

In his collection of essays aptly titled *The Poverty of Theory,* the British historian E. P. Thompson refers to this dialectic in C. Wright Mills's phrase of the clash between "molecular" research and "macroscopic" generalization. Along with Thompson, I believe that "In any vital intellectual tradition this dialectic, this abrasion between models and particular is always evident."[1] Along with Thompson, I look with considerable skepticism at theories which are ungrounded, which are arrived at without that intensive immersion in the world of the particular and the empirical, which are creatures of the mind untainted by corruption with a world of fact. To quote again from Kenneth Burke, who so clearly sees how craft and theory both create vocabularies and languages that imprison:

> I do not see why the universe should accommodate itself to a manmade medium of communication. . . . Perhaps because we have to think of ourselves as *listening* to the universe, as waiting to see what it will prove to us, we have psychotically made the corresponding readjustment of assuming that the universe will abide by our rules of discussion and give us revelations in a cogent manner. Our notion of causality as a succession of pushes from behind is thus a disguised way of insisting that experience abide by the conventions of a good argument.[2]

While I have done research in several "areas" of sociology and the social sciences, much of my work has occurred in relation to the study of alcoholic beverages, of drinking. I have been interested in how alcohol has been an object of law and political action in the United States but have also come to know much about the entire field of alcohol studies. While I have used "molecular" research to provide me with some ideas about American life—with "macroscopic" generalizations—I have been made aware of how complex, ambiguous, and paradoxical are such generalizing efforts. The more I know, the less I can confidently accept a "science" or even a discipline of alcohol studies.

Yet—and I assume you anticipated that there would be a "yet"—the other side of the dialectic cannot be scuttled. As a graduate student exposed to that intensive empiricism which symbolic interactionist research led us toward, the sociologist was somehow exempted from the world he or she studied. The essential model of a social science was adhered to. The subject was human and constructed a world of meaning-

1. E. P. Thompson, *The Poverty of Theory* (New York: Monthly Review Press, 1978), 274.
2. Kenneth Burke, *Permanence and Change: An Anatomy of Purpose* (New York: Bobbs-Merrill, 1965), 99.

ful objects, but operationally the observer could grasp those meanings and arrive at a "true" picture. Paradoxically, it was a humanistic view of the subject but a scientific view of the student.

My research and my experience in other cultures have made me discontented with what Nicholas Luhmann calls "totalizing paradigms." But the same experiences and the ferment of linguistic and epistemological work in recent years has made me see the empirical world of fact as less than clear and consistent. What Max Weber wrote in the early part of this century still rings true. (I quote from a translation by two former College social sciences instructors, Edward Shils and the late Henry Finch.)

> The question as to what should be the object of universal conceptualization cannot be decided "presuppositionlessly" but only with reference to the *significance* which certain segments of the infinite multiplicity . . . have for culture. . . . Order is brought into this chaos [of countless individual events] only on the condition that in every case only a *part* of concrete reality is interesting and *significant* to us, because only it is related to the *cultural values* with which we approach reality.[3]

This insistence that knowledge is always knowledge from some distinctive point of view is lent even wider support in the recent emphases which language studies and symbolic anthropology have produced (and which invaded Soc 2 in the 1960s and 1970s). The social construction of the real world makes the relation between subject and object, between observer and observed, between the sociologist and his or her data a matter of interaction rather than a one-sided affair. This relation between fact and fact finder exists, as Alfred Schutz pointed out, at two levels: in the typologies which the actor uses in defining real events and in the typologies which the sociologist makes in capturing the processes by which his or her subjects create those typologies.

Such considerations have led me, in my recent work, to an interest in how members of society create and construct an orderly and understandable world of moral and cognitive judgments. Grounded in the complexity of alcohol studies and the observations of a real world of police, drinkers, courts, and researchers, I have been trying to examine how auto safety has come to be perceived as a public problem and how drunk-driving has come to be construed as explaining a piece of it. My interest has lead me further: to examine how we, as a collective body, use the literary and rhetorical style of science and the ritualistic and

3. Max Weber, *On the Methodology of the Social Sciences* (Glencoe, Ill.: Free Press, 1949), 78.

symbolic style of law to dramatize, symbolize, and construct a cognitive and a moral order about this mundane topic. What I have been about is interpreting the phenomena of alcohol problems in a manner which reveals the interpretive moral and political and even theological judgments which surround the taken-for-granted quality of our realities; the way in which science and law are utilized in American life.

I have argued elsewhere (as has Richard Brown) that the vital trope of sociology is irony; the revelation of the very opposite and unrecognized elements in our paradigms. Such self-understanding enables us to create and construct alternatives where none were perceived. I think it is in the role played by imagination grounded in observation where best can be seen the uniqueness of social research. It is a mix of art and science that I wish we could still call "the social studies."

That dialectic, the tension between imagination and empiricism, is no more resolvable today than it was in the late 1940s. Graduate education was an attempt to govern if not to eradicate the imagination; to replace it with method, with the search for certainty. Soc 2 implicitly valued the imaginative and glossed over the intricacies of the empirical world. As a scholarly endeavor predicated on the model of positive science, sociology has presented a dialogue which attempts to reach a conclusion to dialogue, to find right answers. A truer vision, which I think the College contributed to, is that the dialogue is itself the answer. "Good talk" is itself a valuable attribute of human life and a way to create and develop the understanding and the alternatives which the human mind can gain from exposure to the world of fact with all its complexities.

When I was a freshman, I was influenced by a statement from John Dewey on the first page of my Social Sciences II syllabus, and which I believed in for many years. "Change," wrote Dewey, "is the fundamental fact in the social sciences as motion is the fundamental fact in the physical sciences." I would now say that the fundamental fact in the social sciences is that there are no fundamental facts in the social sciences. Our study, our craft, is humanistic as well as scientific. It is humanistic in the significant way that imagination must be used to give significance, value, and meaning to what we do. We create as well as discover, and the works that have been of the greatest value have been those that took the demands of craft lightly and created just that order that the empirical world hides. Such works have given us the capacity to be self-reflective and to widen our imagination even though they have often ignored the molecular empiricism which holds them to earth. it is interesting that when I came to list some of the contemporary works which have become part of the materials affecting the reflective conversation of my time many were the works of past Social Sciences 2 faculty: *The Lonely*

176

Crowd (Riesman), *White Collar* (Mills), *The Social Origins of Dictatorship and Democracy* (B. Moore), *The Coming of Post-Industrial Society* (Bell), *The Triumph of the Therapeutic* (Rieff).

The educational atmosphere that existed (and I hope still exists) at Chicago gave the College student, whatever his or her later exposure to social science, a vision of it as a means to make sense out of experience. To participate throughout one's life in the reflective discussion that public and intellectual life presume is its vital aim. Both the consumer-oriented view of education and the preprofessional, pre–graduate-school models make undergraduate education either a terminus that ends with a diploma or a passageway to a journeyman's craft. Either way seems half an education.

The dialectic I have been describing may never have been in anyone's educational plan. It was probably unlooked for and, possibly, not much noticed. Its sources are both in the nature of human knowledge and in the particular campus structure that made such autonomous centers of culture possible.

I realize the partiality and limited accuracy of the contrast I have been describing. Reading this paper in an earlier draft, my colleague and still also my friend, Bennett Berger, remarked that not only was it too reverential but I had used dualities in the very way I was criticizing. He is of course correct, probably in both his remarks.

The tension between craft and imagination, between a scientific and a humanistic vision of what the social sciences are about, was never perfectly or even largely embodied in the two cultures of the College and the graduate school. As my remarks certainly maintain, typologies seldom meet concrete reality. (As the late Gerhard Meyer was fond of saying, "things are not so simple as all that.") It is through our reflections now that we see what could be only dimly seen at the time: that each side of the dialectic has become known to us through dual loyalties and dual tasks. That understanding of different ways of knowing and grasping at knowledge is both deeply valuable and at the same time of highest importance for the educational process and for the scholarly pursuit.

Plato's *Republic* has been described as a "feast without satisfaction" because it begins with a walk and a conversation before dinner but the conversationalists never get to dinner. That never-ending quality to both education and scholarship is a lesson of profound import. It was among the most vital products of studying and teaching at Chicago. It is symbolic to me that this paper began in autobiography and ends in epistemology. Such reflectiveness about first principles is what imagination lends to craft. It is best attained in an intellectual atmosphere which does not shrink from the uncertainties, ambiguities, conflicts, and tensions which are the drama and joy of the mind at work and at play.

9

My Education in Soc 2 and My Efforts to Adapt it in the Harvard Setting

David Riesman

In this contribution I shall say something about the combination of design and accident which brought me in the first place to the College of the University of Chicago, and, thereafter, to Soc 2. That will entail a discussion of a question that has perplexed many of my friends and colleagues: namely, how I came to switch allegiance from the teaching of law to the teaching of the social sciences. Thereafter, I shall turn to the intensive self-education I experienced as simultaneously student and teacher in the College. I shall touch only briefly on the origins of Soc 2 (dealt with extensively in David Orlinsky's and Michael Schudson's accounts); thereafter, in the course of illustrating my efforts to adapt to Harvard College's general education program some of the intellectual perspectives and pedagogic preoccupations of Soc 2, I hope to make more vivid by comparison what was and remains special about the College.

I

My personal experience of life has only reinforced my belief in the large role chance plays in human affairs, whether on the personal or the larger societal level; for many people like myself, a career is a retrospective redefinition of a series of occupations, positions, and opportunities. A great many people who observed my shift away from being a professor of law to being a professor of the social sciences, and of sociology in particular, have wondered why I made such a switch: it is a puzzle especially to law professors, who regard that occupation as vastly superior to being a professor in a supposedly "soft" field and teaching mere undergraduates rather than prospective professionals. There is also some curiosity about how I managed to start as a lawyer and end in a sociology department without passage through the ordinarily requisite terminal training and degree of the Ph.D.

A part of the answer is that I was never fully committed to the law. Like quite a few of my classmates in the Harvard College class of 1931, I drifted on to Harvard Law School in part because I had failed to win a Rhodes Scholarship in which I had planned to read history at Oxford. (I now believe this was a fortunate failure.[1]) At that time, an academic career did not occur to me. My father was an eminent professor of clinical medicine and later of the history of medicine at the University of Pennsylvania, and I thought myself inferior to him in learning and assiduity. My mother's attitude, as an early Bryn Mawr graduate who had led her class but then not pursued the academic career that was supposed to follow upon her receipt of a fellowship to study in Europe, was that the only people who really counted in the world were those she called "first-raters," the creative artists whom she early recognized (Stravinsky, Faulkner, Virginia Woolf, Soutine) and several scientists of such originality that they could be included in her pantheon, primarily Freud and Einstein. Hence by her definition I was not a first-rater. I accepted her verdict and, by implication, the validity of easy and dogmatic divisions of people into first-raters and everybody else.

If I was not a first-rater, it mattered little what I did; it was the non–first-raters, in her view, who did the work of the world as it was carried on day by day. Hence, I might as well become a lawyer (like her brother, who spent much of his time in good causes such as helping the athletic development of impoverished youngsters in Philadelphia).

I had majored in biochemical sciences at Harvard, never with the thought of going to medical school, but accepting my parents' advice that one should study in college what one could not do on one's own, and since one could always read and go to art galleries and concerts, one should use the laboratories. So I studied organic chemistry with James Bryant Conant, and had one truly exciting course, on the physiology of the blood, with Lawrence J. Henderson. But I lacked the physical dexterity for laboratory work, and most of the science courses I took were taught in a routinized way; I did well in all of them, but disliked them. Both my parents and most of my college friends looked down on mere

---

1. The judgment is cryptic. It includes my later experience of Oxford donnish talk, with its brittle gamemanship, its verbal acuity, and the detailed factual knowledge brought by sixth formers from good public and grammar schools to major British universities, and my realization that I read too slowly and was not the sort of detective to do the kinds of work in history which had inspired me when C. K. Webster came to Harvard for a term from the University of Aberystwyth to teach an enormously detailed, erudite, and fascinating course on British diplomatic history in the era of Castlereagh and Canning and their role in the development of the Monroe Doctrine. We shall see later in this account how my being a slow reader affected my attitude toward being a law professor.

commerce, so the idea of the Business School did not appeal to me, although part of my education in social science began when, in my first law school year, I lived in the same residence as Elton Mayo, and came to know him fairly well (and his friend Henderson less well), and admired his patient empirical work for Western Electric Company.

I had recognized intellectually that Yale's Law School was broader than Harvard's, with a reputation for having introduced the social sciences into legal education. But I had many friends in Cambridge of both sexes, and quite a few of my college friends were going on to Harvard Law School. I arranged for two roommates with whom I could share ideas. One was a classmate, James Henry Rowe, Jr., a man with literary aspirations who was bored by law school, seldom got up in time to go to class, and was sure he would flunk out at a time when the Law School was reputed to fail a third of its entering class.[2] The other was Donald Meiklejohn, a graduate student in philosophy from Wisconsin, whom I had met the previous year through his stepmother's niece, one of my closest friends; I already had met his father when, as a Harvard College sophomore, I brought a number of college and university presidents to lecture at Harvard, including Alexander Meiklejohn, Clarence Cook Little of Michigan, Hamilton Holt of Rollins, and others, to tiny audiences who shared my interest in education and in educational reform.[3] By living at the Brattle Inn (which has since given way to a series of boutiques), where Mayo also lived and several other philosophers who were friends of Meiklejohn, I could be sure that talk among the group of roommates would rarely be about the law.

However, the main intellectual influence on me was a young instructor in government, Carl J. Friedrich, who had come from Germany shortly after World War I and had landed at Harvard and become a tutor in the residential house among whose first denizens I was a senior. Friedrich had taken his doctorate under Alfred Weber at Heidelberg and also studied in Vienna, and he introduced me to European social science and to the study of mass communications, which he was trying

2. James Rowe was rewarded for his interest in French novels by being Justice Oliver Wendell Holmes's last law clerk when the Justice had retired and wanted someone as his clerk who would read to him and share literary rather than legal interests; Rowe went on from there to become one of Franklin D. Roosevelt's anonymous assistants, and playing a part in the New Deal, and to end up as a Washington lawyer-lobbyist-politician active as a centrist in the Democratic party, one of Hubert Humphrey's leading advisers and supporters.

3. I was primarily responsible for inviting Donald Meiklejohn to come to teach at the College at Chicago, beginning the year after my arrival. I also recruited a close friend I had come to know during the four years I had taught at the University of Buffalo law School: Reuel Denney, a poet and critic who was then teaching English at a Buffalo high school.

to include within a theoretically and historically oriented government department.

Unlike Rowe, I read my cases and attended classes, but I did not do the kind of diligent study that was characteristic of my more eager classmates, and though I did not expect to fail, I did not expect to do particularly well at law school. I was completely astonished to find that I led my class, automatically became a member of the Law Review stuff, and was asked by Felix Frankfurter during my second year if I would become law clerk to Mr. Justice Brandeis—an opportunity I accepted and that carried with it a postgraduate fellowship at Harvard Law School in which one was supposed to prepare for work with the justice, presumably by study with Frankfurter.

I used the opportunity to study with Friedrich, with whom I had in the meantime bought a rundown farm near Brattleboro, so that we spent much time together on weekends clearing brush and painting and preparing a home for his family and a small tenant farmer's shack for my summer residence. I had begun an introduction to economics through law school courses in antitrust law and in corporation finance; Friedrich encouraged me to audit the economics classes of Edward Mason and others. I began to help him with the textbook later published as *Constitutional Government and Politics.*

It was Friedrich who gave me the confidence that I could make a contribution in academic life. Hence, when offered at the age of twenty-seven an opportunity to become a professor of law at the University of Buffalo Law School, I was able partially to overcome the sense of inadequacy instilled in me by my parents. Furthermore, I liked the idea of going to a city very different from Philadelphia, where I had grown up, or Cambridge, Boston, or Washington, where I had lived, to a city noted for its heavy industry and large Polish and other "ethnic" working-class populations. Unlike the three colleagues who (under the leadership of Dean Francis Shea, a Harvard Law School graduate and former New Deal official) had taken over a practitioners' law school—all of them Harvard Law School graduates who later returned there to teach—I was not primarily interested in the salient policy issues created by the New Deal and the newly developing fields of administrative law and labor law, as well as the increasing interest in constitutional law, but preferred to try to understand the social-psychological significance of decisions in landlord and tenant controversies, or in libel and slander. To put the matter differently, I was curious about the often unintended public consequences of decisions in areas of private law, rather than in commenting on the more obviously significant decisions of the United States Supreme Court. I was not so much a critic or housekeeper of leading decisions as an intellectual looking at seemingly trivial cases for the illumination they might shed on popular attitudes: for example, toward property or toward verbal assault, as refracted through the law.[4]

A study of the legal decisions governing defamation was congruent with my interest in public opinion and the role of the press. It also allowed raising an interesting cross-cultural issue: Why was it that Americans when verbally assaulted were supposed to be able to "take it," whereas in other countries—England, Austria, Argentina, among others—damaging verbal abuse, whether by individuals or by the press, was subject to severe sanctions in the form of civil penalties. I made use of contacts with European émigrés whom both Friedrich and I were seeking to place in American institutions (particularly lawyers, who had to go through an American law school before they could become legitimate practitioners) in order to increase my understanding of the attitudes in other countries toward the impact of words. I also recalled the dueling customs of an earlier era in the South, where gentlemen took words of abuse with deadly seriousness. My interest was in what all this said about American egalitarianism, illustrated in the belief that public figures were fair game for defamatory abuse, a tradition in the American press going back to Revolutionary days.

While my colleagues in the law teaching profession respected me, they did not share these interests. With exceptions, such as the imaginative Karl Llewellyn (who later came to the University of Chicago Law School from Columbia), the older generation of law professors sought to tidy up the law, acting as quasi housekeepers to rationalize the often contradictory decisions in state and federal courts under broader generalizations. In contrast, many of the colleagues of my own generation were preoccupied with issues arising out of the New Deal and large questions of governmental policy and the use of the courts, in ways with which we have become familiar, to promote what they regarded as social justice.

One of the articles I wrote at this time which grew directly out of my work with Friedrich, "Government Service and the American Constitution," I sent to the *University of Chicago Law Review,* whose editor at that time was Reuben Frodin—again, a chance occurrence, since Frodin later turned up as associate dean of the College at the time when I was being considered for an appointment.

4. The first law review article I wrote as a law professor, "Possession and the Law of Finders," *Harvard Law Review* 52 (1939): 1105–34, was an empirical study which compared legal decisions about the rights of finders of lost property ("finders keepers") with the actual practices of department stores, transportation companies, and others who in the course of business acquired large amounts of lost property and held it for the owner and, where possible, made efforts to return it, no matter what the cases held concerning rights of finders in a particular jurisdiction. At that time, studies comparing what cases said with what actually happened in the world were uncommon.

While at Buffalo, I began psychoanalysis with Erich Fromm, an outcome of my mother's close friendship with Karen Horney, who referred me to Fromm; I would travel to New York on alternate weekends and have several sessions of two hours each before returning to Buffalo. Several of my colleagues regarded psychoanalysis with deep suspicion, and anyone who went into analysis as a weakling who could not solve his own problems and stand on his own feet. In general, my law professor friends and colleagues regarded the work I was doing in defamation, public opinion, and a bit later on civil liberties in terms of the hazards as well as the benefits of freedom of speech, as interesting but outside their orbit of concerns.[5] Those who were interested in my work turned out to be friends I made during a leave of absence spent at Columbia Law School: Robert and Helen Lynd; Ruth Benedict and Margaret Mead and some of their circle; Richard Hofstadter; Lionel and Diana Trilling; and others.

Recognizing my restlessness as a law professor doing research on topics I did not consider relevant in any way to my teaching, I was offered the opportunity of joint appointments in law and political science by Lloyd Garrison then dean of the University of Wisconsin Law School, and Wayne Morse, then dean at the University of Oregon Law School; a friend who was dean at Ohio State also offered a joint appointment. But by that time I had concluded that political science as I had come to understand it from Friedrich and his colleagues was almost as abstract and theoretical as much legal scholarship;[6] the movement of empiricism into political science had not yet developed great strength. (It was only after I came to Chicago that I met Harold Lasswell, who exemplified in a brilliant way the combined application of a psychoanalytic approach and historical knowledge to both juridical and political issues.)

II

Friedrich sought to persuade me to take a doctorate in political science, and I believed I would probably have to do some graduate work before I

5. My Buffalo colleagues, notably the late Mark DeWolfe Howe, Jr., were absolutist devotees of the Bill of Rights. However, in law school I had concluded that the Fifth Amendment was a harmful legacy of long-vanished star-chamber practices in England, observing that countries at least as committed to liberty as the United States allowed the examination of criminal defendants by judges as well as by prosecutors. Nor did I share with them what I regarded as an almost vigilante attitude toward church-state separation as applied to aiding church-related schools and colleges, an attitude which seemed to me not conceivably within the purview of the framers of the federal Constitution, but later additions, in many cases reflecting anti-Catholic bigotry.

6. Cf. "The Law School: Critical Scholarship versus Professional Education," *Journal of Legal Education* 32 (1; April 1982): 110–19.

could shift fields completely. But with four small children born between 1938 and 1943, this did not appear to be a practicable course of action.

In 1942 I had published a monograph, "Civil Liberties in a Period of Transition," issued both as a separate brochure and as a contribution to a series of volumes entitled *Public Policy*, edited by Friedrich and Mason. It was an essay which took a critical view of some civil libertarian positions, looking at them in terms of social psychology and the problems of demagogic attack that the rise of Fascism and Nazism had made so evident, not only in Europe, but also in this country. With his omnivorous reading, Edward Shils had come across this essay and was using it as a reading in Soc 3. Realizing that the author was still alive, he suggested my name to Maynard Krueger, then chairman of Soc 3, and to Champion Ward, the dean of the College, and Reuben Frodin.

It was evident in 1945 that, with the returning veterans, colleges were understaffed and would need to expand rapidly. The opportunity to learn some social science in the process of teaching was more attractive than a tentative offer from Yale Law School, or any other likely opportunity. Champion Ward and Reuben Frodin visited me in New York, and I came out to visit the College with Edward Shils as my host and major supporter. (Shils gave a party for me at which he introduced me to a number of the more interesting social scientists at Chicago, including one of his own graduate students, a young man named Morris Janowitz). I met the staff of Soc 3 at a luncheon chaired by Maynard Krueger. I liked the group, which was lively and wide-ranging in knowledge and interests. The upshot of Shils's initiative was that I was invited to teach in Soc 3. Although I had been a full professor of law and was by that time thirty-six years old, it seemed entirely appropriate that I should be brought out as an assistant professor of the social sciences, without any discussion, let alone any assurance, concerning tenure.

I began in January 1946, to teach two sections of Soc 3: one was the second term of the year-long course that had started in the fall; the other was a speed-up course for veterans in which I was teaching the materials with which the course began. It was to Shils's already fabulous erudition that I primarily owed my appointment as an assistant professor of the social sciences in the College.

III

The next six months were among the most intellectually and emotionally stressful of my life. Earlier on, knowing with the impending end of the war that I would in all probability be leaving New York City, where we were then living, my wife, Evelyn, and our four children had moved to our farm in Brattleboro. It was impossible to rent any place where we could live as a family in Chicago. Accordingly, I lived in hotels, by myself, and under the regulations then prevailing, one was required to move every four or five days to another hotel—an agonizing business, since I was never sure I could find a place, and tramped the streets looking for possibilities. Finally, after some weeks of this anxiety-ridden existence, I managed to secure an apartment at the Windermere Hotel where I could stay until the spring term ended. That summer we did manage to buy a house on University Avenue but could not take possession of it until fall. The house was far too large for us but all that was available at the time. We rented out the top floor to graduate students and for part of one year, when our children were away at school, shared the house with Lewis and Rose Coser.

On the personal side, Edward Shils did his best to make me feel at home. He knew the good restaurants of the area, and enjoyed my company; on these occasions, we sometimes talked about the course and the colleagues in it. I met Everett and Helen Hughes and started to attend Everett Hughes's lectures on fieldwork and participant observation, so that Hughes became a significant mentor for me in sociology. I met Robert Redfield, and when Evelyn joined me, we became good friends of the Redfield family.[7]

On the academic side, I felt anxious and besieged. In two different courses I was having to stay one step ahead of my students. Teaching sections in Soc 3 was an entirely different experience from the combination of lecturing and questioning I had been accustomed to in law school.

Since students could wander about and were not definitively assigned to sections, there was always the threat that students would drift off to people who, it was believed, could prepare them better for the comps (even though as individual faculty we had no control over the examinations) or who were thought to be more exciting or entertaining. One day I showed up at a meeting of one of my sections with my worst nightmare realized: there was not a student in sight. I had gone by train to visit my family in Vermont the previous weekend but had returned just in time to meet my class. As it turned out, the ever-helpful Gerhard Meyer, thinking that I had not returned, had come and taken

7. I was working too hard, even frantically, to have much opportunity to make friends, and I missed the regular athletics which had previously helped—as they do to this day—to maintain my sanity. I found no fellow squash players nor adequate facilities for the game. Regular tennis had to wait until the following year, when we were able to bring Reuel Denney to the College to teach both in the humanities and the social sciences; Donald Meiklejohn, a Wisconsin college star, was way out of my duffer league.

my students into his own class—he returned them when he realized that I was there after all and ready to meet the class.[8]

IV

Many students, especially those coming from the Lab School, tested out of Soc 1 and quite a few out of Soc 2. But Soc 3 was thought to be so difficult and taxing a course that it demanded both the most superior faculty the College social science staff could provide, and the attendance of all students who wished to graduate from the College. Those who taught Soc 3 regarded themselves, and were regarded, as the elite of the social science staff. They included two widely read German émigrés, Gerhard Meyer, already mentioned, and Christian Mackauer; the formidably learned and scholarly Edward Shils; the philosophically trained and broadly educated Milton Singer. Frank Knight gave lectures in Soc 3 on economics. Soc 3 was oriented toward public policy, and the readings included some classics of political theory; some Supreme Court cases; Max Weber's *The Protestant Ethnic and the Spirit of Capitalism;* Frank Knight and others on macroeconomic theory. Readings based on fieldwork, whether in anthropology or sociology, were absent. Though the course raised profound issues of policy, it did so in what seemed to me a somewhat overgeneralized manner. That puts it too strongly—I am speaking here of questions of emphasis and degree—but as in the College as a whole, so also in Soc 3, there tended to be a focus on a canon of Great Books.[9]

Maynard Krueger had been a vice-presidential candidate on the Socialist ticket with Norman Thomas. I do not recall any Communists or fellow travelers teaching in the course, and as a group, they were notably absent at the University of Chicago, in contrast to Harvard and a number of other institutions at that period. I am inclined to think that this freedom from what was still a fairly potent ideology among academics and intellectuals in the immediate post–World War II years is a

8. Perhaps I should add that I had a very old-fashioned view of responsibility to meet all classes and still hold to this same attitude. While both Chicago and Harvard have been generous with leaves of absence, I have never missed a class because of a meeting or convention, or any other reason except a highly elevated temperature or a total lack of usable vocal cords.

9. As a brilliant graduate student in political science at Chicago, Philip Rieff had founded the short-lived *University Observer* in 1947. Many years later he was to write a remarkable essay, calling his fellow academics back to scholarship and away from any sort of pandering to students or to the *Zeitgeist*. See Philip Rieff, *Fellow Teachers* (New York: Harper & Row, 1972).

not unimportant element in the fact that the University of Chicago during the late 1960s under the chancellorship of Edward Levi, was able to remain relatively unaffected in its curriculum and its standards. The social scientists at Chicago during my years there were either conservatives, notably in economics, wildly liberal, unfanatical social democrats, or apolitical. We lacked any substantial cohort of ex-Communists who had become violently anti-Communist, or of covert Communists ready to be reignited by the student-faculty revolts of the late 1960s.[10] No concessions were made, whether to the demands of black students and their white allies for special programs of study or for "relevance" in general, nor was there grade inflation, as occurred on most campuses of equivalent selectivity. Having in New York come to know a number of the editors of *Partisan Review* and others such as Dwight MacDonald and Mary McCarthy, deeply involved with battling against the Stalinists, I was grateful for the relative ideological peace and corresponding intellectual disinterestedness that on the whole characterized the social sciences at Chicago in those years.[11]

V

As I have already implied, a good part of Soc 3 was compatible with Robert Hutchins' distaste for "mere" empiricism. Obviously, Soc 3 was very different from the program at St. John's College in its concern with contemporary social, political, and juridical problems—otherwise,

10. What Chicago did have was a group of scientists who had worked on the Manhattan Project in the secret laboratories underneath Stagg Field. Shils and other social scientists, and the historian Alice Smith, joined them in the work of the *Bulletin of the Atomic Scientists* and in their early effort to assure civilian control of the atom—an effort that succeeded with the passage of the McMahon Bill but did not prevent the later victory of Edward Teller, the Strategic Air Command, and Admiral Strauss over Robert Oppenheimer which made final the decision to proceed to build the fusion or H-bomb. There was also a group of World Federalists, including at that time Leo Szilard; I met some of them and admired their aim, but failed to get an answer to my question as to how, with world government, what were once wars between states would not turn into civil wars. Concern with the nuclear issue remained a principal thread of my political concerns, against which all other issues were assessed, from those early Chicago days until the present.

11. Testimony on these issues would be valuable from Daniel Bell, who as a late adolescent had been editor of the anti-Stalinist *New Leader* and left Chicago to work for *Fortune* at the time that journal was helping lead the campaign against Robert Oppenheimer. Also valuable would have been the reflections of the late Reinhard Bendix, who left Chicago for Berkeley, deserting its sociology department for the more sober milieu of political science as an aftermath of the student-faculty protests of the 1960s.

something as contemporary as my essay, "Civil Liberties in a Period of Transition," could not have been made a required reading.[12]

My own attitude toward Hutchins was ambivalent. I regarded him as making an immense contribution to American higher education nationally by his insistence on general education, by his effort to group disciplines into more comprehensive divisions, by his refusal to make any concessions to short-run vocationalism or to allow student consumerism to dictate the curriculum. Consequently, I supported Hutchins against his enemies both at Chicago and elsewhere. However, we had substantial differences concerning the College. For one thing, I was eager to include extensive empirical work in the sequence on the social sciences. When working on the development of Soc 2 in 1946–47, I looked for unprocessed data which students and their mentors could interpret (for example, unprocessed field notes from community studies, or life histories, or the actual questionnaires used in a public opinion survey), all items Hutchins considered trivial and ephemeral. The characteristic arrogance of a bright lawyer was a familiar experience, but nonetheless something of a burden, mitigated by Hutchins' wit and charm.[13] It seemed to me that Soc 2, which included readings in Freud, Ruth Benedict's *Patterns of Culture,* and the recently published work of Gunnar Myrdal, *An American Dilemma,* offered materials of richer empirical substance. I decided to migrate from Soc 3 to Soc 2 and persuaded Milton Singer, Gerhard Meyer, and Christian Mackauer to make the move along with me. Milton Singer was crucial in accepting the leadership of the expanded staff of Soc 2 and in the breadth of intellectual horizons which informed the development of that course. (Naturally, as in all such matters, elements of personality entered, but they are not to the point here.)

12. The St. John's College program includes in readings for the senior year selections from Tocqueville's *Democracy in America;* from Karl Marx's *The Communist Manifesto* and *Capital;* from Freud and Keynes; however, these works are not read in any historical context, but as parts of an ongoing "Great Conversation." Soc 3 took for granted the importance of the historical context of the works that we read.

13. Furthermore, I regarded Hutchins as making a profound mistake both politically and educationally when he insisted that the College program be complete in itself and sealed off from electives in the graduate divisions. When I came to the College, students had the option of taking two courses in one or another of the graduate divisions, which therefore retained the hope that they might acquire some possible Ph.D. candidates who had become attached to a particular specialty while still undergraduates. But Hutchins in his grand manner despised specialists. When he along with those I came to refer to as the "College patriots" added a capstone course in history and what was then known as O.M.P. to the College curriculum, thus closing off apertures for electives, I fought the decision as a mistake—as indeed it turned out to be, since the limited capital of goodwill the College had among the graduate divisions pretty much evaporated at this point. I also believed that students should be exposed to specialists as well as generalists as part of their general education—a judgment that Hutchins, with a certain grandiosity, easily dismissed.

Milton Singer became the chairman of Soc 2 and assigned to me the task of developing a revised Soc 2 in cooperation with the other people teaching in it. Among these, one of the most important, who left his mark decisively on Soc 2, was Daniel Bell. He was thoroughly steeped in the work of Karl Marx. He had strong empirical interests as well. Along with Milton Singer and me, he appreciated the contribution of Freud and the value of reading some of Freud's writings in an undergraduate course.

I should point out that both Soc 2 and Soc 3 differed from other College courses in the balance between formal lectures in Mandel Hall to the entire class and the discussion sections. Some courses had three section meetings and one lecture a week. I found the section meetings so intense that two a week seemed just about right. And the number of lectures we had made it possible for specialists on the staff to exhibit their erudition to their colleagues as well as to students; if they were sometimes over the heads of many of the students, then the section leaders could help interpret what was said in later section meetings.[14]

14. At one point, Donald Meiklejohn, accepting his father's belief that lecturing was an antiquated idea and that discussion with students in the Socratic mode was alone worthwhile, sought to abolish the lectures and have four section meetings a week. I thought as already indicated that this was unwise pedagogically, since the rhythm of lectures and sections in my judgment had worked well. Such a change would have meant a virtual doubling of the responsibility of each instructor, by having to prepare four rather than two section meetings, plus the occasional lecture in the field of one's special interest. If Meiklejohn's notion had carried the day, I believe I would have left the College. I regarded many of the section meetings, conducted along Socratic lines, e.g., "What did Max Weber mean by this particular sentence?" as a kind of ping-pong game between a few bright students and the section leader, and I believed that students should be exposed to the full range of lecturers that the University offered rather than having their experience confined to the particular person in whose section they landed or to whose section they might shift. For example, I brought Milton Friedman to lecture in opposition to rent control to an audience composed almost entirely of veterans. The students booed him. I intervened to say that I thought they should listen carefully to Friedman, that when they came themselves to buy a house, they would find that rent control was an immediate palliative only for those who had already found rented places to live. Rent control had been promoted politically by targeting landlords as great and greedy "slumlords." But I knew that many apartments had been built by working people who had invested in real estate, putting up a three-or four-story flat building with apartments which they could take care of themselves without the resources to pay the "tax" rent control imposed. The veterans were not persuaded, and although I am not a devotee of Milton Friedman in many other respects, I still regard his judgment on rent control as correct and proved so by the experience of cities where rent control has been retained.

I also invited Bruno Bettelheim to lecture in Soc 2. There I also intervened, not to defend a lecturer, but to protect a student. Bettelheim, a brilliant man given to sarcasm, had noticed a young woman knitting in the third or fourth row of Mandel Hall. He told her to stop, remarking that she was really masturbating—a comment I thought uncalled for and outrageous. (Legends have built up about this episode. Some credit me rather

The Chicago quarter system had great advantages for faculty members. There was always a certain attrition after the fall quarter, so that it was possible to teach the fall quarter and take the winter and especially the spring quarter off without imposing excessive burdens on colleagues.

Accordingly, after teaching the fall quarter in 1946, I was granted the next two quarters off to work on the creation of the kind of mixture that came to characterize Soc 2. At the same time, a group of us in the course were actively recruiting faculty colleagues who could contribute to the course by sharing its general concerns and by their special knowledge. For example, beginning with no one trained in anthropology, we brought in Rosalie Hankey, who had been trained at Berkeley and done her fieldwork in the Japanese relocation camps—work that Morton Grodzins, a political scientist and later dean of the Social Science Division, thought was significant, and worked to get published. (It was not our doing, but it was the kind of event that occurs when colleagues work closely together, that Murray Wax—recruited several years later from the University of Pennsylvania and Temple, where, with training in the natural sciences, he had been teaching philosophy—broadened his interests to include our versions of the social sciences, married Rosalie Hankey, and eventually took a Ph.D in sociology with a thesis on magic, ritual, and religion in Viking culture—work that might be thought of as a combination of social history and retrospective, psychologically oriented anthropology.) I do not recall who was responsible for recruiting Alicja Iwanska, the Polish émigré who had taken her doctorate in sociology under Robert Merton at Columbia, and had then done a fine monograph based on fieldwork in a rural hamlet (to which she gave the ironic pseudonym "Good Fortune") in the Pacific Northwest. At that time, happily, the line especially at Chicago between sociology and anthropology was not sharply drawn; the two departments had been united at the graduate level until the 1940s, and Alicja Iwanska was on the border between the two fields. Sylvia Thrupp was already on the scene as an economic historian—the closest to economics Soc 2 ever came.

I was especially eager to bring to the staff someone with experience in survey research. Margaret Mead called my attention to Robert S. Weiss, then at the Institute for Social Research at the University of Michigan, one of the major centers of training in survey research and

---

than Bettelheim with the remark, but these must be people who do not know me, because my antagonism to the use of sarcasm by faculty members toward students is passionate. Some have the student making a comeback she was too crushed to make: "Dr. Bettelheim, when I knit, I knit; when I masturbate, I masturbate!" This is wholly apocryphal.)

analysis. A social worker before receiving a Ph.D. in sociology at Michigan, Robert Weiss brought a broad background of social psychological understanding as well as his survey expertise to Soc 2. Indeed, the staff we sought had to be interested in expanding their horizons beyond their original specialties.

In one area sometimes included in the social and sometimes in the natural sciences, we made no effort to recruit: namely, experimental psychology. But I would have been very happy if we could have found an economist willing to join the staff. In a sense, economics has been the most advanced of the social sciences, and the highly professionalized narrowness of some of its practitioners reflects this very progress. To illustrate: I occasionally would suggest to graduate students in economics that they take a leave of absence to do something akin to fieldwork by taking a position, for example, as assistant comptroller in a small business. They would learn something about microeconomics in a very direct way. Invariably, their reaction was that aggregate statistics were more than adequate for the understanding of microeconomic phenomena—and in any case, while they were sojourning in company which would necessarily be dismissed as idiosyncratic, some disciple of Paul Samuelson would have published four articles in refereed economics journals! It was not a hazard that a bright aspiring economist would wish to take.[15]

After Soc 2 had been given for half a dozen years, the thought occurred to me that we might build another course around Detroit, automobile workers, and the whole automobile culture and its consequences for American life. One could focus on production, both the assembly line and the styling sections (the fads and fashions, annual obsolescence, and the spread and patterning of innovation), on interethnic cooperation and conflict in a metropolis repeatedly studied by the University of Michigan, on the whole development of suburbaniza-

---

15. Herbert Simon, in his Nobel Prize speech for the award in economics, emphasized the importance of studies of disaggregated economic phenomena in minute detail. Indeed, Herbert Simon, with his wit and continuing interest in undergraduate education, and his polymath probing and subtle curiosity, may be regarded as the ideal-typical product of the University of Chicago at that era.

At one point I sought to see whether I could interest Kenneth Boulding, who had moved from Iowa State University to the University of Michigan, in the possibility of coming to the College at the University of Chicago. Trained in agricultural economics, Boulding had a bent for the application of economics, as well as a marvelously fertile imagination throughout the whole range of social sciences and beyond. But he preferred to live with his family in the academic community of Ann Arbor rather than the metropolis of Chicago. The Chicago Department of Economics did benefit from another émigré from Iowa State in Theodore Schultz, with whom I later came to share interests in the assessment of investment in education, but he was never available for the College.

tion and on what the anthropologist John J. Roberts was then studying as "roadside culture," as more and more internal tourism by auto was occurring. In part, it was for want of an economist that this idea never got very far, for I thought one would need in the course an economist familiar with the whole structure of the automobile industry, the pattern of subcontracting, the place of dealerships and the ramifying economic consequences of America on wheels. The notion might not have worked anyway, demanding as it would an enormous amount of work by the staff to develop such a course and then to learn how to teach it effectively so that it would interest undergraduates who were, for worse as well as better, involuntarily captives of the Chicago program.

The Soc 2 staff included wide-ranging political scientists, such as Morton Grodzins, already mentioned, and Alfred DeGrazia; the historian Livio Stecchini; a number of sociologists, notably Joseph Gusfield, Sally Cassidy, and Paule Verdet.

VII

We owed some of these recruits to the support given to the College by some faculty in the Graduate Division of the Social Sciences. The Committee on Human Development, which I was asked to join several years after coming to Chicago, was itself an interdisciplinary group, including anthropologists, notably Lloyd Warner; such psychologists as Allison Davis, Bernice Neugarten, and William Henry; and, for sociology, Everett Hughes. There was also a short-lived Committee on Communication headed by Bernard Berelson, an interdisciplinary group offering a master's degree, on which I also served. Indeed, Robert Hutchins seemed to follow a policy reminiscent of Franklin D. Roosevelt's policy during the New Deal: when Roosevelt did not like the workings of one of the old-line cabinet departments, he appointed a new agency and gave it a similar mission! So, too, Hutchins created new interdisciplinary committees within the Division of the Social Sciences, among them the Committee on Planning, which he brought Rexford Tugwell to head and during whose brief existence some remarkable recruits were gathered: Edward Banfield, Martin Meyerson, and a graduate student, Staughton Lynd (whom I recruited to work with me as a research assistant on a book on Thorstein Veblen). The Committee on Social Thought, of which Robert Redfield was the main inspiration, along with John Nef, added to the climate of interdisciplinary work at the graduate level which both provided graduate student and other recruits to the College staff of Soc 2 and made it possible for me increasingly to divide my commitments between the College and the Graduate Division. (In 1954 I became a member of the Department of Sociology while retaining my allegiance to the College.)

VIII

The University of Chicago had from its founding been a coeducational institution. I took for granted the contribution women scholars could make, and the presence of such outstanding women as Sylvia Thrupp, Rosalie Hankey Wax, Alicja Iwanska, or later Sally Cassidy, was not thought to be anything special. So too I took for granted friendship and colleagueship with Allison Davis, as well as with St. Clair Drake, a black anthropologist teaching at Roosevelt University, or with Horace Cayton, coauthor with Drake of the book, *Black Metropolis,* dealing with the social pyramids among the Negro population of Chicago.

But it did not follow from the presence of women on the faculty that at Chicago shy women students were not often more diffident in section meetings than the assertive young men whom the College attracted and fostered. This was true in spite of Chicago's long feminist record. While shy and sensitive women students in my observation often fare better at the women's colleges, they were far freer at Chicago than at the Ivy League institutions in the East which at first grudgingly and only later eagerly welcomed women undergraduates.

I would like to illustrate the kind of pedagogic experiment our individual section meetings made possible by an example I hit upon to draw out the more diffident women. One of our readings from the very outset had been Freud's *Civilization and Its Discontents.* In a footnote on page 117 of that book, Freud notes that the death instinct must be innate because children of parents who are kindly and benign nevertheless get angry at the parents without reason—hence, hostility must be inborn. When we came to this passage I would ask for a show of hands as to who had ever been a baby-sitter, and generally the majority of women in the class had had that experience. I then asked these women to report on their experiences as baby-sitters in the homes of permissive parents, for example, faculty families in the Hyde Park area. Had they observed anything that the parents did or neglected to do which might make children angry? At first, the question had some of the students perplexed. At that time, there was a kind of sanctity about the readings and especially about Freud. How could a seventeen-year-old student contradict Freud on the basis of mere personal, happenstance observation? I would insist that just such observation was necessary to test Freud's generalizations. Then the stories would come out about ways in which parents who appeared permissive were actually self-indulgent in not wishing to go to the burden of disciplining their children; they would not set up formal rules, but would show disapproval if informal hopes were disobeyed. There turned out to be ample reason why children of such parents would get angry with them; one did not need to posit a "death instinct" to explain children's rage.

This pedagogic device often gave the shyer women confidence that they could draw upon their own experience in other areas, and once having broken the ice of speaking in a section, it was easy to continue. Any such technique is, so to speak, good for this trip only. At a different time and in different milieus, many students came to give almost total credence to what they felt, not to what they thought or what they had carefully observed. They listened to what they believed were their own private and unique feelings and claimed authenticity for these against the claims of others, at least those outside their peer group: claims of the teacher as authority, of the book as authority, of the whole intellectual tradition as authority.

Another pedagogic experiment had a different aim. If my less than adequate memory serves me, we began Soc 2 some years by reading Gunnar Myrdal's *An American Dilemma,* making use of his appendixes dealing with problems of method and of objectivity in the social sciences. The approach of Myrdal was so reasonable and persuasive to the white liberal students in the College that they readily assumed that white Americans regard American race relations as a dilemma, suffering guilt for failure to live up to the ideals of equality. To jar this prevalent view, I would ask my students to make the thought experiment of how a fatalistic Catholic from Spain or Italy would view American race relations. I would note than Gunnar Myrdal was almost ultra-American in his energetic rationality and belief that problems, once delineated, could be solved. This was notable in his finding that the items high on the agenda of American Negroes, such as equal employment opportunity, were more readily granted by whites than items low on the agenda of Negroes, such as integration of neighborhoods or intermarriage. In discussion I would guide the students to the realization that a fatalistic visitor from a non-Puritan country might wonder why some Americans were so vulnerable to guilt about race relations; all societies were stratified in one way or another—and commonly, the world over, by color—and how many Americans really did feel that this constituted a dilemma? The human heart has in any case great capacities for compartmentalization, hence for living equably with what others might regard as dilemmas. Students could come to realize that such a hypothetical visitor would probably have written a very different book. This discussion was not initiated to denigrate Myrdal, whose work I valued, but rather to place it in a broader perspective and make clear that it was not the only approach that one could take, and to lead the students to raise the empirical question as to how many Americans actually experience a dilemma, and at what level of consciousness.

Among the colleague group teaching Soc 2, we would trade such ideas for the conduct of section meetings. We would also struggle, year by year, with the always inadequate efforts at integration of disparate materials—disparate in terms of difficulty and in terms of seeking to draw connections among the different readings. The title we gave the course, "Culture and Personality," included only part of what we were teaching. In *Civilization and its Discontents,* Freud dealt with broad cultural issues, but in other more technical writings, such as the *General Lectures on Psychoanalysis,* which we occasionally read, he stuck pretty closely to what I termed his hydraulic theories of personality, which were quite remote from those to be found in the writings of Ruth Benedict or Erich Fromm's *Escape from Freedom.*

The great writer had to be read on his or her own terms as well as subsumed under the integrative impulse. Hence there was an inevitable dicontinuity in the readings and in the course itself, just as there was in the lectures. For example, my four lectures on Freud (later published in *Psychiatry* and collected in *Individualism Reconsidered*) were a critical effort to elucidate some themes of Freud's thinking and then to interpret and clarify these—hoping to avoid reductionism—in terms of his own era along lines that have since then become much more familiar and even taken for granted. In contrast, the lectures on Max Weber were more expository, dealing with the inherent difficulties of *The Protestant Ethic and the Spirit of Capitalism*—a book not easily included as a work of culture and personality, since it is in large part a brilliant, though speculative, historical interpretation. Contemporary community studies, such as August Hollingshead's *Elmtown's Youth,* or a book drawing on that and similar studies, *Who Shall Be Educated?* by Lloyd Warner, Robert Havighurst, and Martin Loeb, lacked the grandeur of Freud or Weber. And it was not easy to subsume them under a "culture and personality" rubric, since they were primarily concerned with social stratification in the educational system of a small community and the question as to whether class lines in America were growing more rigid or not—a question of salient importance to sociology and to society, but not one which had direct bearing on questions of personality and intrapsychic functioning.

IX

In my remarks for the Soc 2 fiftieth-anniversary celebration held at the University of Chicago, I dealt with the marvelous hubris which allowed us to range over such large territory in a way that would have been much more difficult as knowledge accumulated and specialties multiplied. I also touched upon the way in which the term "interdisciplinary" began to attract followers who had no discipline and who, by attacking specialization, laid a false claim to superiority. In the course itself, we consciously sought to avoid such a polarization, making clear that interdisciplinary work was only one genre among others, the effort toward which could be, but was not inevitably, fruitful.

In retrospect I have asked myself what made the venture at least the limited success that I believe occurred. One element already adumbrated was the mutual good will among the staff of the course, who were willing to read works in fields in which they did not feel fully at home, subject to the guidance of those who were somewhat more expert, knowing in most cases that their turn would come as we moved to other topics and readings. More important was the willingness of the students to make the efforts at connection with the materials and the discussion of them that the course required. A great majority took it for granted that it was up to them to seek to master the materials. They were argumentative about particular readings, and preferred some to others, but they did not object to the idea of required readings—let alone, as so many students do today, to any substantial assignment of readings at all. They were willing in an extraordinary way, as it looks from the vantage point of the 1990s, to postpone gratification in terms of learning how they had done on the examination. Though there were trial-run examinations at the end of each term, the grade that counted was the grade on the comprehensive examination at the end of a full year. More recent generations of students have not been willing to wait that long, in a style more characteristic of the United Kingdom than of the United States, for a verdict on their performance but have insisted on more immediate feedback. To be sure, at that time the occupational future did not look so hazardous as at present, and studies were not as driven to seek top grades as they have since become.

Correspondingly, students were willing to open themselves up to new materials even beyond the readings in the syllabus. I often found that if I mentioned a particular book, for example, Thorstein Veblen's *The Theory of the Leisure Class*, students might dig out the book in the library, rather than simply let the matter go by as a bit of name-dropping on the part of the professor.

Indeed, to return to my pedagogic device vis-à-vis *Civilization and Its Discontents*, students sometimes seemed almost too bookish, too willing to accept the authority of the esteemed authorities who were read in the course. I could make the point by another illustration. When we were reading Piaget's *The Moral Judgment of the Child*, I would ask students to describe for me how they had actually played marbles when they were in school. This was an area where the young men generally had far more experience than the young women. Some would describe how they could come to a game of marbles with a crony who would back them up as the group of boys got into a wrangle over efforts to alter the rules of the games—often ending up in physical combat. I would observe how different was the ganglike behavior described by some of the students from that of the mild Genevan working-class children observed by Piaget, thus making a cross-cultural anthropological point concerning a reading ostensibly focused on the development of moral judgment and cognition.

I did not intend by such examples to suggest that our readings could be dismissed by students because they did not jibe with their own experiences of daily life. Rather, I intended to have students take seriously both the reading and their own experience, and to make serious efforts to reconcile the two without discarding either one. In many instances, each ought to qualify the other. The reading might be overgeneralized, or the student's experience might be misapprehended or quite idiosyncratic.

The effort of such teaching was to help students learn to read more carefully, and at least as far as I was concerned, to approach heated issues with a combination of concern and detachment. In terms of any grand integration of the social sciences, I doubt if for many students the course was more than the sum of its parts. Whatever notions of integration we members of the staff possessed, severally and collectively, could only be unevenly conveyed in a single course. Still, that is a good deal more than happens in most undergraduate liberal arts colleges where distribution requirements permit a student to select, let us say, either an economics course or a history course (allowing an enormous roster of choice among epochs and places and themes), or a course in sociology or anthropology which might be quite specialized.

Soc 2 provided two great advantages over such a pattern. I have already referred to the principal one: namely, that students were all reading the same books and listening to the same lecturers in Mandel Hall, and thus what happened in the curriculum could spill over into conversations among students and faculty outside the classroom. And then for the lecturers in Soc 2 we could take for granted what students had learned on the basis of their whole experience in the College, whereas in other institutions one would be dealing with students about whom one could take nothing for granted, some of whom would already have had intensive work in an area whereas others would not know who James Madison was or whether the Renaissance preceded or followed the Reformation. In a student body selected meritocratically (granted the limitations of tests, including the Chicago multiple-choice examinations),[16] one could pitch one's discourse at a level which would not bore the ablest for the sake of salvaging the least adept and the neophyte. Another advantage that Soc 2 possessed and still possesses over the typical distribution requirement is the exposure of students through the lectures to a great variety of styles of presentation: students were not permitted to select lecture courses on the basis of who was more entertaining or whether the class met at a convenient hour, as is so common elsewhere. Because the number of lectures any one of us presented in Soc 2 was small, almost lapidary care could be devoted to the lectures in a way that only the most gifted lecturers manage at other institutions.[17] Indeed, I do not know if it is true of others who are graduates either of the staff or the student body of Soc 2,

16. Against their many critics, I have been a strong defender of the Educational Testing Service and the much maligned SAT (or ACT) examinations as one basis for admission to college and for students to decide where they will be well matched at college. (See "The Onslaught on Standardized Testing" in David Riesman, *On Higher Education* [San Francisco: Jossey-Bass, 1980], 123–36.) This is because, like democracy, these tests are flawed in many ways, but are better that the alternatives generally offered, such as counselor or teacher recommendations, or admissions interviews. One type of flaw, perhaps particularly significant for Chicago-type students, became evident to me when I analyzed the answers to a fall term trial multiple-choice test for students in a section whose members I knew quite well as individuals. I brought copies of the examination to class and asked particular students why they had given the answers they did, which were not the answers marked correct by the examiner. They could not believe that so simple an answer as the intended one could be correct; there must be a trick somewhere. They therefore found abstruse but plausible reasons for another answer—something I had surmised by studying the patterns of their answers. I think I helped these students by pointing out to them that the College examiner was, like *l'homme moyen sensuel*, not out to trick students, and that they should not assume that obvious answers were invariably mistaken ones. For it was often the most brilliant students who had been led astray by their very ingenuity. I proposed as a remedy that there be a line on the examinations in which a student could explain an answer, and if the explanation were intelligent, be given credit, even if the student's choice was other than the one intended to be the answer. The hazard of this scheme was the time it took while going through the examination, so it was not an ideal solution, but my little experiment did show that coaching helped at least that group of Chicago students who envisaged examiners as more devious than was the case. Indeed, Christine Maguire, a psychologist who served as examiner, was in no way devious.

17. Only a rare person of great energy, ingenuity, and capacity for organization is capable of innovative teaching when the teaching load itself is as large as it commonly is in liberal arts colleges and many research universities. Today in many public institutions, faculty members are required to teach a certain number of "contact hours," based on the populist judgment that faculty members have an easy life and do not deserve to teach, let us say, a "mere" six hours a week. To be sure, perhaps the majority of faculty would not do better teaching if they did less of it, and there are surely differences among disciplines in this as in many other respects. But in a staff-taught course, vanity as well as scrupulousness may compel the lecturer to reread and rethink the text every year when it is used in successive years, discarding old notes and incorporating more recent scholarship.

but for many its virtues are most apparent from the perspective of other institutions, whereas to those who were struggling with the course at the time, its problems of coverage and cohesion could appear utterly intractable.

X

On the whole, I found it an advantage to be able to teach both graduate and undergraduate students at Chicago. But I was troubled by the fact that I could see bright undergraduates whom I had known in the College become more timid and less exploratory when they entered the Ph.D. program in sociology. Furthermore, a certain contamination is likely to creep into the relation between a graduate student and his or her academic mentors—the contamination that placement of the graduate student will depend heavily on the mentor's recommendations, and in a polarized field such as sociology, there may also be involved attitudes toward particular "schools" of thought or method and, recently, of ideological persuasion. Such "contamination" is not wholly escaped in undergraduate teaching, but at the College or in the voluntary choice students make at Harvard, one's undergraduate students are for the most part not dependent on any one instructor, for it is their overall record, their GRE scores, or LSAT, or MCAT scores, and in Ph.D. programs, the verdict of their professors in their major field, which can influence their later fates. I decided that I preferred primarily to teach undergraduates even though this meant a certain divorce between the areas of my teaching and the shifting areas of my research interests.

If I could find a place with able students where I could primarily teach undergraduates, I decided to leave Chicago, particularly when I discovered that the graduate students working with Everett Hughes or me or others who were regarded in a stereotypical way as "merely" qualitative, were anxious lest their theses not pass muster. With a not uncommon paranoia, they concluded that no thesis without tables in it would receive the imprimatur of the department, even though I would repeatedly send them to the library to look at the dissertations recently done in which there were no tables—not that I myself had anything against tables: indeed, I believed students should be able both to create and to understand tables or other modes of presenting quantitative data succinctly.

XI

What Harvard offered were two attractions: the opportunity of a special chair which would permit me to delineate my own program and thus to teach undergraduates almost exclusively, and the interdisciplinary excitement of the former Department of Social Relations, which brought together sociology and cultural anthropology, along with personality and clinical psychology. The department attracted first-rate undergraduates and, at the graduate level, adventurous graduate students and junior faculty who, though specializing in one wing of the joint department, would be exposed to all the wings. In the days of Florence Kluckhohn and the late Clyde Kluckhohn, no one could get through without anthropological exposure and, at the graduate level, a fieldwork requirement.

When I decided in 1957 to leave Chicago—a sad and difficult parting—I had arranged to offer a course in Harvard's general education program which at that time was oriented, in the fashion described in the famous "red book," to a generally historical transmission of the Western heritage—a program into which a course that would emphasize empirical work in contemporary America would fit only if it were given a historical backdrop. As most readers probably know, Harvard never did achieve a true core program in the sense that all students would be taking the same course and doing the same readings; indeed, the chance that a student would have as a roommate or a table companion a friend who was taking even one of the same courses out of the smorgasbord of two thousand courses was both random and rare.

The historical focus was not a problem for me, since I intended to begin the course with an intensive study of Tocqueville's *Democracy in America*, focusing primarily on the second volume, which deals with the cultural and social-psychological aspects of American life as envisioned by Tocqueville, rather than the more geographic and political descriptions of the first volume. Tocqueville would remain the staple to which we would return throughout the course, as, for example, when we came to read Robert Lane's detailed interview study of fifteen men in a New Haven housing project, *Political Ideology*, which explores Tocquevillean themes of equality, class envy and resentment, political participation, and passivity as the chief focus of his repeated interviews.

One major interest we had in Tocqueville was to view him as an early, untrained but imaginative ethnographer, spending a nine-month field trip in America with his companion Gustave Beaumont, writing with an eye to a French audience whom he was seeking to persuade that, given freedom of association and the ability to form many voluntary associations, a free press, and a British-style judicial system, democracy would not be anarchy, or ruinous to men of property. It would, he envisaged, have a leveling effect on the heights of culture and conduct, but it would also avoid degradation and submissiveness (except for the condition of the Indians and especially the Negroes, for Tocqueville feared the worst in race relations).[18] We asked ourselves in lecture discussions and sections how Tocqueville translated the information and misinformation he collected and pondered over, often close to despair, for five years in Paris, and almost by inventing an American that he built out of fragments, presented us with a picture of ourselves more recognizable to the mid-twentieth century than were the accounts by such observers as Dickens, Harriet Martineau, the Trollopes, or George Grund, a German émigré who wrote, contra Tocqueville, *Aristocracy in America*. We asked whether it is not an optical illusion for Americans to see ourselves as in constant perpetual motion, at least in geographic if not in status terms, because our eyes are captured by the movers and not by the stayers—although the latter are affected by the movers who enter their turf, bringing different values, churches, aspirations for themselves and for the locale from which they might soon move again. We saw Tocqueville as a cultural and political conservative, fearful of the negative consequences of reactionary efforts in Europe to stem what he saw as the providential further development of both democracy and equality, yet aware that both were threats to individual liberty which might yet in some measure be preserved by accommodation and vigilance.

When we read Alicja Iwanska's "Good Fortune"[19] we sought to be equally alert to the hauteur of a Polish visitor to a provincial farming community, of course far more self-consciously acting as an ethnographer, analyzing the sexual division of labor and leisure, the still influential religious attitudes (Tocqueville seemed almost unaware of the American pattern of religious revivalism, though he did devote a small chapter to the "fanatic spirituality" of a minority of Americans), and the lack of cooperation for example in pooling farm machinery among the inhabitants.

In earlier years we also read Thorstein Veblen's *The Theory of the Leisure Class*, with its vivid and witty caricature of American life as viewed by a sardonic Norwegian immigrant's son at the turn of the century. I might add that we dropped Veblen in later years when the students themselves became so extraordinarily critical of American society that Veblen, despite his pioneering view concerning the role of women in maintaining the species while men engaged in idle games of warfare

18. George Wilson Pearson, *Tocqueville and Beaumont in America* (New York: Oxford University Press, 1938). Some of us immersed ourselves in Tocqueville's other writings, especially those on the *ancien régime* and his recollections: *The Recollections of Alexis de Tocqueville*, ed. J. P. Mayer (New York: Meridian Books [paperback edition], 1959), and the critiques of Tocqueville both by contemporary and by later writers. See also cf. my essay, "Tocqueville as Ethnographer," *American Scholar* 30 (1961): 174–87.

19. "Good Fortune: Second Chance Community," published by the Agricultural Experiment Station of Washington State University, 1948.

and conspicuous production and consumption, prefiguring some of the themes of the women's movements, was no longer appropriate.

XII

Unlike the collegiality of Soc 2, the Harvard pattern in the general education program, established in the social sciences by a splendid course taught by Samuel Beer, was to have a star lecturer recruit a group of junior faculty and graduate students to teach sections and to work individually with students, at least at the minimum to grade their examinations. In contrast, I shall indicate, the course I directed demanded considerably more, but only for a single term rather than a full year.

In recruiting a staff, which varied over the years from eight to eleven—the maximum being set by the number who could get around the Riesmans' dinner table—I had a head start which proved indispensable in the trial year of the course. Michael Maccoby, who had taken his undergraduate degree in the Social Relations Department, had come after a year at Oxford to the Sociology Department at Chicago to work with me. He then returned to Harvard to take a doctorate in Social Relations and helped recruit staff for the course. My own mentor from my student days, Professor Carl J. Friedrich, recommended for head of the staff a graduate student, Paul Sigmund, then completing his degree. His place was taken later by Susanne Rudolph, also a student in the Government Department, now, as many readers will recognize, one of the mainstays of the Chicago College programs in the social sciences; she and her husband Lloyd Rudolph, who also worked with me for a briefer time, had had the advantage of experience in Samuel Beer's course already mentioned.

To recruit the staff of the course, I drew not only on the diverse graduate students of the Social Relations Department, but also, as already indicated, on Political Science, as well as Social History, the Law School, and the Graduate School of Education. A number of former students from the College at Chicago taught in the course, among them David Gutmann, Thomas Cottle, Richard Sennett, Susan Tax Freeman, and also Robert S. Weiss, who had moved to the Division of Community Psychiatry of the Harvard Medical School from having taught in Soc 2. In the course of time, a number of older faculty members volunteered to take a section in the course because of the opportunity it offered for intellectual colleagueship in an academic environment that, by comparison with Chicago, seemed solipsistic. Such senior faculty included the late anthropologist Dorothy Lee; Richard Hunt, professor of modern German history and, for a time, chairman of the undergraduate program of the Committee on Social Studies—an interdisciplinary major;

Doris Kearns (now Doris Kearns Goodwin), then an associate professor of government; Dean Whitla, a psychologist, director of institutional research and associate director of admissions at Harvard; Charles Bidwell, a sociologist and student of higher education, now at the University of Chicago, where he has taught in Soc 2.

A large proportion of the staff I gathered over the years were graduates of the good small liberal arts colleges—Swarthmore, Oberlin, Antioch, Sarah Lawrence, many of them holders of Danforth or Woodrow Wilson Fellowships; but I did not exclude graduates of the Ivy League (including Stanford), and there were a number of these. I canvassed faculty colleagues who became aware of my interest in finding and then nurturing dedicated teachers for undergraduates, and sought to establish contact with graduate students early, recruiting them several years in advance when this was feasible, and when they would bring to the course some experience as section leaders in their own departments.[20] Given teaching ability and conscientiousness, what I particularly sought were people with some non-American experience, for I thought that in a course dealing with American society one requisite was a cross-cultural perspective on America. For example, Kenneth Keniston had lived for several of his high school years in Argentina, when his father, on leave from the deanship of the College of Arts and Sciences at the University of Michigan, was teaching in Buenos Aires; and Michael Mandelbaum's father, a Berkeley anthropologist specializing on India, had taken his sons to live in India with him during part of their adolescence. I recruited John Padberg, S.J., a specialist on France with extensive non-American experience, and Ricardo Zuñiga, S.J., a Chilean who had received some of his training in Montreal.[21] The Rudolphs, already

20. Occasionally, colleagues recommended brilliant students who turned out to be too arrogant for a staff-taught course. Also, in the initial years, some traditional and powerful faculty members in government and in American history warned their preferred graduate students not to become involved with an enterprise that in their minds was both novel and dubious. I took upon myself the responsibility of seeing to it that the special demands of teaching in the course did not unduly delay completion of the dissertation, although in general it was my experience that the colleagueship of the course helped counterbalance the frustrations many graduate students experience when they work in isolation on a dissertation. But of course this varied with the subject and with the particular individual's stamina and self-confidence.

21. In what was to the shocked dismay of my wife and me still an anti-Catholic milieu when we returned to Cambridge in 1958, it was sometimes said to me that it was good thing for the minority of devout Catholic students to have a Jesuit teaching in the course. I explained that the Catholics had ample opportunity to meet Jesuits through the chaplaincy and the several Jesuit houses in Cambridge, and that the real purpose, in addition to their individual quality, for recruiting Jesuits was for the non-Catholics, to help overcome their bigotries—to find, for example, in Ricardo Zuñiga, someone who knew

mentioned, had done fieldwork in India. Hanna Papanek had done fieldwork in Pakistan and Indonesia. John Atherton, son of a foreign service officer, had lived in France (he is now professor of American studies at the Université François-Rabelais in Tours). Glen Fukushima, a Japanese-American, had married a Japanese and lived in Tokyo. David Gutmann had done field studies in Mexico and among the Druses in Israel. Jane Mansbridge, who later taught in the Chicago social science core, had as an undergraduate at Wellesley majored in French history.

XIII

My principal mission with graduate students was to make it possible for them to become broadly educated teachers of undergraduates in liberal arts colleges; this involved both enhancing their substantive knowledge and adding, since college and university instructors have generally had no training as teachers, assistance in becoming less awkward and more discerning as instructors. Hence, the course was innovative for Harvard in that teaching and mutual learning were proceeding on two levels at the same time: we were teaching the students and we were teaching each other how to teach the students and how different students learned or failed and/or refused to learn. At the weekly and sometimes semi-weekly luncheon and dinner meetings of the staff, I took it as my responsibility, especially for the advanced graduate students, to help them become aware of some of the dilemmas of undergraduate teaching by urging mutual observation of each other's sections and by lengthy discussions of questions arising from their class discussions and experiences.[22]

Also, we were attentive to feedback from the students. They were

---

more about Marxism than most of our radicals (he had to be rescued from the hazards of the anti-Allende coup, no easy task, when some years later, he was teaching at the Catholic University of Santiago).

Similarly, I was often praised in the years before the women's movements for having a staff which included on an average 40 percent women members on the ground that these were good "role models" for the women students; again, I would make the point that they were still more important as role models for male students and staff who did not expect in the Harvard stag setting to find brilliant and capable women who often carried the responsibility of being the head section person in the course.

22. Our discussion adumbrated many of the themes dealt with in a special issue of the *Journal of Higher Education* devoted to ethics and the academic profession (vol. 53, no. 3, May/June 1982), notably Everett K. Wilson, "Power, Pretense, and Piggybacking: Some Ethical Issues in Teaching," pp. 268–81, and Emily Roberson and Gerald Grant, "Teaching and Ethics: An Epilogue" (Grant was formerly a teacher in the Harvard course), pp. 345–57.

sometimes critical of the lack of coherence of the course. Things did not always fit nearly together or follow each other like A, B, C.[23] And we were to some extent affected by the changing focus of their interests. One other form of learning we sought for in the course was that in section meetings students would learn from each other. One of the most striking differences between my experiences at Chicago and at Harvard concerned the willingness of students to listen to one another. Harvard students often resented those who asked questions in class, because as some of them bluntly put it, they were paying tuition to hear from the professor, not from some damn fool student. Indeed, it took great effort to overcome students' disdain for teaching fellows, "mere" graduate students, even though the latter were often not only more attentive but professionally more au courant than their seniors. Section meetings were by their very nature unpredictable, and dependent upon a lucky mix of students—to spark discussion which would engage the class as a whole and not a few hand-waving monopolists. Sometimes section leaders would find that a set of questions about a reading which had elicited splendid discussion in one section would fall completely flat in another. Section leaders who were teaching fellows could take a maximum of three sections, while the older volunteers and some advanced graduate students took but a single one.

Neither my more senior colleagues nor I were experts in the art and incipient science of teaching when the course began (nor would we claim so now). While we made an effort in the section meetings to repress the narcissistic filibusterer and to inspirit the shy, the former task was too much for many of the section leaders, and, at times, too much for me. Sometimes we would take such a person aside and talk to him— such individuals in earlier years were almost invariably male—and ask him not to raise his hand, that we would call on him when we felt it appropriate. But such a tactic with a rebellious and individualistic student

23. Since the course had no examination, I sought to persuade students not to take notes in the way they were accustomed to doing, getting down everything which might be on the exam. Rather, I suggested to them that they listen attentively, perhaps make a few free associations in the form of notes, and then after the lecture-discussion, keep a kind of diary in which they would mix their own thoughts about the material, with the substantive matter presented in readings and lectures. However, most students could not break the habit of assiduous note-taking, and for some (I know this is occasionally true for me when I attend an American Sociological Association or other professional session) taking notes is a way to keep awake! Furthermore, even with Harvard undergraduates, it proved difficult, and in earlier years especially for the Radcliffe women, to learn that different kinds of readings required different kinds of attention. For example, we read Tocqueville with detailed *explication de texte*, but did not expect community studies or certain other contemporary works (such as Willie Morris's autobiography, *North Toward Home*, which we periodically read) to be read in the same fashion.

body was not always successful. After visiting a section, I could offer the section leader comments which would seem simplistic to a student of teaching but which were nonetheless novel to that person. I would, for example, observe that (quite apart from political orientation), some section leaders would call on students sitting on their left and not on their right, or vice versa. We all would have liked to have snapshots of each student. Our section leaders went into class with the advantage of a questionnaire (resisted by some students) which gave background, or what survey researchers call "face sheet" data, on the students. (Explicitly, we did not ask for a student's grade point average, for we wanted it to be clear that neither admission to the course—which was done by lottery when it was oversubscribed—nor assignment to sections depended on grades.) But it would have been quicker and easier for section leaders to memorize the names of all their students if they had also had snapshots to attach to the questionnaires for the first few section meetings.[24]

Another equally simple injunction I would draw from visits to sections was to avoid using sarcasm—which indeed is rampant at Harvard among both students and faculty. Even junior faculty who had been teaching for ten years were often astonished when I would say to them that sarcasm stings, and that they often humiliated students; they still saw themselves as young and, as it were, weightless; how could anything they said hurt anybody? But sarcasm is almost never weightless. In dealing with filibusterers, however, it was sometimes an essential tool.

The structure of the course consisted of the usual formal lectures, most often given by me, sometimes by visitors or by staff members (if the subject was in their special domain), twice a week. And sections were held once a week by each staff member. Section meetings in general have had low status at Harvard, not only because of the students' belief that teaching fellows are by definition not big shots, but also partly because of the drill-like character of some sections in large courses. In this course, however, the sections were at least as highly regarded as the lectures, and better attended.

Sections met nominally for an hour and a half, but generally ran for

24. When I recently offered what our Sociology Department terms a "conference course," in effect a proseminar, in American higher education, I carried to each session two-sided "place cards" for each student, in the hope that students would come to speak directly to each other by name and not only conduct dialogues with me. (It is something taken for granted at the Harvard Graduate School of Business Administration, where students at large lectures sit in a horseshoe-shaped amphitheater with assigned seats, as in first-year basic classes at Harvard Law School, but in an undergraduate course in Harvard College, this repeated action of bringing in and distributing the cards, as one would at many kinds of conference, had symbolic as well as practical utility.)

two hours. Though we tried to find seminar rooms—no easy task—and to have sections no larger than the nineteen or twenty that could sit around a single table and face each other, scheduling and space problems could mean that we would sometimes have as few as eight or as many as thirty students in a section.[25] Though there were rarely that many, when there were, we almost necessarily arranged them in inner and outer rows—and in so doing we gained, if we did not already have, a greater appreciation of the importance of "architecture," what Martin Trow terms private space, in the quality of learning and teaching that is feasible in a classroom.

As time passed, some section leaders came to have their own reputations, but we made every effort in the generally relaxed flux at Harvard not to permit switching of sections; on the contrary, we built sections as we built the staff, seeking a variety of students, in terms of background, in each section, and scattering older people, such as Nieman Fellows, (who held one-year fellowships in journalism), foreign visitors from the Center for International Affairs, and so forth. As the number of black students increased markedly after 1968, we sought to hinder the efforts some of them made to group themselves in one or two sections (as they soon came to group themselves residentially and in noncurricular activities). We did not invariably succeed. I recall visiting one section where six blacks, mainly—as is the Harvard norm—from private schools and fairly affluent backgrounds, intimidated a dozen whites until I brought out by questioning that several of the whites came from working-class backgrounds—one was the son of a lumberjack in the Northwest—far more modest than that of blacks, who pretended to be, in the early years of black power, authentic ghetto types.

Along with the substantive knowledge contained in readings, lectures, and section meetings, our staff sought to draw on personal qualities among students in terms of what they could contribute and, while these remained reasonably constant, the shifting character of student outlooks necessitated different strategies. Above all, we sought to cultivate curiosity, so that the physical and human world around a student would become more vivid. Rather than approaching the *Umwelt*

25. Most teaching fellows preferred small sections, certainly no more than ten, and preferably fewer. But I stressed that there were compensating advantages in a larger group: learning to keep alert and attentive to what was going in such a group, making notes immediately after class concerning who spoke and who did not, and through individual conferences, learning to recognize and use the broader resources of the larger group with regard to differing interpretations of text and different experiences of life. Handling the larger group required a greater alertness and a faster ability to identify individuals by name, background, and capacity to contribute or to disrupt or wander, and these were valuable acquisitions for a young instructor.

with either the deadpan diligence of many of our students at that time, or the residual cavalier insouciance of the gentleman's C, which later turned into the antigentleman's B, we wanted our students to be capable of observing and understanding more, through ability to relate readings to observation. This included the willingness to be surprised, as against a temptation to assume a blasé attitude—and a willingness to change and to be self-critical.

When I came to Harvard, a mid-term and a three-hour final examination were required in all large courses. I had to defend before the Committee on Educational Policy the justification for dispensing with examinations and substituting instead a long term paper, plus shorter papers which were often assigned by section leaders as exercises to assure that students had done and understood the readings.[26] The grade in the course depended on the long paper, as well as the student's performance in the section meetings. The section leader had the task of seeing to it that outlines of these papers were submitted early, and we continuously urged students to spend less time in data gathering and more time in analysis and writing than they were inclined to do if left to their own devices. Indeed, staff members and I were torn by ambivalence concerning the degree to which we departed from the announced Harvard norm that students should stand on their own feet and not be protected against failure resulting from procrastination or poor judgment. If students missed a section meeting, some staff members would telephone them or send postcards; was such concern unduly parental and inappropriate? In fact, we often did rescue students who had become paralyzed by their own anxieties, and in extreme cases we might suggest that students consult the Bureau of Study Counsel, which offers psychological as well as pedagogic support. And at times, the non-attender turned out to be, for example, a cavalier *Crimson* editor, convinced of his ability to turn out an elegantly written paper in a few all-night sessions.[27]

The section leader graded the students' papers, consulting others and me where appropriate, and also wrote letters to students evaluating their papers—an extent of comment not infrequent in smaller liberal

26. I should make clear that I am not in principle opposed to written examinations; many can be quite illuminating. See, e.g., my essay, "The Impact of Examinations," and that of Thomas Schelling, in *Examining in Harvard College: A Collection of Essays by Members of the Harvard Faculty,* ed. Leon Bramson (Cambridge: Harvard University Faculty of Arts and Sciences, 1963), 71–87.

27. Cf. David Riesman, Joseph Gusfield, and Zelda Gamson, "Conflicts over Academic Standards and Personalism at Monteith," in *Academic Values and Mass Education: The Early Years of Oakland and Monteith,* (Garden City, N.Y.: Doubleday, 1970) chap. 9—a discussion based largely on the work of Zelda Gamson.

arts colleges, but at that time (and still today, though there has been some change)—a rarity at Harvard. The section leader's role in facilitating the work of students made for close relations, and I continually run into former students of the course who have kept in touch with their section leaders since graduation.

At the beginning, I read all the papers myself after they had been graded and letters written, putting the grade and letters aside until I had formed my own judgment, and then writing to the student in a way that took account of the section leader's comments and avoided redundancy. If I had any doubts about my letter and its possible effect on the student or its possible unfairness in the light of the section leader's greater knowledge of the student, I would share a draft of the letter with the section leader before sending it to the student, and of course always sent the section leader a copy. I regarded these letters as a form of teaching both for the section leader and for the student—I made clear to the students that they were to make two copies of their papers, one of which would be retained in my file and another for them to keep. Eventually, my responses were often so delayed as not to mean much to the student who had gotten the paper in and gone on to other things, or who was embarrassed that I had expended time and thought on a paper that he or she had not expected me to see. I realized that I could not maintain the task I had set myself of reading all the papers.

Thereafter, I read papers which were recommended to me by section leaders, or where I had myself served to advise the student concerning some particular topic where the section leader had felt less adequate to help. For me, reading papers was more interesting and valuable an enterprise than reading an occasional examination paper. It gave me a better sense of what our students were concerned about, what their intellectual and personal vitamin deficiencies were, toward which we might address ourselves, as against their strengths, which the competitive atmosphere of Harvard College encouraged them to nourish at the expense of taking chances in areas where they felt less self-confident.

When our course began, Harvard College students felt reasonably at home in the library and, in many instances, in the laboratory; there was no other large course which dispensed with a final exam and which encouraged students to choose a topic themselves. We did not insist that they do a small-scale empirical study, but we did our best to persuade students of the value of this; those who continued to demur could do theoretical and library-based papers. But with the majority who were willing to take a try at fieldwork of some sort, we had to overcome the misapprehension that, for empirical work, one needed either a large number of survey-type interviews or, in more recent years, some kind of project making use of a computer. Since we drew students from all fields of interest in the College, including many students who had not yet decided on a major, we needed to redefine the presuppositions many of them had concerning what "science" is. Frequently this was a misapprehended natural science model. An empirical paper would have to be a "sample," for example, of a hundred random interviews with fellow students. I would explain that the fellow students were not a universe whose boundaries were known, that one did not know what questions to ask if one started with little knowledge and only minimal preconceptions, and that in any case students rarely lived as isolates. Rather, one might want to get at student social networks and explore the definition, for example, of what friendship meant, making an initial foray on a small, nonrepresentative group—something which might later become, and sometimes did become, the basis for a senior thesis or even a dissertation.[28]

We defined "science" to mean pretty much what Martin Trow suggests in his discussion of the moral discipline of the academic disciplines: namely, doing what was appropriate in the circumstances, with as much objectivity as possible, while recognizing that this was a goal and not something one could attain. Methods included looking for negative evidence and reporting negative or uninterpretable findings, as well as writing down clearly and exactly what one did: for example, in gaining access or describing as fully as possible what the setting was like in an interview, and how the interviewer's own reactions might perhaps have influenced responses.[29] We made amply clear that this was not an introduction in a formal way to "sociological methods," as these might be taught in a course for prospective majors.

At the beginning, as my experience in Soc 2 suggested, our students were awed in the face of the authority of books they read. Or they were diffident and did not believe that they could venture out on their own, do interviews, or engage in participant observation, when they were not

28. Perhaps I should make clear that, although the course served as a de facto introduction to sociology for a number of students interested in the field, our efforts did not aim to enlarge the number of sociology majors. At the graduate level my colleagues and I have been inclined to believe that as a field of scholarship sociology is only rarely eight years deep and that undergraduates are better prepared for graduate work in sociology by any number of other subjects: classical studies and history in general; economics; one of the natural sciences; any sufficiently demanding program of broad liberal education combined with specialized work. Fortunately, this was not a time when FTE or "body count" determined the fate of departments, individuals within them, and whole institutions.

29. See Martin Trow, "Higher Education and Moral Development," *AAUP Bulletin* 62, (1; April 1976): 20–27.

trained social scientists. In other words, our effort was to persuade students that it was legitimate in a general education course to undertake what might be thought of as a kind of pretest or prolegomenon to a longer study such as one might do if one had ample time and resources, and that they could make a contribution certainly of some interest, even of originality.

Having decided that we ourselves should publish some of the student papers, we brought out three volumes in the first years of the course, one of them containing papers based exclusively on educational settings. It was a way of proving to students that they could do publishable bits of work, and we picked a great variety of papers for the volumes so that students would not be overpowered by the most talented.

I have already indicated how, in reading Tocqueville, one of our emphases was on his "anthropological" notebooks and letters, stressing the nature of the journey itself, the biases of a number of his conservative, Federalist informants, and his ability to use episodes from people met on his travels who were not leading citizens, whether a Michigan frontiersman-farmer or a boatbuilder. Further to help the students prepare themselves for potential fieldwork on their papers, we then read Alicja Iwanska's "Good Fortune," as I have already mentioned. We turned next to William F. Whyte, Jr.'s *Street Corner Society*, emphasizing the appendix in which Whyte so beautifully describes his own problems as a fieldworker, including his ethical dilemmas. (Herbert Gans has a short appendix on just such problems in *The Urban Villagers*, a frequently assigned reading.) We often read Robert Lane's *Political Ideology*, to show how much one could find out concerning Tocqueville's themes by interviews with fifteen men in a New Haven housing project. For those considering fieldwork, we recommended portions of Rosalie Wax's admirable book, *Doing Fieldwork: Warnings and Advice*.[30]

As I have already said, we did not insist that students do papers based on interviews or fieldwork of some sort, but rather that this provided a relatively cost-free opportunity to explore and, under supervision, test oneself in a new kind of skill. Interviewing, moreover, especially outside of one's own familiar orbits, requires courage as well as skill: the courage to knock on a door, not sure how one will be received or what kind of interferences (television, dogs, crying children, etc.) one may have to cope with; there is the further courage one needs to persist despite the fear that the material one is acquiring is mostly worthless chaff—hazards

30. University of Chicago Press, 1971. See also William F. Whyte's "On Making the Most of Participant Observation," *The American Sociologist* 14 (February 1979):56–66; also comments by Robert A. Stebbins and by this writer and others, "Toward Amateur Sociology: A Proposal for the Profession," *The American Sociologist* 13 (November 1978): 250–51.

which beset all but the most case-hardened fieldworkers or survey interviewers. We encouraged students to turn in drafts of their final papers well ahead of time, on which the section leader could then make comments and suggestions, giving the student an opportunity to rewrite and improve the paper—but not many left themselves enough time to make use of this option.

While many students jumped at the chance to develop a paper which took off from personal experience, for example, in tutoring or in the civil rights movements, others were stumped by the abundance of options, and had no idea of a possible topic. To forestall last-minute papers, and lessen the possibilities of plagiarism which had been feared by some of the members of the Committee on Educational Policy when we argued for the privilege of dispensing with a final examination (as if cheating could not occur in formal, proctored examinations!), students had to decide on their paper topics early, and, where the section leader had any reason for misgivings, the issue would come before our full staff. Thus, we vetoed papers that seemed tinged with voyeurism, or the many which were obviously overambitious and would not give students a feeling that they had accomplished some small, manageable bit or work. (Even so, in all short-term empirical undergraduate work, there is always the chance that students will at the last moment be turned away from a research site or will otherwise end up with negative results. This is a relatively riskless enterprise in the natural sciences, where such results are often publishable, but a hazard for an undergraduate in the social sciences, and one against which we sought to provide protection. This could be in the form of backup projects, or we might permit the student to write a full description of the original project and the reasons for its miscarriage.)

To summarize: the course proceeded on three tracks, whose congruence was seldom tidy. One track was the lectures, which I gave or presided over, in which I discussed readings and materials supplementary to the lectures. Questions and discussions during the lecture were encouraged and, even with three hundred or more students, proved feasible if we had a proper sort of place to meet. By meeting at the noon hour we could continue with students who cared to stay on for additional discussion, sometimes continuing the discussion over lunch in one of the residential houses. In such an instance we would reserve a small dining room for the hour following the lecture, where students—and often several tutors and myself—could continue the conversation. This might also occur with sections which were held in the late afternoon and followed by supper in one of the houses, a supper to which I would sometimes be invited.

The second track was the section meeting for discussion of lectures and readings. We sought to teach the course almost entirely from paperback books which students could bring to class, and in the best instances a spirit of eager mutuality developed from this practice. Sometimes questions about lectures and readings raised in section meetings would be brought back to me for further treatment in a lecture. It was not uncommon for me to devote a full hour's lecture to a question that a student had raised, thus departing from the planned outline and syllabus and making the course still more untidy. A secondary gain from responding in this way to a student's question was dramatically to illustrate, in the face of Harvard students' hostility to those who interrupted by asking questions, that professors could learn from students' questions and comments.[31] The sections would also give students a chance to outline orally their prospective term papers for criticism and comment by fellow students; we sought to create a noninvidious atmosphere in which students would not hesitate to bring up tentative plans, failures, and mistakes.

And, as already made clear, the third track was the term paper itself. The diverse interests and experiences of the staff of the course made it possible for us to refer students among ourselves, myself of course included, when a student was pursing a specialized topic for which the particular section leader did not feel especially competent.[32]

31. The reluctance of students to expose themselves by asking questions prevails in many academic settings at many levels of size and selectivity. However, in comparison with students in Soc 2, Harvard College students are in many cases especially guarded, Harvard now being the most sought-after of any undergraduate institution in the academic hit parade, and in consequence often attracting those for whom it is a very poor match in terms of the students' fields or personal qualities: hence the frequent assumption that all the other students must be brilliant. The fear to be thought naive is often overpowering.

32. We followed a similar practice when it came to grading and evaluating papers, where maintaining any degree of equity among the grades given in the different sections was always an issue of discussion and exchange of papers and views. Zelda Gamson and others have written about "personalism," and how difficult it is, when one has gotten to know a student well, to give a low grade on the basis of institution-wide norms, particularly if the student has made notable progress and worked indefatigably. But a senior simultaneously writing an honors thesis might, by poor timing, do a makeshift job on the course paper, and yet be so talented and write so well as to turn in a paper far superior to the average. Here "personalism" could work in reverse, with the disappointed section leader tempted to grade the paper down because of recognition that the student could have done a more taxing and significant piece of work. (We never suffered from the kind of teaching-assistant revolt where all students were given A's to discredit "the system" that Richard F. Tomasson describes during the time he was department chairman at the University of New Mexico. See "Report of the Department of Sociology, 1972–72" [Albuquerque: University of New Mexico, 1973]. Mimeographed.)

Because students did on the whole extend themselves, the course gained a reputation for giving high grades prior to the time of grade inflation. Thus, while scaring away some highly grade-conscious students who knew they could get an assured honor grade on an exam and were uncertain about how they would fare on a long paper in a low-consensus field, we also did attract a relatively small number of students who saw the course as a

While, as I have noted, some students wanted to undertake overambitious projects or suffered from a surfeit of options, there were others who had no idea of a possible topic. An illustration will help. I remember talking to a shy Radcliffe student who came from a small New Hampshire town and could not see what she could do for a paper which might produce new knowledge. It turned out that her father was a small businessman, and that through him she knew the other small businessman of the community. I suggested to her that she examine an essay by Martin Trow in the *AJS* on the attitudes of small businessmen toward Joseph McCarthy in Bennington in the 1950s,[33] and that she interview the businessmen she knew concerning their ideologies about politics, the state and federal governments, the chances they had in life. She did just that, managing a few really searing interviews, and doing a paper that made a

---

"gut." Sometimes they would deliver papers late to section leaders with whom they had not in fact worked to develop a topic. In rare cases, we suspected and then tracked down plagiarism, often a paper written for another course (which might have been legitimate if agreed upon in advance with both instructors); we reported all such cases, a practice many instructors and even senior professors have now abandoned out of a cowardly fear of "hassles," including the chance of litigation. We would refuse to accept the paper and fail the student. When, as was frequently the case, these were graduating seniors, failing grades created tension for some during the Vietnam War—tensions which, in discussions with the senior tutors (in effect, decentralized deans) of the residential houses, appeared to be unfounded, since virtually no Harvard student went involuntarily to Vietnam, although a few braved the general campus climate to go voluntarily. One student threatened to shoot me, a white Virginian who had gotten by, according to his senior tutor, to the last term of his senior year despite repeated assaults on tutors and other similar actions, and I will not say that I was not frightened. The fact that, in cases of doubt, several of us would read a paper was some defense against an increasingly adversarial and litigious atmosphere in the later 1960s and 1970s. At the same time the number of such controversies and general problems of oversight grew as the number of students taking the course grew (feasible only when section leaders were willing to take two or three sections), so that at one time we had over six hundred students in Sanders Theater, then our largest lecture hall and one in which discussion from the floor was almost impossible. I then limited enrollment because the load on me of having to deal with a certain proportion of "difficult" cases had proved to be too great and also because we preferred a more intimate setting where questions could be asked at lectures. I also consciously reduced the charismatic potential of a lecture, refusing, for example, to end the hour on a neat summary or epigrammatic remark. I became more matter-of-fact in the late sixties as some of my more politicized colleagues became more passionate. In particular, I held to my belief that students should hear complex sentences that contained words many did not know, hoping, perhaps quixotically, that they would look them up in the dictionary or not be afraid to ask what they meant. I thus avoided what became among some sociologists and psychologists outside the experimentalist fields a kind of rap session argot which highly educated students used to demonstrate their egalitarianism.

33. Martin Trow, "Small Businessman, Political Tolerance, and Support for McCarthy," *American Journal of Sociology* 64 (1958): 279–80.

contribution. (With her permission, I sent the paper to Professor Ivar Berg, who found it illuminating; the result for the student was a dramatic increase in her self-confidence.)

The letters section leaders wrote to their students, of which I always received a copy, concerning their papers and often their general performance in the section, were responsive both to the paper's contributions and to its limitations. These letters, the staff meetings and memoranda, and the visits I would pay to sections when their leaders felt sufficiently secure to invite me, gave me a sense of the abilities of individual staff members as teacher-scholars and generally also as potential or actual researchers, which proved useful to many in helping them in the postdoctoral job search.[34]

My sense of what students needed (as distinguished from what they wanted) changed as we moved into the period of the 1960s, the era of the cry for "relevance." Not only the readings but the papers students chose to write changed considerably. It no longer took enormous effort to get students to go out into the field. Many preferred the field to the library, especially if some kind of activisim were involved. It was at this point that I concluded it was necessary to encourage students to do, for example, small bits of social history based on bibliographic sources rather than oral history, which had in the meantime become popular. We sought consciously to be "countercyclical," insisting on the unattainable ideal of objectivity as students grew more politicized and ideological in the late 1960s. For example, if Elliot Liebow's *Tally's Corner* was a popular reading, as it occasionally was, I insisted that it be read only if we read conjointly Horace Cayton's autobiography, *Long Old Road*. This book gives an account of a black whose father had been a Republican newspaperman in a city (Seattle) which then cruelly shipped Chinese out to sea, much as happened recently to the "boat people," but where eminent Negroes were not aggressively discriminated against; I was opposed to the implicit determinism of *Tally's Corner*, as many blacks have also

---

34. I am referring here not only to the detailed letters of recommendation I would write to the many liberal arts colleges and comprehensive state colleges which sought young men and women gifted in teaching (a quality which, contrary to legend, research universities also sought, in addition to promise as a researcher), but also to the self-confidence those looking for positions might have in facing the prospect of teaching two or three courses per term outside their area of specialization (on which they might be able to teach a course for a few students every second year). Some could then enter the crucial and stressful years prior to the decision on tenure with some leeway to prepare for publication all or sections of the dissertation, or to do other writing. This issue was perhaps especially exigent for the increasing number of two-career families in which a more equitable division of domestic labor was sought between the spouses (a few such couples taught in the course, either simultaneously or in sequence).

DAVID RIESMAN

been.[35] I also did not want our black students to have to suffer with a certain kind of somewhat specious envy from our hard-working, generally upper-middle-class, highly educated and affluent white students (and we had highly educated and affluent upper-middle-class blacks as well), who obtained vicarious enjoyment from reading about apparently spontaneous lower-class black life.

Similarly, our effort to enhance curiosity had to take different forms among undergraduates (and graduate students also) in those years. At the outset, student curiosity was limited by inhibition and self-mistrust. But by the late 1960s, curiosity was inhibited by a cynical or nihilistic attitude toward society and its institutions: everything was corrupt, everything was a "sell," and since we already knew that, what was there to find out about it?[36] In this conclusion by students that they already knew what society was like, and it was rotten, they were encouraged by some senior scholars and younger faculty, as well as by events, and it became difficult to sustain an uninhibited curiosity which would subject their now conventional radicalism to scrutiny. Especially perhaps among Harvard College undergraduates, the narcissism which led to the conclusion that one already knew what was worth knowing became a more serious and more difficult obstacle to overcome than diffidence had been earlier.

These changes in student temper were of course not universal—one had to be careful that one did not take the vocal students as the voice of "the students." One had to individuate and to distinguish among students in terms of what would be helpful in the development of each one's curiosity—perhaps the quality above all which I sought to encourage as a lifelong outlook.

35. One of the leaders in taking this position is a former colleague in the course, Orlando Patterson, a Jamaican trained at LSE (Patterson's wife, Nerys Patterson, also taught in the course). See, e.g., Orlando Patterson, "Toward a Future That Has No Past—Reflections on the Fate of Blacks in the Americas," *The Public Interest*, spring 1972: 25–62.

36. One of my most depressing experiences in these later years was repeatedly to encounter students who would come to confer about their curricular program and complain that all the courses were so boring, unaware of the degree to which this was a verdict on themselves. I found such students particularly trying, since for myself I capitalized on residence at a university to audit a course every year (something I had also frequently done at Chicago), and there were usually a dozen courses which I would have liked to audit but could spare time only for one. (I made use of this opportunity to go slightly beyond amateur standing as a student of Japanese history and contemporary culture.)

216

10

Comment on "My Education in Soc 2," by David Riesman

Harold S. Wechsler

David Riesman's essays and reflections upon American life, especially upon American higher education, are always illuminating and provocative. His autobiographical approach in "My Education in Soc 2" prompted me to think about individuals strongly identified with the University of Chicago who influenced his outlook and scholarship.

The chapter suggests many parallels between Riesman's biography and that of his sometime ally, Robert Maynard Hutchins. Riesman and Hutchins came from academic families. Riesman's father taught at the medical school of the University of Pennsylvania, while Hutchins' father, a minister, first became professor of theology at Oberlin and then president of Berea College. Riesman's mother attended Bryn Mawr, which bore the strong stamp of M. Carey Thomas, while Hutchins' mother attended the only slightly less demanding Mount Holyoke. Academic rigor was not an unknown virtue in either family.

Both Riesman and Hutchins report unsatisfactory educational experiences in institutions still committed to a classical liberal arts curriculum. "My formal education [at Oberlin]," wrote Hutchins, "had given me no understanding of science, mathematics, or philosophy. It had added almost nothing to my knowledge of literature. I had some facility with languages, but today I cannot read Greek or Latin except by guesswork."[1] Nor did Riesman's work in Greek and Latin at William Penn Charter School go much beyond rote memorization.

Riesman next went to Harvard to study the biochemical sciences. Hutchins enrolled at Yale to study history. But neither scholar offered a compelling rationale for his major, and both found their way to the law schools of their respective universities. (Riesman would not have overlapped with Hutchins if he had ended up at Yale.) Both found their stays rewarding *despite*—not because of—the curricula of the law

<hr/>

1. Robert Maynard Hutchins, "The Autobiography of an Uneducated Man," in his *Education for Freedom* (Baton Rouge: Louisiana University Press, 1943), 4.

schools. At Harvard, Carl Friedrich and Karl Llewellyn exposed Riesman to the social sciences. He continued his metamorphosis from the law to the social sciences at Columbia and completed the transformation at Chicago after foregoing a chance to teach at Yale Law School. Hutchins discovered the trivium, the syllogism, and the Adlerism while at Yale. When they finished their formal studies, neither Riesman nor Hutchins possessed a Ph.D., a nearly inescapable credential for an academic career, and both made a virtue of what was a liability in the eyes of many colleagues.

Given the similarities in background, as well as the key point at which they diverged, Riesman's expressed ambivalence about Robert Maynard Hutchins is not surprising. Both found their way to the groves of academe probably more from nature than nurture. Their negative academic experiences at institutions with world reputations led them to a concern for curriculum and to recognize that academic reputation had become a function of knowledge generation, not dissemination. Both confirmed an adage about the law: namely, that it is the one generalist profession. If the law led Hutchins to a search for first principles, it led Riesman to a search for the general through the particular.

Both Hutchins and Riesman would agree with Daniel Bell's conclusion that general education before 1950 aimed for consensus, civility based upon an appreciation of tradition, antispecialization, and integration rooted in an interdisciplinary approach.[2] Finally, both Hutchins and Riesman understood that most of the world ignored both Soc 2 and the "Gospel According to St. John's"; that Chicago offered something unique to its undergraduates despite internal schisms.

A digression: Daniel Bell and others suggest that early advocates of general education wished to socialize the increasing number of immigrant students who appeared at Harvard, Columbia, Chicago, and other metropolitan universities. But these colleges would not likely design a curriculum for the supposed needs of a constituency they were simultaneously seeking to exclude. Columbia, for example, hoped—but failed—to segregate the professionally oriented Jewish students from their more genteel Protestant counterparts and to restrict the contemporary civilization sequence to the latter group. Harvard, Columbia, and Chicago all had a "Jewish problem," and all three resorted to rather unsavory means to "solve" it.[3] But the general education move-

2. Daniel Bell, *The Reforming of General Education: The Columbia College Experience in its National Setting* (New York: Columbia University Press, 1966), chap. 2.

3. Harold S. Wechsler, *The Qualified Student: A History of Selective College Admission in America; 1870–1970* (New York: Wiley-Interscience, 1977), chap. 7, 9.

ment arose from a deeper impulse—a concern about the general course of American culture and the American university.

To return to the main theme, Riesman's overall evaluation of Hutchins is positive. Indeed, Riesman's comparison of Hutchins to Franklin Delano Roosevelt, for example in their creation of parallel agencies and committees, prompts us to look at Riesman's other writings on the academic presidency.

"The reading of academic history . . . and my own observations," Riesman wrote in *On Higher Education*, "led me to believe in the 'great man' (today we would say 'great person') theory of academic change or reform." He added: "Although individual faculty members might seek to make changes, they were almost invariably unsuccessful without support from the top, and it was often in fact the academic leaders, especially those in an earlier era who had authority and long tenure, who had a view of the whole and wanted to leave their stamp on an institution as well as to keep up with its rivals and thus were less provincial than their faculties.[4]

Riesman thus defended—even vindicated—that superb Veblenian characterization, the captain of erudition. Indeed, much of Riesman's writing on higher education is as much contra Veblen's *Higher Learning in America* as it is influenced by Hutchins' volume of the same name.[5]

In 1953, David Riesman published his interpretive biography of this other Chicago influence.[6] Carl Friedrich had introduced Riesman to Veblen's writing twenty years earlier; Riesman testified that his thinking about Veblen matured in the presence of his Soc 2 colleagues. His comments on the damage which sarcasm inflicts upon a student seem to me prompted by Veblen's legendary use of this device. Riesman also noted that Veblen and Hutchins shared certain dispositions: antivocationalism, separation of teaching and research, and the subordination of the "student culture" to the life of the mind.[7] Riesman also pointed to differences in their attitudes towards the classics and toward dialectic.

But Riesman noted that Veblen and Hutchins differed fundamentally on the faculty's centrality to the academic enterprise. Riesman respected Hutchins' strong presidency, but Veblen would have no greater

---

4. David Riesman, *On Higher Education: The Academic Enterprise in an Era of Rising Student Consumerism* (San Francisco: Jossey-Bass, 1980), 293.

5. Thorstein Veblen, *The Higher Learning in America: A Memorandum on the Conduct of Universities by Business Men* (New York: B. W. Heubsch, 1918); Robert Maynard Hutchins, *The Higher Learning in America* (New Haven: Yale University Press, 1936).

6. David Riesman, *Thorstein Veblen: A Critical Interpretation* (New York: Scribner's, 1960).

7. Ibid., 102.

respect for Hutchins than he had for William Rainey Harper. A strong presidency, Veblen believed, inevitably diminished the faculty's ability to pursue ideas that arose from idle curiosity—disinterest. In the modern university, the norms of the business community had supplanted academic norms, and the college or university president was the medium for imposing these alien norms.

Riesman viewed this depiction as simplistic, if not wrongheaded. If anything, he wrote in the Veblen book, "university careers were becoming increasingly attractive for purposes of social and career mobility as an alternative to business; their growing competitiveness and loss of generality was due less to their conquest by trustees chosen from the ranks of the fatter vested interests than to the fact that young men were beginning to find a career in natural or social science rather than in banking or wholesaling. In fact, it is the greater prestige of universities which has lured the young seeking prestige—and at the same time has allowed them to pose as gentlemen amiably superior to businesslike conduct both within and without the ivied walls."[8]

Riesman went no further in the Veblen book. But he subsequently developed this insight into a full critique of American higher education, the best statement of which is contained in *The Academic Revolution*—a book that might better have been entitled *The Revolution of the Academics*. Here, Riesman and Christopher Jencks, his coauthor, argued that the maturation of academic norms—especially the prestige attached to the research function of the modern university—had "academized" nearly all aspects of the higher education enterprise. Imposing these questionable norms on professional education and especially on undergraduate education had negative effects. "If this book has any single message," the conclusion stated, "it is that the academic profession increasingly determines the character of undergraduate education in America. Academicians today decide what a student ought to know, how he should be taught it, and who can teach it to him. Not only that— their standards increasingly determine which students attend which colleges, who feels competent once he arrives, and how much time he has for non-academic activities." Resistance by various groups "may help persuade the academicians that they are a beleaguered minority and thus help them rationalize continuing efforts to extend their influence, but it has not provided much basis for creative initiative or reform in undergraduate education."[9]

8. Ibid., 109.
9. Christopher Jencks and David Riesman, *The Academic Revolution* (Garden City, N.Y.: Doubleday, 1968), 510.

If William Rainey Harper, Chicago's first president, proved to Veblen that a president could subvert idle curiosity to business norms, Robert Maynard Hutchins proved to Riesman that a counterrevolutionary chief executive could disentangle academic norms from places where they did not belong.

Coda: William W. Watt, who recently retired from the faculty of Lafayette College, wrote a poem in 1943 that reflects a viewpoint that I think David Riesman, who questions facile characterizations of individuals and ideas as "first rate," may appreciate.

On the Gospel of St. John's

*(After Reading the Catalogue of St. John's College
And Its Prescribed List of Great Books")*

My knowledge of Lucian
Is quite Lilliputian,
I'm feeble on Gibbon and Hume,
I couldn't finagle
A study of Hegel
From now to the trumpet of Doom—

Do *I* have a true education today?
Nay!

The course at St. John's is the liberal par,
All other other curricula foreign,
Say Hutchins and Adler, Buchanan and Barr,
And Van Doren

My stock of Plotinus
Is shamefully minus,
I've never consulted Justinian,
My notion of Grotius
Is worse than atrocious—
So how can I have an opinion

That's worthy to enter the brain of an ant?
I can't

So say with the confident tones of a czar
And not with the peep of a straddler,
Van Doren and Hutchins, Buchanan and Barr,
And Adler

221

My store of Lucretius?
Now don't be facetious
I'm rusty on Darwin and Dante
Racine? Apollonius?
Vague and erroneous
Bentham? Thucydides? Scanty.

Whether-to-pity-the-Germans-or-hate books,
Fighting-will-end-at-a-definite-date books,
Private-initiative-vs.-the-State books,
Can-we-control-them-or-must-we-inflate books,
How-to-get-on-with-a-difficult-mate books—
All of them second-or-third-or-fourth-rate books—
Not Great Books!

Such trash couldn't possibly sully or scar
The bright intellectual scutcheons
Of Adler, Van Doren, Buchanan and Barr,
And Hutchins

—W. W. Watt[10]

10. William W. Watt, "On the Gospel of St. John's," reprinted by permission; © 1944, 1972. The New Yorker Magazine, Inc.

Part IV

Enduring Controversies in Changing Times

11

Why Read Freud? Psychoanalysis, Soc 2, and the Subjective Curriculum

Bertram Cohler

Understood both as a means for the study of lives over time, and as a particular approach to study of the interplay of person and culture, psychoanalysis has long played a significant role in Social Sciences II. As early as 1932, the staff had arranged to reprint Freud's *Civilization and Its Discontents,* whose first translation, by Joan Riviere, had appeared nearly simultaneously with Freud's initial publication of the German version of the essay. The title page of the syllabus including Riviere's translation acknowledged the assistance of Virginia and Leonard Woolf in arranging permission to reprint the translation. Students in Social Sciences II were reading one of Freud's most significant intellectual statements well ahead of either the English-speaking psychoanalytic community or the general public!

From the early years of the course to the present time, Freud has remained one of the three or four major social theorists whose work is studied across the year. The significance of Freud's writings for the course has also changed over the years in response both to changes in the College curriculum and in response to changing conceptions of the social sciences. Particularly during the past two decades, there has been increasing interest within our own university in psychoanalysis as a perspective informing such disparate fields as study of ritual and myth, political leadership, and criticism. Faculty reliance upon psychoanalytic inquiry in their own scholarly study has contributed to the prominence accorded Freud's writings in general education courses within both the humanities and the social sciences. This chapter considers the place of Freud and psychoanalytic scholarship in the general education social science course currently entitled Self, Culture, and Society, and the significance of the encounter with psychoanalytic texts for the lives of students and faculty alike.

Psychoanalysis and General Education

Often regarded simply as a therapeutic technique, over the past two decades psychoanalysis has increasingly been recognized as a significant intellectual perspective with broad implications for study in both the humanities and the social sciences. Within the disciplines of the humanities, psychoanalysis is increasingly recognized as an important tool of criticism. This use of psychoanalysis goes well beyond a simple, reductionistic formula for explaining an author's work in terms of presumed biographical events of early childhood. Rather, concepts of wish and intent outside awareness assist in understanding construction of the work, from poetry and novels to works of art.

A similar appreciation of psychoanalysis has informed study of social life as well, from ethnographic inquiry to study of political leadership and historical events. Again, as contrasted with more traditional, reductionistic psychoanalytic approaches to the study of person and social context, this recent, more innovative use of psychoanalysis emphasizes the importance of understanding intentions in a broad perspective which encompasses not only sexuality but also maintenance of self-regard and personal integrity, and psychological use of others as a source of solace and support, not just during the years of early childhood, but throughout the course of life.

Interestingly, this widening scope of psychoanalysis is based not on the metapsychology, or general psychology theory, dealing with what Freud portrayed as the realm beyond consciousness, but on so-called "clinical" theory, derived from study of lives within the domain of clinical psychoanalysis. It is ironic that much of the impact of psychoanalysis upon arts and letters stems from appreciation of the role of psychological conflict as a determinant of life history and social context, whereas the use of psychoanalysis within both the social sciences and the humanities has largely focused on study of metapsychology, which may be understood better as a reflection of Freud's scientific world view, than as his singular contribution to the understanding of wish and intent. There is no way of "testing" Freud's assumptions which are based on his scientific world view. Efforts to use the approach of experimental psychology as an analog to concepts of psychic structure and energy have succeeded in being little more than a translation of experimental psychology into other terms. After listing a dozen so-called ego functions said to govern human action, Klein wryly observes that this list is more characteristic of a university psychology laboratory than a psychology of human intention.[1] The approach of metapsychology, particularly as

1. G. Klein, *Psychoanalytic Theory: An Exploration of Essentials* (New York: International Universities Press, 1976), 152.

enshrined in the ego psychology characteristic of study of Freud's work over the past half-century in the American university, offers a pseudo-scientific approach to the study of psychoanalysis which makes psycho-analysis acceptable to contemporary Popperian models of social science study, but does little to increase our understanding of the integrity and coherence of action.

Contemporary psychoanalysis has attempted to extend Freud's initial concern with the "why" of behavior, so well exemplified in the case studies reported in *Studies in Hysteria* and the more extended reports on Dora and Lorenz (the "Rat-Man") through exploration of psycho-analysis as a means for studying meanings expressed through wish and intent. This focus on meaning is consistent with important intellectual perspectives reflected in the concept of human science inquiry, and places psychoanalysis within the same intellectual tradition as reflexive ethnography—Crapanzano, Rabinow, and Sullivan—and analysis of both interview and text within the social sciences.

Understood as a means for study of intention, psychoanalysis has a place in social inquiry. The question is whether this mode of inquiry properly belongs in a program of general education. At the outset, as Clarence Faust observed in *The Idea and Practice of General Education*,[2] it is important to differentiate between general and liberal education. General education reflects a concern with questions most worth asking in the arts and sciences, rather than with a narrower, more discipline-based focus upon preparation for occupation or profession. General education courses are taught as discussion-style seminars in which texts and written assignments focus on issues of enduring significance. These courses have been explicitly designed to avoid the more paro-chial concerns characteristic of disciplinary concentrations, although students completing these general education courses often find them-selves as well prepared for advanced work in a discipline as beginning doctoral students several years their senior.

The goals of general education courses are realized through a series of year-long courses taught by a staff concerned more explicitly with questions than with particular texts. Course faculty are well versed in the past and present controversies within their own scholarly disciplines and well acquainted also with issues spanning the disciplines of the hu-manities and the social sciences. While a Great Books approach, pi-oneered by Mortimer Adler and realized through the curriculum of St. John's College, has much the same goal, the St. John's program avoids the larger question of why a text is studied at all, or of how to regard the

---

2. C. Faust, *The Idea and Practice of General Education* (Chicago: University of Chicago Press, 1950).

many different ways in which a text may be read. Studying texts in this way makes them accessible only through other texts and, more vaguely, through their relevance to the times in which they were written. Read this way, the texts are more difficult for students to use as a foundation for understanding a broad range of contemporary problems.

General education courses in the social sciences stress issues and problems common across disciplines. However, the curricula of these courses show significant change over time, reflecting changes in questions posed within the disciplines of the social sciences (and to some extent, the humanities also). At the same time, the nondisciplinary character of these courses is essential if they are to speak to the need of educating men and women as citizens, reflexively informed regarding the human condition. As Milton Singer observed in *The Idea and Practice of General Education:* "What can be done in the classroom is to provide a background of relevant historical and scientific knowledge, an analysis of general principles, and some concrete exercises in deliberative thinking about well-prepared specimen cases on which history has already passed some judgment.[3] Recognition of the concept of the "other," through the study both of history and of ethnographies, assists in fostering an appreciation of the diversity of cultures and of the variety of solutions to common human dilemmas which may be possible. This comparative cultural and historical study plays a central role in fostering deliberative thinking.

Selection of issues to be addressed in general education courses is important in realizing the overall goal. There is a continuing and necessary tension between issues, whether enduring or emergent, in the social sciences and humanities, and particular topics serving as the focus of a general education course in a particular quarter. This creative tension is fostered by encouraging participation in the general education courses by faculty more accustomed to working within a specifically defined discipline. Faculty may be able to use this opportunity as a way of broadening their own scholarship, while the course in turn profits from continuing contact with the leading edge of knowledge in an area of study. The presence of younger scholars in the course, still conversant with issues in their own doctoral education, further insures that the course will reflect contemporary as well as enduring issues of study in the human sciences.

As important as it is for the course to reflect contemporary scholarly study, there is also a danger in exclusive concern with contemporary concerns of the disciplines. For example, there is the problem that a general education course in the social sciences may be focused too much on the philosophy of social science inquiry rather than on more

3. Ibid., 131.

general efforts to understand person and social institution. While questions of doing social science must necessarily inform the scholarly study of the faculty, these issues may be less of a concern among students, for whom a particular general education course may be their only social science course and who are necessarily less concerned than faculty with issues of social science epistemology. There is also the problem that such enduring questions as determinants of social position, constructions and transformations of meaning within culture, or freedom and authority in political life, become submerged in a focus which reflects merely passing concerns within particular social science disciplines. Students and staff should be conversant with means used to decide which enduring problems are important to study, rather than becoming "experts" in an area of study justifiable only because it is currently the concern of a number of scholars within a discipline.

The Soc 2 course has been constructed to reflect the issues common to the human sciences, particularly anthropology, sociology, and psychology. Writing about this course 1950, Singer observed:

> The task of examining the possibilities and limitations of studying human nature and society in a scientific spirit falls largely on Social Sciences 2. This task is focused on the relation of an individual's personality to his culture, a problem which naturally interests the student at this stage of his life. And so it happens that this is one of the liveliest fields in the social sciences, with many established classics available on our own and other cultures and many relevant works appearing in cultural anthropology, psychology, and sociology. Moreover, it is a field in which scientific analysis can and does lead to better human understanding of interpersonal and intergroup relations.[4]

Singer notes that the course has traditionally considered such questions as the concept of human nature, what is the nature of cultural difference in personality, the relation of social and cultural changes to personality, and the question of normal and abnormal. The goals of the course include both careful reading and analysis of critical texts in the human sciences, and also the ability to apply understandings obtained from these texts in understanding self and others. Forty years later, Singer's characterization of the course and of the principal issues considered over the three quarters, has a contemporary sound. While the significance of "science" as a mode of inquiry in the social sciences has been further clarified in the intervening time, the concept of systematic study, informed by evidence, remains a foundation of Soc 2. For exam-

4. Ibid., 128.

ple, we may use texts such as those concerning ceremonies marking the transition from childhood to adolescence, reports on relations within the family in our own society, reports on lives over time, or those of persons with psychological distress.

Psychoanalytic study, from Freud's initial observations regarding the course of hysteria, through studies of Winnicott, Khan, and Kohut concerning attainment of the capacity for solace, all fit within the goals of the Soc 2 course. Indeed, it is not just Freud's pioneering concern with the determinants of meaning which is of significance within the course: Freud also pioneered the application of a particular understanding of wish and intent to the study of social institutions. Freud's formulation ·regarding the determinants of religion clearly contrasts with those of such other social theorists as Durkheim, Weber, and Levi-Strauss. Comparative study of the work of these four theorists provides students with contrasting perspectives on the study of religion and social life.

Psychoanalysis, Curriculum, and the Classroom

If a general education course is to succeed in its mission, it should speak to issues both of intellectual and personal development in the lives of students. Ultimately knowledge is personal, uniting subjective and objective. Helping students to "own" their knowledge (a term initially posed by a former student in the course) and to make it a part of their own life, continues to be a major goal of the course. Indeed, it is difficult to distinguish between intellectual and personal development, and students gradually appreciate the extent to which idea systems and personal concerns are intertwined. In the present incarnation of our course, the potency of idea systems is introduced early in the first quarter, for example, with the discussion of Marx and the place of alienation in social and personal life. Precisely because of its concern with the foundation of meaning systems, additionally informed by the study of learning and going to school, psychoanalysis plays an important role in the curriculum. Not only are psychoanalytic concepts important in the study of culture and social life, they are also important in informing the process of instruction itself and in increasing the role of the course as a means of fostering intellectual and personal development in quite parallel ways among both students and course staff. While psychoanalysis shares this means for facilitating personal and intellectual development with historical materialism and cultural analysis, it may be unique in its capacity to speak to the quite personal concerns of course participants with their own distinctive life experiences.

Weber's classic study *The Protestant Ethic and the Spirit of Capitalism* provides an example of a text fostering both personal and intellectual development. The man in an "iron cage," separating reason and passion, is both an ideal type for our own time and a problem of particular relevance for university students. Too often efforts to understand are viewed as necessarily conflicting with personal concerns. Weber's text deals both with the origins and the present expression of a particular world view which most students share with Weber, with their instructor, and with each other. The text raises issues concerning work and vocation, commitment to idea systems beyond mere mechanical conformity, and the basis of personal satisfaction.

Beyond the objective curriculum, and the intellectual challenge of understanding Weber's view of objectivity and reason within the West, there is another, implicit, concern regarding the place of these texts in students' own lives (and the lives of faculty as well). It is difficult for students to read this text without recognizing its immediate relevance to their own lives and appreciating the problems posed for us all by the "this-worldly asceticism" described by Weber. Teaching Weber has a pedagogical advantage over Freud since, while Weber is also concerned with issues of intention and action, the argument is posed in a more general manner, less explicitly concerned with the content of wish and intent than *The Interpretation of Dreams*. Students are able to consider the historical origins of the ethic which has become so central in the lives of all of us within the Occident while, at the same time, reflecting on both the benefits and the problems posed by adopting "this-worldly asceticism" as central in their own world view. This is particularly relevant to our university, where it is common for students to seek courses more difficult and challenging than those required for the degree.

The Subjective Curriculum

While Weber introduced the concepts of intention and the complex interplay of meaning and wish, Freud makes this connection explicit. Particularly in his discussion of sexuality and inevitable conflict between the generations, Freud speaks to issues salient in the lives of university students. Parallel to the explicit curriculum, there is an implicit or subjective curriculum running along a parallel track which, too often, may not be explicated as a part of instruction. Further, psychoanalysis speaks not only to the content of the material that provides the basis of the curriculum in Soc 2 but also to the very process of instruction itself, including the relationship between student and instructor, and the parallel, continuing personal and intellectual development among all participants in this shared learning.

B E R T R A M   C O H L E R

This model of the determinants of thinking suggests that all secondary process, or formal, logical, thought, is determined by need or wish.
The model is consistent with the clinical theory in which Freud maintains
that persons understand experience in terms of wish and intent. Study of
what interests us may be understood both in terms of satisfaction of wish
or intent, and also in terms of enhancing the sense of personal integrity.
This perspective on learning and education, distinctive of psychoanalysis, has been portrayed by Richard Jones in *Fantasy and Feeling in
Education* as the "subjective curriculum."[5] Jones maintains that parallel
to the so-called objective curriculum, or what is presumed to be learned
in school, there is a subjective curriculum which, if properly employed,
may actually enhance learning.

Jones's observations regarding the curriculum stem from his participation in Jerome Bruner's project for a junior high school social
studies curriculum based on Bruner's concept of education. Called
as a consultant when it became clear that students were not profiting
from Bruner's *Man: A Course of Study,* Jones observed that the curriculum was so personally threatening that students protected themselves
from recognizing its relationship to their own lives. The classroom
teacher focused almost exclusively on the objective curriculum. Empathic observation of student discussion of the filmstrips led Jones to
recognize the intense and personally painful content reflected in such
lessons as that showing Eskimo families leaving their elders behind to die
when harsh winter conditions made it difficult to feed a large family.
Jones realized that many students reacted powerfully to issues of care for
dependent and helpless family members. In the absence of an opportunity to discuss these feelings, students were forced to block out particularly personally painful and frightening scenes. This observation led
to efforts to talk about the meaning of the filmstrip for students, after
which it was possible to reflect on the intellectual significance of the
lesson.

Focus on the personal or subjective experience of the curriculum
should not be regarded as a substitute for study of the formal curriculum; concern with issues of meaning (the subjective curriculum) further
enhances the power of what is learned in school by removing potential
sources of resistance to learning new and possibly threatening material.
Prior to the discussion of student's own response to observing the film-
strips in Bruner's social studies curriculum, classroom discussion of the
material was tentative and superficial. Following acknowledgement of

5. R. Jones, *Fantasy and Feeling in Education* (New York: New York University Press,
1968).

232

the subjective meanings inherent in the filmstrips, students were able to become much more engaged in the discussion of the material. Jones's point is that recognition of meanings latent in the formal curriculum enhances rather than interferes with the goals of learning the formal curriculum.

Anne Roe's studies regarding the significance of personality in career choice has pointed to the importance of matching personal history and career interests.[6] Her work implicitly recognizes the concept of the subjective curriculum: students are motivated to seek particular careers based both on normatively defined expectations and particular life experiences. For example, a college student who has lost a parent through death due to cancer may be motivated to seek a career in scientific research or in clinical medicine in order to make reparation for angry feelings consequent upon parental loss, or in order to seek solace for such a loss, passively suffered, through activity on behalf of others. Student selection of particular undergraduate concentration programs may be dictated by the subjective meaning attributed to a particular program. In an effort to foster a sense of personal and collective integrity, students from various ethnic groups may select concentration programs in areas related to their own ethnic group. These students seek to learn the language and cultures of their family's tradition, often denied to them in the family's zeal to realize acculturation and success for offspring of immigrant parents.

One of the consequences of reading psychoanalysis within Soc 2, accompanying increased awareness of less explicit concerns, is increased understanding of the many factors accounting for intellectual interests. For example, as a result of reading *the Interpretation of Dreams*, an undergraduate student from a southern community who had relatives on both sides of his family fighting for both the North and the South in the Civil War was able to decide upon a concentration in American history. Following his parents' divorce when he was in high school, this student had developed a passionate interest in the Civil War and, particularly, the origins of the conflict in the preceding decades. The student wrote a senior paper on Henry Clay, described by one instructor as publishable in a scholarly journal, and went on to a distinguished career in American history. He reported being further helped during his doctoral studies by a personal analysis which clarified both the sources of his intellectual interests and his difficulties interpreting Lincoln's prewar situation.

6. A. Roe, *The Psychology of Occupation* (New York: John Wiley, 1956).

BERTRAM COHLER

The Subjective Curriculum and Both Personal
and Intellectual Development

Jones argues that both developmental and educational timing must be considered in planning the curriculum. For example, he states that Bruner's social studies curriculum demanded a level of abstract thinking which could not be attained by the junior high school students for whom the curriculum was designed. While undergraduate students generally have attained the capacity for logical thought, wish and intent may interfere with the capacity for learning the material; Piaget viewed wishes as playing a part in thought by maintaining egocentric perspectives derived from early childhood. Psychoanalytic perspectives suggest that intention is always present as a determinant of thought and that making these implicit wishes and concerns explicit, through introspective study, fosters increased understanding. However, just as in the therapeutic setting, timing of curriculum may be essential in fostering introspection. Little is to be gained from asking students to master concepts which pose issues for personality development unless consideration is given to timing and to provision of support for both instructors and students dealing with these issues. (At the present time, this is a major issue impeding the effectiveness of educational programs concerning such sensitive social issues as substance abuse and AIDS.)

In discussions of personal development across the college years there has been little attention paid to the significance of timing within the curriculum. Issues which third- and fourth-year students are able to discuss with a degree of personal comfort may be particularly difficult for first-year students to consider (more than half of the students in our general education course are in their first collegiate year). The unique problems posed for students in the first years of college have seldom been discussed. Away from over an extended period of time, first-year students are often homesick and may be overwhelmed by the variety of life styles around them, by lack of parental supervision, and by their new-found freedom for personal expression. Second-year students confront yet other problems in adjusting to life at college. While many colleges provide support programs for first-year students, they assume that the second-year student has made this adjustment to college life. However, with the excitement of the first year now having worn off and the need to make such important career decisions as selection of a major or of a concentration program, the second year presents particular challenges for these students. Problems similar to those of first- and second-year students are also common among students transferring from other colleges.

Issues of subjective curriculum and timing across the academic year

234

have been among the factors relevant to continued revisions of the Soc 2 curriculum. For example, in the 1950s and 1960s, it was common to teach Durkheim's book *Suicide*, Freud's case studies, and *Interpretation of Dreams* in the first quarter of the course, which often is the first college term for our beginning undergraduate students. Common sense alone would suggest that students just beginning their career in a residential college might find it difficult to discuss topics which are so personally relevant and potentially painful. Further, students must gain some degree of comfort with their instructor and with fellow students in order to be comfortable discussing the emotionally loaded topics explicit in the work of both Durkheim and Freud.

Even the subject of religion, and Durkheim's demonstration that religious worship is ultimately the worship of society itself, may pose problems for students from families in which religious commitment is a major aspect of daily life. Particularly at a college like Chicago, where many of our students may be the first to attend an elite college, in a community characterized by traditional values, the suggestion that religion and society are one is difficult for students to entertain. Across the weeks spent discussing this text, students become increasingly aware that Durkheim is concerned with larger issues than the rituals and beliefs of the Arunta. Realizing that turn-of-the-century France was similar to aboriginal Australia in the place of religion within social life, students may become personally threatened by this challenge to cherished traditions. Readings may threaten important family values: reading Todorov's analysis of Cortez's and Columbus's impact on American Indian peoples, one student began to question the impact of his own religious tradition, which required several years of missionary work among people adhering to so-called primitive religions. This student was thrown into a personal crisis as he began to question the value of conversion to Christianity and his failure to appreciate "local knowledge" during the time he spent as a missionary.

As difficult as such topics as religion and gender are for students when introduced in the winter quarter of the course, it would be virtually impossible for students just beginning college to confront such personally threatening topics. If the goal is for students to master the curriculum, it may be better to discuss these possibly threatening topics later in the academic year, when students feel more comfortable with their place in the classroom and the college, rather than to deal with them immediately at the beginning of the fall term. With appropriate regard for such concerns the entire Soc 2 curriculum was redesigned in the early 1970s: the autumn quarter now begins with the issue of work and economy, the winter quarter considers issues of symbol and meaning, and while the spring quarter focuses on concepts of meaning and person, or self. Since issues of vocation and career are central in the lives of students, while being less painful to discuss, it seemed particularly appropriate that the year begin with these issues. The works of Adam Smith, Karl Marx, and Max Weber, together with such historical studies as those of E. P. Thompson on time and formation of the concept of discipline at work in the Industrial Revolution, are important in helping students deal with issues of vocation and management of time in their own lives.

Having worked together across the academic year, often with the same fellow students and (less frequently today) the same instructor, by the spring quarter students have acquired enough self-confidence and have sufficient experience within the College to be able to talk about issues regarding sexuality posed by the study of Freud's work. The goal in each instance is not to pander to student interests, or even to regard students as emotionally fragile and in need of protection. Just as in *Man: A Course of Study,* the goal is to teach the curriculum and to have students profit both intellectually and personally from having studied the material. Developmental and instructional timing is critical in realizing these curricular goals.

Efforts to force students to question themselves and society may produce overwhelming feelings of confusion and uncertainty. This is certainly not to say that controversy should be avoided or that we should abandon the goal of enhanced understanding and personal freedom uniquely possible through higher education. Rather, the significance of the subjective curriculum must be explicitly acknowledged so that these challenges are not so overwhelming as to produce disorganization or, more likely, to call into play those means of protecting oneself against recognition of psychological conflict which may preclude real learning. Writing about the captivating power of Sophocles' tragedy *Oedipus Rex,* in a way relevant to the curriculum, Freud argued in *The Interpretation of Dreams* that the continuing power of this classical drama for our own time is founded in the larger conflict which it portrays. However, without acknowledgment of the personal power of this message, intense feelings are elicited which may interfere with full appreciation of this tragedy.

One student reading *The Interpretation of Dreams* in Soc 2 gained increased understanding of a problem in his own life: he was always attracted to women who were unavailable, either because they were about to graduate from college and leave town, or because they were going out with a friend or roommate. He had lost friendships with roommates or best friends by becoming involved with their girl friends, women who by common understanding were "off limits" to him. Working on an assigned paper discussing a recent dream, this student became aware of some of the reasons for this attraction. As a consequence, he has been shifting his romantic interests in a direction which offers the prospect of more satisfying intimate relationships and continued friendships. Another student, an avid sailor, became aware of feelings of resentment regarding an intrusive father who had been inappropriately involved in his older brother's achievements in world-class tennis. Reading Freud's *Interpretation of Dreams,* he realized that his interest in sailing emerged, at least in part, because it was an activity which his father could hardly observe, let alone not take an active part in. This student was able to talk about his disappointments regarding his father, particularly in connection with the father's efforts to relive, through his sons, his own mid-life personal and career crises, which had followed early social and business success.

At the present time, about one in three marriages ends in divorce, very frequently preceded by conflict between the principals which is potentially more destructive than the actual divorce upon the lives of their children. Particularly among upper middle-class families, if the divorce does not take place within the first five years after marriage, before the advent of parenthood, it is most likely to occur after children have left home for college. One student, still shaken by his parents' announcement of their impending marital separation the night before he was to leave for college, found *Oedipus Rex* particularly compelling. An essay written about the play proved important in resolving intense feelings regarding his parents long-standing marital conflict. Failure to attend to meanings implicit in texts which are assigned, and to make these meanings explicit in discussions with students, may lead students to protect themselves against the full impact of the drama, encouraging students to keep the play at a safe distance without having to confront its personal significance.

Just as Jones's revision of Bruner's junior high school science curriculum enhanced understanding of the goals which Bruner had attempted to realize in *Man: A Course of Study,* discussion of personally significant texts increases student appreciation of these texts. A student from a wealthy, politically connected family became fascinated with Beulah Parker's social psychological study of a multigeneration family, *A Mingled Yarn: Chronicle of a Troubled Family.* He readily recognized the salience of Parker's life-history report for himself and his own family, using Parker's portrayal of conflict in values across the generations as a means of increasing his understanding of the problems faced by his own family. Ultimately, he was able to reconcile long-standing differences with both his grandfather and his father as a result of the study of this text. Another student, taking a humanities common year course, reported being assisted in dealing with grief resulting from the sudden death of a parent shortly after beginning college as a result of reading Plato's *Phaedo,* a dialogue focusing on the question of the immortality of the soul.

Teaching and the Subjective Curriculum

Jones did not ask why senior, well-regarded, classroom teachers failed to observe students' experience of often personally threatening film-strips used in Bruner's curriculum. Well educated, with advanced study in educational psychology at one of the nation's most distinguished uni-versities, these teachers failed to respond to student concerns regarding this curriculum in their usual thoughtful manner. Too often, from ele-mentary school to university, empathy fails in the classroom. Joseph Katz and Nevitt Sanford have noted the increased impact which could be realized by the curriculum if instructors were able to attend more directly to their student's feelings about what they learn.[7] Sometimes the curriculum affects the instructor in ways which parallel the effect of curriculum upon students. Temporary lapses in the instructor's capa-city to respond empathically to student concerns likely represent the intersection of student and faculty anxieties.

Other factors may also interfere in the faculty's capacity for empathy with students. For example, instructors may regard student absence from class as personal criticism, even to the point of being unable to teach the course because feelings of self-worth and competence are compromised by the failure of students to attend class. Their usual em-pathy with students appears to be derailed by these absences from class. While in no way condoning student's absence from class, instructors must recognize that students have their own lives to lead and that there are inevitably times when they cannot attend class. Students are often surprised to learn that their absences have such an unintended impact upon their instructors or even that they are missed when they are not in class. The dynamics of student (or faculty) absences for the subjective experience of the class is an issue requiring further study.

Texts such as Freud's case studies, much of modern drama, or partic-ular ethnographic accounts, are especially likely to challenge the in-structor's capacity to respond empathically to student concerns. One of my colleagues, well versed in cross-cultural accounts, teaching with me in a quarter devoted to issues in the cultural construction of gender, pronounced as "disgusting and revolting" an observational account

7. J. Katz and N. Sanford, "The Curriculum in the Perspective of the Theory of Per-sonality Development," in *The American College: A Psychological and Social Interpretation of the Higher Learning,* ed. N. Sanford (New York: Wiley, 1962), 418–44.

within a nonliterature culture of homoerotic practices and ingestion of semen through fellatio as a necessary protection against pollution by women. Clearly, this account elicited personal concerns which made it difficult for this course staff member to make explicit the implicit meanings contained within the text.

Instructor and student each contribute to the construction of meanings within that "intermediate space" described by the psychoanalyst D. W. Winnicott, which is the classroom. Just as in all relationships, each participant enters into this discussion with particular wishes, fears, and experiences across a lifetime. A teacher growing up in circumstances of poverty may find it difficult to teach in an affluent suburb. An instructor unsure of his or her own scholarly abilities may find it difficult to be supportive of the fledgling scholarly efforts of college students. Bettelheim has observed that, as child and teacher meet each morning, they enter a world in which even experiences of the present day influence life in the classroom. In a similar manner, the student encountering the instructor in the college classroom brings the experiences of daily life into the discussion in a manner parallel to that of the instructor. A fight with a roommate, a difficult phone conversation with parents the previous evening, or a difficult examination in an earlier class, all contribute to the student's response to the curriculum, the group, and the instructor. In a similar manner, a disagreement with a colleague or an administrator, or even conflict with one's own young adult offspring, all may contribute to the instructor's mood and produce an at least temporary break in empathy in responding to student struggles with a text.

Meeting in the classroom, instructor and student jointly construct shared meanings based on separate and shared life experiences. If the student feels quarrelsome as a result of something that happened before school, or if the instructor feels particularly impatient because his or her own experiences that morning, the conditions are ripe for conflict between them. It may be best to acknowledge such tensions explicitly, as during mid-terms, when students are likely to devote much of their time to quizzes in those courses where the mid-term examination is important for the overall grade. (It is a reflection on our own problems in maintaining a sense of personal integrity that we should assume our course is the only important one in the lives of our students and that our course should always receive preference in allocation of study time!)

Campuswide and community events also help to determine the meaning of the classroom discussion on a particular day. At the most commonsense level, students in Soc 2 enjoy using their increasing understanding of social life in reviewing a national election or international event taking place concurrently with the course. However, more difficult campuswide or community events, from racism to homophobia and sexism to suicide, may be implicitly a part of the discussion and may need to be made explicit. A few years ago there was a series of unrelated suicides on our own campus. On the morning following the third suicide, during the winter quarter, by a student who was close to several of the students in that particular section of the Soc 2 course, the instructor acknowledged this event at the beginning of class and invited discussion of feelings regarding the suicide. The student who had killed himself had been well liked in his college house and had held major positions of responsibility both within the house and in a number of campus organizations. The fact that the student was known to so many of the class, and so well liked, made it particularly difficult for students to make sense of the tragedy.

Since the suicide took place during the winter quarter, when students already felt some sense of colleagueship, several students were able to talk quite openly of their feelings of guilt at not having recognized their friend's depression, their own concerns regarding feelings of alienation and lack of interest in their work, and their own struggles with depression. The very effort at shared understanding enhanced the feeling of closeness among students and with the instructor. Indeed, several students later commented that this class was a turning point in understanding the goals of the course and in helping them increase their own sense of personal integrity. Students and instructor shared in the common effort to make sense of their feelings, additionally relying upon course readings in Marx, Weber, and Durkheim. The instructor attempted to integrate personal and intellectual concerns in a discussion which assisted students both to make better sense of their own feelings about their friend's suicide, and to make the readings more a part of themselves, rather than simply required reading.

The task of dealing with the suicide reflects both the concept of subjective curriculum and the instructor's own continuing self-scrutiny parallel with that of the students. Clearly, the dilemmas of modernity as presented by Marx and Weber are important in understanding the sense of personal despair leading to suicide, while discussion of Durkheim raises issues of social solidarity and anomie. The interplay of personal concern and social context is also highlighted by class discussion of the suicide. For the instructor, this was a painful issue as well. Memories of the suicides of a family member and two close friends initially made it difficult for the instructor to summon the courage to talk about this issue in class. This reluctance was initially expressed as concern that the students should be protected from having to confront their feelings, and that this discussion would take valuable class time away from discussion of the text (students were reading Durkheim's *Elementary Forms of the Religious Life* at the time of the suicide). Discussion with a colleague helped to clarify these issues and made it possible to broach the subject in class.

The Personal Impact of Student upon Instructor

Many of the issues of concern in precollegiate education are heightened in university teaching. Self-esteem, concern with issues of competition, and concern with issues of identity all are brought into particularly sharp focus during late adolescence and early adulthood. The complex interplay between student, faculty, and curriculum often become entangled in ways difficult to distinguish. Student expectations regarding accomplishments of faculty may threaten the self-esteem of those faculty who question the value of their own contributions. Other faculty may feel threatened by student accomplishments or experience feelings of competitiveness with students whose research may call their own contributions into question or who may succeed in resolving an issue whose solution has eluded them.

All too often, university teaching is viewed as a burden or obligation which interferes with scholarly study. This is an often-voiced concern among departmental colleagues reluctant to join in teaching general education courses such as Soc 2. The very fact that students so often make the curriculum a matter of intense personal and intellectual concern only adds to the discomfort which university faculty may experience at the thought of undertaking instruction in general education. Students relish the opportunity to work with distinguished scholars, and to bask in the glow of the faculty member's enjoyment of scholarly study and the recognition accorded him or her for scholarly accomplishments. However, faculty are not always comfortable with this admiration and may flee from the classroom and from feelings of grandiosity, ill at ease with the discrepancy they perceive between their goals and accomplishments. Regardless of "real world" attainments, faculty self-regard may be so great that even Nobel prize accomplishments may be minimized when contrasted with imagined success and desired attainments.

All too often, problems in recruiting faculty to teach general education courses are attributed to organizational factors, including faculty overcommitment to departmental matters or conflicts with time and energy for their own scholarly work. However, beyond these often legitimate factors, and seldom consciously, faculty may also be concerned with trying to live up to those student idealizations just mentioned. As a result of working with students, instructors' personal doubts may lead to increased feelings of depression or personal depletion which, in turn, may be covered by increased arrogance and diffidence regarding student concerns. Discussion-style instruction may evoke a teacher's worst fears and self-doubts, and disappointing response of the class to a discussion leader's efforts may so exacerbate these doubts that faculty avoid any participation in general education.

The propensity of students in general education courses to ask pointed intellectual questions regarding the assumptions of academic disciplines may be a further source of discomfort for faculty. It is not enough to teach a text because it is a part of a particular discipline's tradition or the source of present controversy. The text must also speak to some larger issue, and the instructor must be able to convey both the promise and the problems posed by a text to be discussed in class. Research university faculty experiencing conflict between teaching and scholarly work, and liberal arts faculty feeling overwhelmed by heavy teaching schedules, may find it difficult to maintain an empathic stance. Obviously, students look to faculty for guidance in understanding the curriculum. Less obviously, students seek assurance from faculty about their talents and skills, an assurance that abets continued learning.

Letting oneself be used by students in their efforts to maintain self-esteem when confronted by challenging situations is an important element of what Daniel Levinson and his colleagues, in their study of career development, term "mentoring," the care and concern expressed by senior members of an organization for their juniors. In his portrayal of career development, Levinson describes a phenomenon characteristic of organizations as diverse as universities and businesses, in which persons in established positions commonly support the development of those just beginning their careers. In follow-up studies of the mental health of college men at mid-life, more successful men were also more explicitly concerned with mentorship and mentoring.[8]

In the academic situation, Thistlewaite has shown that mentorship, defined as devoted faculty concern for student careers, is a better predictor of whether students will obtain a doctorate than such school characteristics as quality of laboratory facilities or library size. In the natural sciences, the instructor's collegial manner and expectation of intellectual rigor and, in the social sciences and humanities, concern for student welfare, enthusiastic teaching, and fostering controversial discussion, all are associated with student completion of the doctorate.[9] Clearly, this men-

8. D. Levinson, C. Darrow, E. Klein, M. Levinson, and B. McGee, *The Seasons of a Man's Life* (New York: Knopf, 1978); D. Levinson, "Toward a Conception of the Adult Life Course," in *Themes of Love and Work in Adulthood,* ed. N. Smelser and E. Erickson (Cambridge: Harvard University Press, 1980), 265–90; D. Levinson, "A Concept of Adult Development," *American Psychologist* 41 (1986): 3–13.

9. D. Thistlewaite, "College Environments and the Development of Talent," *Science* 130 (1959): 71–76; "Rival Hypotheses for Explaining the Effects of Different Learning Environments," *Journal of Educational Psychology* 53 (1962): 310–15.

toring is difficult to provide when the instructor feels competitive with students or when the mentor, often inadvertently, becomes involved in reenactment of conflicts regarding authority and competitiveness parallel to those of childhood.

The mentor may be particularly important in fostering a student's determination to succeed in spite of adversity, or in giving the student the courage to try. The skillful instructor is able to give the student courage to work on a problem of particular difficulty, perhaps one even at the growing edge of his or her own academic competencies, and to stick by the student during times of difficulty in realizing new learning. As the psychoanalyst Haskell Bernstein has observed, in every effort to learn new material there are those "dark moments" when the concept is particularly confusing or when the answer eludes the student's best efforts at comprehension. A valued mentor can assist students with low self-esteem to evaluate their own talents and skills more accurately and arrive at an appreciation of themselves more in line with the reality of previous attainments and potential for the future. In this manner, the mentor is able to facilitate new learning and to give students the courage to try.[10]

Despite evidence that faculty mentors are important for student growth, college faculty often find it hard to tolerate student admiration. For students such idealization may provide important psychological support, permitting them to feel they can achieve great things through association with admired teachers, but faculty often feel unequal to students' admiration, for the reasons discussed above.

On the other hand, some instructors are disappointed when students do not admire them enough or assume their values. These faculty seek a mirror for their own interests and attainments among their students and are disappointed in students who fail to adopt their own interests and concerns in just the manner which they had initially sought. For example, an instructor who tries to foster rebellion against adult authority may be disappointed when students fail to adopt his cause as their own. Instructors who were activists in the sixties and seventies commonly feel discouraged that most contemporary students appear to be uninterested in issues which so moved them in their own youth. Women instructors who have worked actively for feminist causes may feel dispirited when young women of another generation appear to be less identified with the feminist cause or may be more concerned with issues of marriage and family formation than with career.

10. H. Bernstein, "The Courage to Try: Self-Esteem and Learning," in *Learning and Education: Psychoanalytic Perspectives,* ed. K. Field, B. Cohler,and G. Wool (Madison, Conn.: International Universities Press, 1989), 143–58.

The emergence of the academic professions in our own country shifted faculty identification from education (especially in a broad sense that includes moral development) to the concerns of particular disciplines. Promotion and tenure came to be determined primarily by disciplinary contributions. Geographic mobility became an important part of academic career development. Always seeking to move to institutions with the greatest social and academic prestige, faculty grew more concerned with professional success than with the lives of students. At the same time, concerned with getting the most prestige for the dollar, administrators offered research facilities, reduced teaching loads, and academic leaves as recruitment incentives. Contact with students was believed to interfere with academic prestige.

There need be no tension between faculty scholarship within a discipline and student needs for effective teaching and availability of role models and counselors. Scholarship, in the sense of deep interest in the field, and teaching are inseparable. Effective instruction requires, in addition to knowledge, an understanding of the emotional process of learning. Both a concern for student well-being and empathic responses to fledgling scholarly efforts are critical to teaching. They are the "silent carriers" which facilitate learning across the course of life. Effective university education should engage students in a lifelong process of learning that will be sustained in spite of fears that efforts will not live up to internal and external standards, the fears of success that characteristically attack women, or the fears of failure that characteristically attack men.

Conclusion

Psychoanalysis is the study of subjectivity, including both wishes and intents of which persons are aware and those which are kept out of awareness because of their potential social or personal reprehensibility. Parallel with what is formally learned in school, students attribute personally relevant meanings to all aspects of schooling, from the emotional climate of the classroom to characteristics of the teacher and fellow students and the subject matter which is being taught. Traditionally, it has been assumed that attention to the subjective curriculum interferes in realizing educational objectives. However, rather than distracting students from that degree of concern with the formal curriculum that is presumed proper, focus on the subjective curriculum may actually enhance educational objectives. This concern with the personal meaning of what is learned in school permits students to discuss fears and wishes related to life in classrooms and creates a classroom optimally attuned to learning. As a consequence, students feel increasingly comfortable, integrated, and able to remain engaged in curriculum and instruction.

Concern with the relationship between student and instructor is also of critical importance for understanding life in classrooms. Just as students attribute meaning to the curriculum that are based on their own life experiences, meanings are also attributed to the instructor. At a commonsense level, a student who rebels against imposition of "arbitrary" authority will find it difficult to learn in school. Recognition of the variety of wishes enacted in the relationship between student and instructor increases the student's ability to understand and to resolve factors such as competitiveness, resentment, or personal attraction which might interfere in this relationship. Greater attention must be extended to the reciprocal roles of student and instructor within the classroom. The instructor's own wishes and concerns are played out in the classroom in a manner parallel to those of students.

The persistence of psychoanalytic perspectives in the Soc 2 curriculum testifies to the inseparability of the intellectual project of constituting a unified vision of social science and of the pedagogical project of effective general education teaching. It has also long demonstrated the value of this intellectual perspective as a means of fostering increased understanding of the relationship of person and cultural context and as means for understanding the relation of intention, meaning, and action in social life. However, in addition to the place of psychoanalysis within the curriculum of the general education course, inclusion of this view of life informs the process of learning and teaching, and enhances curricular goals. Recognition of a subjective curriculum, parallel with the objective or formal curriculum, makes it possible to appreciate text and discussion in ways that increase the salience and value of instruction. Recognizing that students attribute particular meanings to what they read and what they discuss in class, we can make these meanings an explicit aspect of the discussion and so increase the sense of immediacy which we hope students will encounter in reading and talking about texts. Increased recognition of the concept of the subjective curriculum within the Social Sciences 2 course shows that this use of psychoanalysis is able to increase the significance of general education for the personal and intellectual development of both students and course staff.

12

The Portable Soc 2; or, What to Do until the Doctrine Comes

Marc Galanter

> You are not expected to complete the work,
> but you are not free to desist from it.
> —Rabbi Tarfon, Pirke Avot 2:16 (first century)

When David Orlinsky told me in 1982 that his research revealed that Soc 2 was then really in its early fifties rather than its early forties, I felt an even greater sense of affinity to it. But the forty motif emerged even more clearly, for I was with Soc 2 up to its fortieth year—which was my own. So I clung to the image of "notable forties," as I shall for a moment now, though the course enters its early sixties as this volume appears.

There is a long association of forty with the idea of a period of arduous preparation and testing, with ordeal and endurance followed by renewal, even rebirth.[1] In that first deluge, "the rain fell on earth for forty days and forty nights" (Genesis 7:12), the same period that Moses labored on Mount Sinai (Exodus 24:18). The people of Israel were condemned to wander in the desert for forty years (Numbers 14:33–34). The fortieth year marked their triumphant entry into the promised land and a new beginning. But the forty years were necessary, we are told, to allow for the disappearance of those who had been slaves and retained slavish habits of mind.[2]

If we think of Soc 2's forty years (any of its several forty years) as a crossing we may ask ourselves what is the desert? Conventional views of social life? Normal disciplinary social science" The fashionable ideologies of the time? And what is the promised land? There have, it

---

1. We refresh ourselves with forty winks; life begins at forty. Forty is the maximum number of lashes permitted as punishment by Deuteronomy 25:3. Forty is the number of days allowed Ninevah in which to repent (Jonah 3:4).

2. I.e., all but Joshua and Caleb who had been tested during the forty days that the Israelite spies spent in the land of Canaan (Numbers 13:25).

seems to me, been many separate journeys to separate destinations. What, if anything, they share is explored in various ways in this volume and in the wider expanse of conversations it represents.

I want to tell you about the land to which I crossed over—without claiming that it is the land of milk and honey. I want to talk about the kind of intellectual enterprise I have been engaged in since leaving Chicago and to explore how it relates to the Soc 2 project.

How I Got Here from There (or There from Here)

My connection with Soc 2 came about through Soc 3, a cognate enterprise called "Freedom and Public Policy" which was merged into (or swallowed up by) Soc 1 and Soc 2 in the early 1960s. In my later years of teaching in the College, my connection took the form of teaching a variant of Soc 2 entitled "Law, Justice, and the Social Order," which is the direct ancestor of much of the teaching I do today.

I ended up in a sister inter- or multidisciplinary enterprise which goes by several names—"law and society" studies, the sociology of law, sociolegal studies, law and behavioral science. Let me call it social inquiry on law or SIL for short. By this I mean a second kind of learning about law, one that seeks explanation rather than justification, that emphasizes process rather than rules, and that tries to appreciate the distinctiveness of law against the background of larger patterns of social behavior rather than as autonomous and self-contained. What I have been doing in SIL, it turns out, is working through some of the themes that were central to Soc 2.

As I look back to see how I arrived here, I undoubtedly absorbed some of these intellectual dispositions during my time in the College during the Late Hutchins Age (although I never took Soc 2) and during my three years in the Philosophy Department which in my case amounted to extending my stay in the College from two years to five. Then I went to law school, for reasons that are still obscure to me, from which I emerged with an ample portion of the law school view of the world. In this view, law is an integrated purposive system comprising a hierarchy of agencies moved by and applying a hierarchy of norms. It draws on the power of the state but disciplines that power by its own autonomous and internally derived norms. The central legal institution is the court, and the central and typical activity of courts is adjudication. With some slippage and friction, social behavior is aligned with and guided by legal rules. Moreover, that behavior can be deliberately modified by appropriate alterations of these rules.

When I went off to India on a Fulbright scholarship in 1958 to study the abolition of untouchability, I encountered a world vastly different from what my training had led me to expect. Viewed through the lenses of my American legal education, the profound dissociation between legal norms and social reality in India violated my sense of how law was supposed to be. Looking back, I see there were at least two ways to react: one, to regard the Indian case as pathological and deviant and to take my model as a prescription for its cure. (This option was taken by the "law and development" movement.) The other was to consider the possibility that there might be something amiss in the law school view of things. My emphatic identification with India (much stronger then than now) and perhaps a residue of skepticism induced by my earlier training inclined me toward the latter path, but it was a slow cumulative process of constructing an alternative way of making sense of that Indian experience. It was my association with the College that provided the opportunity for constructing that alternative. I came to the College in 1959 after a frustrating year at Stanford Law School, working on a program for South Asian government lawyers (thus starting out on the law and development tack). I returned to the College for a year to teach Soc 3. One thing led to another and I ended up spending the next ten years teaching Soc 2 (and Indian Civilization).

What did Soc 2 teach me? Beyond all the things, true and false, that I learned from texts and colleagues and students, there is a residue of intellectual disposition that has remained with me. I suspect it is partly shared, partly idiosyncratic and misremembered. Let me try to set out my catalog of the components of the Soc 2 project. My version of the party line may strike you as the worn commonplaces of general education, but looking from the professional school, they retain for me a freshness and critical power (as evidenced by their continuing power to provoke unease in law students).

The first commandment was not to take too seriously the claims of the disciplines to exclusive possession of any methods, subject matters, or theories. Indeed, one suspected that loyalty to these claims was purchased at the cost of disablement from rendering social life in its full complexity. We learned to cross disciplinary boundaries freely, but to respect them as convenient features of the landscape, not likely to be dissolved soon into a universal social science. We learned to appreciate the disciplines not as domains of knowledge, but as campaigns of inquiry attached to job markets. We were respectful of their accomplishment and disrespectful of their claims for turf.

Second: We were also disrespectful of the boundary between student and teacher, novice and expert. We were colearners, and if we were more advanced than our students, we were as acutely conscious of our nakedness in encountering what we didn't know. We argued that any inquiry, if pursued far enough, arrived at questions of perspective, meaning, and principle that could be informed but not resolved by expertise. We were committed to pushing on to those questions where we could not wrap ourselves in the garments of expertise and could not make arguments from authority.

Third: We tried to convey an appreciation of the accomplishments of social science. But we erected imposingly high standards. We brought to bear on the claims of social science all the critical scrutiny that social science itself could muster, exposing the hollowness of received wisdom and the pretensions of daring new formulations, turning solutions into problems. We were critical of explanations at any level of analysis, but we were not reductionists who thought there was a single set of fundamental elements by which everything could be explained. It was an article of faith that everything was connected, but in some more complex way. Until the arrival of the Messiah, we were resigned to a world of incomplete and inconsistent explanations.

Fourth: Similarly, we took policy seriously. We thought that the design and implementation of policy has to be informed by the multiple and complex reality that theory reveals to us, but they were different enterprises or at least distinct moments of a common enterprise. We rejected the notion that science could supply neutral technical solutions to social problems. We eschewed any notion that practice could be derived deductively from theory.

Fifth: We practiced loyalty to the text. The avoidance of textbooks in favor of original texts implied that reading of the big world out there depended on mastery of the world of the text. Probably nowhere has a group devoted to the understanding of the world out there lavished such attentive regard on a series of texts—not because the text contained the truth about what was out there, but because it was the unavoidable instrument of our understanding. Since there was no single text, we were propelled into a world of plural understandings. There was no single amalgam in which jarring views were united, conflict resolved. We lived with alternative readings that didn't fit together. In this world of plural understandings, we were constantly reminded of the stratagems of interpretation and choice that were involved in knowing about the world.

In short, the Soc 2 line was to learn to live with a set of permanent and intractable oppositions, to accept the open texture and problematic character of knowledge about society, without despair—to cultivate an appreciation of what we do know while recognizing its flawed and contingent character.

The Received Paradigm of Legal Learning

I mentioned that social inquiry into law was a *second* kind of learning about law. In order to see these Soc 2 themes being played out in SIL, it is necessary to appreciate that SIL is a minority taste. It exists at the periphery and in the interstices of a formidably established realm of legal learning, a realm which includes both academic and practice precincts as well as its own suburbs of popular culture. Let me try to sketch this realm of learning. In doing so I shall overgeneralize outrageously and omit many needed qualifications and disclaimers. I argue that, for all its protestations of its lack of theory, contemporary American legal learning proceeds on the basis of a discernable "paradigm"—i.e., a series of assumptions about the major contours of "law" and the major regularities in the relation of law to social life. Legal scholars and professionals, while accentuating various differences with one another, display a broad agreement about the nature of legal phenomena. I refer not to concurrence in some body of tested propositions, but to adherence, usually tacit, to a set of presuppositions which,[3] taken together, provide a cognitive map, or paradigm,[4] of legal reality. This paradigm provides a lens through which legal phenomena are perceived and suggests how these perceptions are to be arranged.[5] By suggesting what are worthwhile and important questions and what are suitable answers, it shapes our view of what are worthy scholarly endeavors and educational experiences.

For purposes of this discussion, I have artifically isolated the "model" component of the paradigm from consideration of the exemplars (literary and pedagogic) in which these assumptions are embodied (e.g., the

3. These assumptions or basic perspectives are sometimes explicitly articulated, but usually are present as what Alvin Gouldner, in *The Coming Crisis of Western Sociology* (New York: Equinox, 1971), 29ff., refers to as "domain assumptions," i.e., tacit background assumptions about the characteristics of a class of phenomena in which explicit theory is embedded.

4. The paradigm concept is taken from Thomas Kuhn, read in Soc 2 for a time in the 1970s, who uses it to denote "the entire constellation of beliefs, values and techniques and so on shared by the members of a given [scientific] community (*The Structure of Scientific Revolutions* [Chicago; University of Chicago Press, 1970], 175)]. The paradigm constitutes a "disciplinary matrix"—a constellation of group commitments made up of conventions of symbolism, shared values for judging scientific work, exemplars of successful problem solution and shared commitment to a variety of models, ranging from heuristic to ontological, that "supply the group with preferred or permissible analogies and metaphors, . . . help to determine what will be accepted as an explanation and as a puzzle solution [and] assist in the determination of the roster of unsolved puzzles and in the evaluation of the importance of each."

5. I emphasize that the paradigm need not be articulated as "theory"; rather I suggest that it functions as the tacit theory in most "untheoretical" legal research.

appellate opinion, the brief, the law review article, the casebook, "Socratic" teaching) and from the shared values by which these are judged (e.g., comprehensiveness, fidelity to sources, concreteness, relevance to policy, moderation, etc.).

The components of the received paradigm are familiar and by no means startling.[6] They are not so much affirmed as assumed: not assumed to be literally true—their inapplicability in particular instances may be conceded—but to partake of a general correctness that is usually thought to require neither explanation nor investigation. But they are not assumed to be merely a set of normative propositions. They have a composite character, fusing both descriptive and normative, to which we shall return.

The common paradigm, if stated in propositional form, would include inter alia, something like the following:

1. Governments are the primary (if not the exclusive) locus of legal controls; that part of the legal process which is governmental is the determinative source of regulation and order in society.

2. The legal rules and institutions within a society form a *system* in the sense of a naturally cohering set of interrelated parts articulated to one another so that they form a coherent whole, animated by common procedures and purposes.

3. The central and distinctive element of this system is a body of normative learning, consisting, in various versions, of *rules,* and/or standards, principles, policies—and of procedures for discerning, devising, and announcing them.

4. Legal systems are centered in and typified by *courts,* whose function is to announce, apply, interpret (and sometimes

6. Much of this portrayal of the paradigm was anticipated by Llewellyn's 1930 critique of received thinking about law, "A Realistic Jurisprudence—The Next Step," reprinted in his *Jurisprudence: Realism in Theory and Practice* (Chicago: University of Chicago Press, 1962). He attacks the use of rules as the central reference point of thinking about the law; the "tacit assumption" of correspondence between rules and behavior (i.e., both that rules describe behavior and that they control it); the separation of courts from other officials and from lay practice, etc. Curiously, after a devastating critique aimed at expanding the field of legal study to include "everything currently included and a vast deal more," organized in a series of concentric circles: official behavior, views of what the law is, social arrangements, social philosophy, etc., he remarks: "At the very heart, I suspect, is the behavior of judges, peculiarly, that part of their behavior which marks them as judges—those practices which establish the continuity of their office with their predecessors and successors, and which make official their contacts with other persons; but that suspicion may be a relic of the case law tradition in which we American lawyers have been raised" (pp. 40–41). For an assessment which emphasizes carryovers of paradigm assumptions in Llewellyn's critique, see Carl J. Friedrich, "Remarks on Llewellyn's View of Law, Official Behavior, and Political Science," *Political Science Quarterly* 50 (1935): 419–31.

change) rules on the basis of or in accordance with other elements of this normative learning.

A. The basic, typical, decisive mode of legal action is *adjudication* (i.e., the application of rules to particular controversaries by courts or courtlike institutions in adversarial proceedings).

5. The rules (authoritative normative learning) represent (reflect, express, embody, refine) general (widely shared, dominant) social preferences (values, norms, interests).

A. Broad participation in rule making (by adjudication and by representative government) insures that the rules embody broad social interests.

6. Normative statements, institutions, and officials are arranged in hierarchies, whose members have different levels of authority.

A. "Higher" elements direct (design, evaluate) activity; "lower" ones execute activity.

B. Higher elements control (guide) lower ones.

7. The behavior of legal actors tends to conform to the rules (with some slippage and friction).

A. Officials are guided by the rules.

B. The rules control the behavior of the population.

C. Conformity is the result of assent and the (threat of) application of government force.

8. If the above obtain, then

A. the authoritative normative learning generated at the higher reaches of the system provides a map for understanding it; and

B. the function of legal scholarship is to cultivate that learning by clarification and criticism.

C. Legal scholarship directs itself to remedy imperfections—to bring legal phenomena into conformity with paradigm assumptions.

It may justly be asked "How do you *know* that is what American legal scholars believe? My treatment of these as a single cluster may seem a perverse refusal to make important distinctions among legal scholars. For example, I make no distinction between believers in the model of rules and instrumentalists; nor between formalist believers in autonomous rule development and their realist critics. Thus, where some observers detect a radical break, I see a striking continuity. For present purposes at least, if the mix has changed, the basic ingredients are the same. I am not talking about a set of theoretical propositions but about a set of intellectual commitments.

No one is likely to affirm these propositions, or all of them, quite so baldly.[7] If forced to be explicit about one or another, taken as factual propositions, they are subject to qualifications and exceptions. But their distinctive character is missed by regarding them simply as a series of descriptive generalizations. They are not simply asserted as factual generalizations, nor are they taken to be merely a set of normative prescriptions. They have a dual, composite character, fusing both descriptive and normative. They are thought to state what is normal and typical in legal systems—to reflect the inherent and proper shape of legal reality. This fusion of factual and normative assertion (made explicit in some of the items listed, but implicit in all) establishes them as ideological statements—statements about what a legal system and a society (and a scholarly career) ought to be like.[8]

Constructing a Second Learning about Law

These affirmations don't "fit." Although each has some power to describe some areas and strata of legal activity in the contemporary American scene, they are unsatisfying depictions of what is typical and normal in it. Let me take just two examples: the exclusive predominance of official law and the treatment of bargaining.

Mainstream legal learning embodies a kind of "legal centralism"—a picture in which state agencies (and their learning) occupy the center of legal life and stand in a relation of hierarchic control over the regulation that goes on in other social settings. The institutional-intellectual complexes that we identify as national legal systems did indeed, as Weber saw, consolidate and displace the earlier array of normative orderings in society, reducing them (in theory) to a subordinate and interstitial status.

But of course, these other orderings continue to exist. Counterparts or analogs to the institutions, processes, and intellectual activities that are located in national legal systems are to be found at many other locations in society. Some of these lesser legal orders are relatively independent, institutionally and intellectually, of the national legal system; others

7. Indeed, I am not sure they would be explicitly affirmed at all. For present purposes it is sufficient that legal scholars tend to act "as if" they affirmed them.

8. I employ "ideology" here in the sense of an assertion with both descriptive and normative referents. The ideology is not of course confined to legal scholars or to lawyers but is widespread in our society. Here, the stress is not on legalism as a consciously held moral philosophy, but on many of the same features as components of a cognitive map.

are dependent in various ways. That is, societies contain a multitude of partially self-regulating spheres or sectors, organized along spatial, transactional, or ethnic-familial lines, ranging from primary groups in which relations are direct, immediate, and diffuse to settings (e.g., business networks) in which relations are indirect, mediated, and specialized.

The enunciation of norms and application of sanctions in these settings may be more or less organized, more or less self-conscious, more or less consensual and so forth. For convenience I use the term "indigenous law" to refer to social ordering that it familiar to, and applied by, the participants in the everyday activity that is being regulated. By indigenous law I refer not to some diffuse folk consciousness, but to concrete patterns of social ordering to be found in a variety of institutional settings—in universities, sports leagues, housing developments, hospitals, etc. People experience justice (and injustice) not only (or usually) in forums sponsored by the state but at the primary institutional locations of their activity—home, neighborhood, workplace, business deal, and so on (including a variety of specialized remedial settings embedded in these locations).

Official institutions then are not the only sources of normative messages, just as they are not the only arenas in which controls are applied. To examine the rivals and companions of official law we must put aside our habitual perspective of legal centralism, a picture in which state agencies (and their learning) occupy the center of legal life and stand in a relation of hierarchic control to other, lesser normative orderings, such as the family, the corporation, the business network.

Legal centralism has impaired our consciousness of indigenous law. The mainstream of legal scholarship has tended to look out from within the official legal order, abetting the pretensions of the official law to stand in a relationship of hierarchic control to other normative orderings of society. Social research on law has been characterized by a repeated rediscovery of this other hemisphere of the legal world. This has entailed repeated rediscovery that law in modern society is plural rather than monolithic, that it is private as well as public in character, and that the national (public, official) legal system is often a secondary rather than a primary locus of regulation.

Let me elaborate another example. Shortly before this essay was originally composed, I attended a workshop, sponsored by the Association of American Law Schools, on Negotiation and Alternative Dispute Resolution. The title of the workshop reveals something about the picture of the legal work that permeates American legal education. It links negotiation with alternatives and implicitly juxtaposes them to something unspecified! Alternatives to what? To adjudication, to courts. Even while affirming that negotiation is important, it reflects the view that negotiation (and mediation and so forth) occupy the outer edges of the legal realm—they are the soft periphery as opposed to the hard core of legal doctrine. Negotiation is something apart from the real law that occupies legal educators.

This picture misleads in several ways. It implies that negotiation (and other so-called alternatives) are infrequent, new, unproved, marginal. But the gravitation to a mediative posture by judges and other decision makers armed with arbitral power is surely one of the most typical patterns of disputing on the American scene—as an examination of our courts and administrative agencies will attest. The linking of negotiation to "alternatives to litigation" is misleading in another sense. On the contemporary American legal scene the negotiation of disputes is not an alternative to litigation, it *is* litigation. There is a single process of disputing in the vicinity of official tribunals that we might call "litigotiation"—that is, the strategic pursuit of a settlement through mobilizing the court process. Full-blown adjudication of a dispute—running the whole course—is one infrequently pursued alternative, the cost and risk of which are compelling presences throughout.

The settlement process in not some marginal, peripheral aspect of legal disputing in America; it is the central core. Over 90 percent of civil cases are settled (and of course many more disputes are settled before reaching the stage of filing). Lawyers spend more time on settlement discussion than on research or on trials and appeals. Much of the other activity that lawyers engage in (e.g., discovery) is articulated to the settlement process. Even in the case that departs from the standardized routines of settlement, negotiation and litigation are not separate processes, but are inseparably entwined. Negotiation is not the law's soft penumbra, but the hard heart of the process. The so-called hard law turns out to be only one (often malleable) set of counters for playing the litigation game.

The courts are central to the litigation game not only because of what they do in specific cases, but because of the "bargaining endowments" that they bestow on the parties. That is, what might be done by or in or near a court gives the parties bargaining chips, or counters. Bargaining chips derive from the substantive entitlements conferred by legal rules and from the procedural rules that enable these entitlements to be vindicated. But rules are only part of the endowment conferred by the law—the delay, cost and uncertainty of eliciting a favorable determination also confer bargaining counters on the disputants.[9] Everything

9. Delay, cost, and uncertainty may themselves be the product of rules—e.g., a discretionary standard involving the balancing of many factors and requiring detailed proofs is more costly, time-consuming, and uncertain in application than a mechanical rule. But

that might affect outcome counts—all of the outcome for the party, not just that encompassed by the rules. The ability to impose delay, costs, embarrassment, or publicity comes into play along with the rules. Rules are important but they interact with a host of other factors in ways that do not correspond to the neatly separated background and foreground of the law school classroom.

In short, there is a lot of stuff out there that legal learning doesn't account for very well. Legal learning's ventures as explanation track the law's assertion of "hierarchic control" over other social institutions. That these aspirations for control are frequently thwarted is no secret. Actual patterns of legal activity depart from the authoritative learning of the law. The presence of the departures is commonly acknowledged under the rubric of the "gap" between "the law on the books and the law in action" (a locution that has endured since first formulated by Roscoe Pound in 1910). I shall use the term "gap" as shorthand for this perceived dissociation between legal learning's model of what is supposed to be and what is experienced. There are a variety of things we can do with these perceptions. I want to sort them into three major approaches. For short I will call them denying the gap, filling the gap, and crossing the gap.

Denying the gap does not mean denying that it exists, but that it requires us to question our received view of legal reality. Particular anomalies may be interpreted in ways that forestall challenge of paradigm assumptions: they may be regarded as inevitable frictions; they may be relegated to interstitial status; they may be read as a list of unmet needs; they may be regarded as atypical pathology. Within the perceived paradigm, each instance of the gap tends to be dismissed as an exception—something atypical, peripheral, and transient. That is, awareness of such discrepancies does not induce professionals (or others) to relinquish their model of the legal system. Rather it spurs them to add ad hoc explanations to account for these irregularities.[10] As Jerome Frank

---

cost, delay, and uncertainty also result from such nonrule factors as, for example, the number and organization of courts and lawyers. The meaning of the endowment bestowed by the law is not fixed and invariable but depends on the characteristics of the disputants: their preferences, risk-aversiveness, ability to bear cost and delay, etc. A different mix of disputant capabilities may cause a given endowment to take on very different significance.

10. Llewellyn (ibid., 18) observes that when votaries of conventional legal thought are presented with instances of the gap between the "law-in-books" and "law-in-action": "any one of them will proceed to remodel his emphasis *ad hoc;* he will, for a moment, fix his stress on the remedy, even on the effects of the remedy, as used in life. *But* it is an *ad hoc* remodeling. It is forgotten when the immediate issue is passed. It is no part of the standard equipment of investigation, discussion, synthesis; it is a part only of the equipment

once said of Morris Cohn, "he shut his eyes to the usualness of what he desired to think the unusual."

Those who find this unsatisfying seek a revised or second body of learning about law. The response that I call *filling the gap* takes seriously the notion that there are major parameters of legal life unaccounted for in legal learning and that it is necessary to extend and enrich traditional legal scholarship by adding an empirical dimension. If the basic cartography is sound, what is needed is exploration into uncharted territories and detailed surveying. The routes of exploration are set by legal doctrine. But this filling-the-gap response has itself been challenged for its dependence on received notions of legal learning and for inhibiting the development of alternative theoretical formulations. The perception of a "gap" proceeds from and expresses an expectation of harmony or congruence between authoritative normative learning and patterns of action. As Richard Abel has written:

> This continuing preoccupation with the gap problem has had unfortunate consequences for the development of a social theory of law. Scholarship is confined to a single question, seen from two perspectives: why does behavior deviate from law; why does law mandate a conformity which is not forthcoming? We are thus directed to particular gaps between law and behavior, and how we may close them. But we cannot entertain the possibility of another relationship between law and behavior, or begin the construction of a more complex model in which law and behavior interact without a one-to-one correspondence.[11]

The "gap" perspective circumscribes the search for regularities or patterns by elevating the authoritative normative learning—"the law on the books"—into a map to guide our exploration. It is as if we attempted to understand language behavior by focusing on the differences between written and spoken English, assuming harmony or congruence as the normal condition and devoting our attention to explaining the special cases in which we found some discrepancy. Indeed, the visualization of the "law in action" as representing a deviation from or debasement of the "law on the books" parallels folk belief about language usage.

---

of defense. When used apart from combat . . . it flares like a shooting star, and disappears. Always the night of words will close again in beauty over the wild, streaked disturbance."

11. Richard Abel, "Law Books and Books about Law," *Stanford Law Review* 26 (1973): 175, 189.

The poverty of the "gap" as a way of describing our legal experience is suggested by a comparison with the much more differentiated way we, as amateurs, have of recording and remembering language usage. We recognize the coexistence of formal literary language, colloquial varieties along local, class, and ethnic lines, occupational jargons, not to mention in-group argots, pidgin, slang, sign language, baby talk. Even these crude folk taxonomies suggest the possibility of formulating a variety of questions about regularities in the way the common code is refracted by different groups and in different settings, about patterns of mutual influence (or lack of it) among these sectors, about their change and persistance. We need to supply ourselves with concepts for a differentiated description, or mapping, of the legal process. But the "gap" perspective is an obstacle to this: the "law in action" collapses an immense variety of phenomena into a single undifferentiated mass; the "law on the books" provides an inadequate map to that mass; and the underlying expectation of harmony narrows the range of questions that we ask.

Among those unsatisfied by a project of filling the gap, some imagine a second (or revised) body of learning about law that would construct the word of law on lines independent of the professional paradigm. I refer to this response as *crossing the gap*. But to where? There are several destinations.

One destination is a pure scientific positivism which would build a science of legal behavior quite independent of both consciousness of the actors and the institutionalized learning of the law. Another road across the gap is what might be called left insurgency, which would link the construction of new learning about law to the dismantling of repressive legal institutions and to the fostering of new legal (or nonlegal) institutions that would express a new (or refound) state of community. Each of these shares some affinities with a third path that, for want of a better term, I shall call liberal eclecticism, and of which I confess to being a practitioner.

Let me try to locate it by thinking of these three as rival ways of dealing with the perception that mainstream legal studies fail to account for much of the life of law in contemporary society. We may think of legal learning as the affirmance of one term in each of a series of oppositions or polarities. It upholds the official law of the state as opposed to indigenous regulation; it views law as self-contained and autonomous rather than socially situated and permeated; it views law as imposed rather than interactive; it affirms adjudication as central and bargaining as peripheral.

Scientific positivism proposes to chart from afar the actual patterns and discover the laws underlying them; left insurgency would abandon differentiated formal law (or reconstitute it by making it responsive to truly popular or indigenous elements). The approach of liberal eclecticism shares with the positivists a drive toward explanation detached from the imperatives of prescription and policy. It shares with the left a drive to rediscover and resuscitate the suppressed, discreditable side of each of these oppositions. It embraces them not only to acknowledge that they retain operative force, but because they may be a source of value.

Legal Studies, Social Theory, and General Education

This embrace reflects one enduring theme in social science and in the Soc 2 course at Chicago: the theme of unending hierarchic systems, showing that what appears to be top down is really bottom up, that it is the unconscious, the folkways, the proletariat that are the dwelling place of the forces that move (or should move) and shape the social world. It is the romance of the underside: the less formal, the less organized, the less respectable is seen not as mere material to be ruled, shaped, tamed, but as another, perhaps principal, source of value and meaning. I see this in my own inclination to attack the pretensions of legal centralism and argue for openness to the value of indigenous regulation, and in the insistence that the results of bargaining are not inferior to those of adjudication. At the same time, I am aware of the dangers of romanticizing the bottom—there are lots of nasty things about indigenous regulation and many reasons to doubt the fairness of many bargaining outcomes.

Once we acknowledge that the answer is not to be found in our authoritative learning about society, then what? As we turn from the narrowness and abstraction of that learning to embrace the world, we may be tempted to think that uninstructed flesh has answers. (Are we sure these are good proletarians who will go to workers' education classes rather than staring at the TV and swilling beer?) It is not unlike an old Soc 2 problem. We want to throw off the yoke of the repressive superego without giving free reign to anarchic id; we want the form, direction, acuity of ego. We want to be rid of tyrants without loosing mobs— we want to create constitutional monarchies with broad participation and responsible citizenship.

The liberal eclectic program—which some have called postmodern law—turns out to be a similar bourgeois compromise. It seeks to recapture the energy, participation, and variety of indigenous regulation, of bargaining and so forth, but wants them informed, monitored, and refined by a continuing dialogue with formal legal institutions, who become teachers rather than controllers.

Alongside its other roles, general education may provide a vital function as a repository of skeptical regard from which to mount challenges to the received wisdom and ruling paradigms of the professions. In it can be institutionalized stances that enable people to gain distance, stand outside the ruling paradigm. Among such stances are some closely related to the kind of intellectual commitments that I earlier labeled the Soc 2 party line. It involves the maintenance of ironic distance from the claims of the profession—an ability to see it as another indigenous system of learning, one that deserves appreciation without granting its claims for hegemony.

Soc 2 was certainly not the only road to SIL. My companions arrived there by many other paths, by breaking out of the textual tradition of legal studies or broadening a tradition of empirical study to encompass the inescapably normative world of law. In retrospect Soc 2 proved a remarkably auspicious path. One who traveled by that route was untroubled by the absence of a disciplinary catechism, by the marginality of the enterprise, or by the dizzying spiral of text and context. Like Soc 2, SIL was moved by a genuine hunger to know about the world out there, combined with an awareness of the frailities of the enterprise of knowing about it. Soc 2 provided a model for appreciating the achievements of positive social science without ignoring the imperfections and ironies that prevade it. It showed how to be mindful of the problems of the enterprise without sinking into hermetic absorption with the enterprise itself.

Reflecting on my own course over the past years, I am struck by a series of recurrent zigs and zags—between law and social science, between domestic and comparative interests, between the detached quest for explanation and concern with policy. I like to think that this restless movement mirrors some duality lurking in the subject matter that continues to absorb me: the tension between the aspiration for a universalistic and inclusive legal order and the varied normative life of composite societies. If so, perhaps these zigs and zags can be counted as gropings upward along a spiral of understanding rather than as blind oscillations between fixed poles. My moments of optimism are animated by a feeling that my years of immersion in India emboldened me to discard much of the law school view of the world and to develop a fresh perspective from which to view the legal process in America. Similarly I think that my "frolic and detour" into Soc 2 prepared me to contribute to the construction of a second body of learning about law.

Social inquiry on law has aspired to promote the emergence of legal doctrine that is informed and inspired by systematic knowledge of its context. Now, in the early 1990s, there are signs that, as legal life has expanded and the system of knowledge about it has changed, the hold of the paradigm of legal thought described here has loosened. Much professional discourse proceeds as if the paradigm were intact. At the same time lawyers are awash in information that does not fit comfortably into the received picture of legal normality. The paradigm is surrounded by increasingly diverse and assertive rival views of the legal process.[12] Whether and how it will be transformed or displaced remains to be seen.

12. Some of these developments are traced in M. Galanter, "Presidential Address: The Legal Malaise, or Justice Observed," *Law and Society Review* 19 (1985): 537; and in M. Galanter and T. Palay, *Tournament of Lawyers* (Chicago: University of Chicago Press, 1991).

13

Alternative Social Sciences

McKim Marriott

Around the year 1950, the Soc 2 staff achieved a radarlike advance in intellectual technology—a literary device for multiple-choice exam questioning based on words that might have been spoken by the greatest authors of social science. The new device transcended time: by its use the staff were able to test students by presenting them with imaginary debates on culture, personality, and society among any five past masters, such as Karl Marx, Max Weber, Emile Durkheim, Sigmund Freud, or others, as well as among living luminaries. However, the transcendent new technology produced opportunities and difficulties that continue to confound and challenge the social sciences today.

The Traveling Seminar

Attending to voices from the past was hardly a new intellectual development, but the examiners of Soc 2 used their device also to transcend social and cultural space. By doing so, they paralleled some of the social sciences' most significant adventures and misadventures during the middle of the twentieth century. Originally constructing dialogues only for imaginary cocktail parties in Hyde Park, the examiners went on to invent debates that might have taken place in the mansions and slums of Chicago's Near North Side, and then in suburban Park Forest. The masters seemed to be catching Tocqueville's taste for travel: over the next two decades they maintained a regular itinerant seminar, voyaging to each of the increasingly remote locales studied by the course, and ultimately spreading their analytic ideas across five continents. Exam records show what Marx, Durkheim, Weber, Freud, Tocqueville, George Herbert Mead, and other greats might have said about worker motivation at a factory in early nineteenth-century Manchester, about sociality in a twentieth-century village of southern France, and about religion while canoeing across a lagoon in Papua–New Guinea. Possible remarks by factory workers, peasants, and Papuans were not systematically recorded, apparently because Soc 2's staff and students agreed with Max Weber that only Western social scientists' thoughts deserved serious attention: they alone appeared to have "universal significance and value."[1]

The Western seminarians did not see eye-to-eye on every matter—otherwise they (and we in the course) would not have kept on debating. But they did travel together, year after year, and their different comments usually seemed to complement each other. Students felt (as they showed in numberless essays) that syntheses of the several masters' analytic concepts were desirable and possible. If theorists could just combine Marx's analyses of material factors with Durkheim's typology of social forces, with Weber's perceptions of rationality and shared subjectivities, and with Freud's understanding of unconscious dynamics, they would produce a truly general social science—one which could dissect any complex problem of human behavior into its elements, then reassemble those common elements into logically related, testable propositions.

The hope for such a complete and universal science was of course not original among or limited to participants in Soc 2. For centuries before, philosophers had essayed general theories of human nature. Contemporary scholars such as anthropologist Robert Redfield at Chicago and sociologist Talcott Parsons at Harvard, like others elsewhere during the 1940s, were at work on syntheses of recent major European theorists. Beginning about 1946, Chicago's departments of anthropology and Sociology together had instituted a year-long introductory graduate course called, "Culture, Society, and the Individual"; and several graduate committees of the university paralleled much of what Soc 2 was attempting. At Harvard, faculty from Anthropology, Sociology, and Psychology joined to form a new Department of Social Relations and to write collaboratively, as in the influential book *Toward A General Theory of Action* (1952), edited by Parsons with Edward A. Shils. If generalists could carry one such body of theory to all academic fields, then the differences between disciplines as well as those between peoples might be transcended.

American power was also enjoying global expansion in those same years, and like the explorers and missionaries of earlier empires, the behavioral scientists of mid–twentieth-century America found themselves making imperial intellectual designs. As opportunities expanded

1. M. Weber, *The Protestant Ethic and the Spirit of Capitalism,* trans. Talcot Parsons (New York: Charles Scribner's Sons, 1952) 13.

for teaching and researching abroad, more and more behavioral scientists began observing everyday life in societies culturally far removed from those in which their own sciences had originated.

Students were naturally eager to join all in these expansive ventures, but felt unprepared to do so. In 1950 undergraduates (who in Soc 2 had been reading about the nonliterate educational methods of the Papago, a Native American tribe) protested to the dean of the College that the existing all-Western curriculum was itself culturally "tribal." They complained that the staffs in the social sciences, like tribal elders, had been indoctrinating Chicago's own youths in an ethnocentric manner, restricting them to a narrow range of historical experience and to parochial ways of thinking about that experience. They demanded ecumenical knowledge—knowledge that could be developed only from broader perspectives.[2]

Transcending the "Tribal Curriculum"?

At the apogee of this universalizing and expansive thinking, the College took two extratribal steps that reflected world developments by transcending Western society while extending the range of Western culture: (1) in 1956 it created a new set of year-long, non-Western civilization courses to accompany the year-long requirement in Western civilization; and (2) having added these courses to the social science curriculum, it watched them return more and more during the 1960s and 1970s to the agendas of the self-confident universalists among the Western theorists. As envisaged by the recommending faculty committee, the core of each new course's staff did in fact consist of scholars who were expert in that civilization's unique history and culture. But each course inevitably also recruited humanists and social scientists who had been trained in Western analytic categories and were intent on carrying forward the ideas of Western masters. (The courses might study the works of Confucius, Ibn Khaldun, or Manu, but would not use their analytic categories or test their theories.) The Western civilization course lent some of its staff members to the non-Western courses to serve as civilizational generalists, while several University programs at advanced levels urged comparisons among the economies, polities, or cultural products of different civilizations. Most aimed to distill (implicitly in Western terms) the common essence of all.

During the 1960s, students who voyaged to the non-Western civilizations were thus often guided by followers of the same masters who had

2. F. C. Ward, "What *Did* Confucius say? Animadversions on the Tribal Curriculum," *Journal of General Education* 11 (1958): 3–6.

constituted Soc 2's traveling seminar. Some guides urged students to compare class conflicts in other lands with those Marx had analyzed during Western Europe's Industrial Revolution. Enthusiasts for Max Weber's sociology proposed measuring China's and India's ideologies against the principles of Western theologians, statesmen, and bureaucrats. Followers of Durkheim's tradition asked Africa-bound students to note evidences of failure to move from "mechanical" to "organic solidarity"—evolutionary types which that master had formed from myths supporting European colonialism. Without benefit of couch, Freudian guides suggested applying to Arabs or Hindus analyses developed from the fantasies of Viennese elites.

Such expanded parochialisms as these could not then have been avoided by reading other social scientists, for the flowering of social science is only recent and all of its roots are culturally Western. Thus, when the Soc 2 staff had before 1950 decided to discuss data from non-Western societies, it had chosen works by cultural anthropologist Ruth Benedict, psychological anthropologist Margaret Mead, and cross-cultural psychoanalyst Erik Erikson. Benedict had applied European typologies to diverse tribal peoples, interposing Western assumptions of ideal and impulse for which she presented no native evidences.[3] Mead and Erikson in their exotic descriptions frankly sought answers to current American questions, using schemes of personal development that expressed distinctively American values.[4] Even in the 1980s, when Soc 2 joined the cruise to India, it was still psychoanalytically guided by a disciple of Erikson.[5] Similar difficulties continued when anthropologist Claude Lévi-Strauss became a Soc 2 author: he analyzed tribal myths as permutations of the distinction between "culture" and "nature," a dichotomy rarely found outside of recent European thought.[6] Since all these authors reported their data in Western categories, none could really be of much help in detribalizing the mind of the West. Indeed, the Western tribal curriculum was extended, rather than transcended, by such Western operations on extra-Western data.

Abstraction, like a wider range of data, was then also much employed for wider theorizing, but seemed unlikely to guarantee a theory's wider appropriateness. Thus some instructors in both Soc 2 and the non-

3. R. F. Benedict, *Patterns of Culture* (Boston: Houghton Mifflin, 1934).

4. E. H. Erikson, *Childhood and Society* (New York: W. W. Norton, 1950) and *Identity: Youth and Crisis* (New York: W. W. Norton, 1968); M. Mead, *Growing Up in New Guinea* (New York: Morrow, 1930).

5. S. Kakar, *The Inner World: A Psycho-analytic Study of Childhood and Society in India* (Delhi: Oxford University Press, 1978).

6. C. Geertz, "The Cerebral Savage: On the Work of Claude Lévi-Strauss," *Encounter* 28 (1967): 25–32.

Western courses attempted to describe the world using one or another of the five "pattern variables" which Parsons and Shils had distilled from the works of the Western social science masters.[7] The variables concern affectivity vs. affective neutrality, ascription vs. achievement, diffuseness vs. specificity in personal dealings, particularism vs. universalism, and self-orientation vs. collectivity-orientation. However universal these abstract variables sound, they force their users to perceive and to distinguish what few people from non-Western cultures were then known to distinguish at all.

Abstracting further, comparativists striving for a more neutral and possibly universal scheme tried using distinctions such as the "means-end" and "actor-action" dichotomies on which Parsons and Shils base their whole scheme of pattern variables. But from these distinctions arise still more peculiarly Western values and usages, such as equality before God and the law, privacy, independence, self-sufficiency, and neolocal postmarital residence; and many other peculiarly Western distinctions, such as body vs. mind, matter vs. spirit, secular vs. sacred, individual vs. society, and rural vs. urban. Content aside, the more one employs abstract forms of statement, the more one may exaggerate the peculiarities of any system of thought—here the Western penchant for absolute values and for dichotomous, yes-or-no distinctions that exclude all middle terms. Although abstracting made any Western scheme's cultural origins less obvious, it also seemed to produce analytic ideas that were less neutral, less likely to prove universal in their applicability.

Anomalies of the Imperial Venture in India

While preliminary considerations raised such doubts about the applicability of Western theories and methods, the results of field research were to present definitive tests. When I and others from the staffs of Chicago's South Asian Civilization course and from Soc 2 had begun to pursue research in India, we intended our projects to be compendious with and to extend the putatively world-embracing Western disciplines in which we had been trained. Comparisons were in our plans.

We sought comparable data, but often obtained anomalous results. For example, Weber had led us to expect that we would find Hindu elites disdainful of this-worldly achievements and concerned mainly with their future rebirths. Weber had led us also to expect a status system supported by fixed "traditional" rules, these either being main-

7. T. Parsons and E. A. Shils, eds., *Toward a General Theory of Action* (Cambridge: Harvard University Press, 1952).

tained in a rigid manner, or breaking down under the stresses of capitalism and bureaucratic "rationality."[8] Marx and Engels had given us, as analysts, the tasks of exposing the hidden material bases of all ideologies, such as those of feudal India, and of thus liberating the exploited rural masses for revolutionary social change.

But we found these expectations to be false or misleading and these tasks to be redundant. The getting of wealth and power were positively sanctioned aims for most Hindus, many of whom told us that morality is always necessarily material, is subject to continual normative flux, and should be pragmatically adjusted. Rural workers in India had long practiced strikes and boycotts, and now Milton Singer found economic rationality to be highly cultivated within families of the Brahman elite—where Weber would have least expected it.[9] We did find "revolutionary" sentiments (although the Indian words for "revolution" refer primarily to astral cycles!), but least among the most dependent workers, to whom food and other elite properties descended and among whom emulative hopes prevailed. Revolutionary sentiments were most often expressed by elites who felt the guidance of change to be their own natural duty.[10] No doubt Marx and Weber had been badly informed about India, but they seemed also to have been operating with inappropriate and irrelevant analytic ideas.

Durkheim's types of social solidarity were observably evolving backwards in India: his primordial "mechanical" type (relations of communal equivalence or similarity, requiring conformity by individuals) I found exhibited best not among peasant castes and kin groups, but among uprooted and politically mobilized migrants to India's growing towns and cities. Conversely, Durkheim's "organic" type (exchanges among nonequivalent persons and groups, having the effect of differentiating individuals) appeared to constitute the strongest ties among family members and also among the rural castes. India's urbanization was destroying many such organic exchanges, and in Durkheim's evolutionary terms would have to be called socially and individually retrogressive. Durkheim's false leads required us to question his types, his logic, and his assumptions.

Freud had assumed conflict to be universal between psychic organs that Hindus would not think of trying to perceive or to distinguish—mind and heart, Ego and Id. He had hypothesized that patriarchy pro-

<hr>

8. M. Weber, *The Religion of India* (Glencoe, Ill.: Free Press, 1958).

9. M. Singer, *When a Great Tradition Modernizes* (New York: Praeger, 1972) and M. Singer, ed., *The Modernization of Occupational Cultures in South Asia* (Durham: Duke University, 1973).

10. S. H. and L. I. Rudolph, *The Modernity of Tradition* (Chicago: University of Chicago Press, 1967).

motes a generalized repression of impulse life, especially for women, but this also seemed inaccurate: observers were confronted with systematic, often florid Hindu enactments of sexuality and aggression by married women, and with men's complaints about women's harassing them.[11] A. K. Ramanujan found oedipal fantasies working vigorously in reverse: in major myths and often in dreams, too, Hindu parents were seen as overwhelming their children and as appropriating to themselves their children's sexual and other vital powers.[12] Adolescent male Hindus saw themselves as growing up by taking more and more orders from male superiors, rather than by cultivating Erikson's American-style independence from authority.[13] Hindu understandings about interpersonal relations in families were evidently as different from Western ones as were Hindu understandings about life in communities; Western ideas seemed unlikely to be of help in deciphering either.

Even the common Western psychological assumption that mature personalities should have "identities" and act as whole and stable entities was notably missing from the findings of researchers among Hindus. In the city of Madras, Milton Singer found that the egalitarian attitude of the "generalized other" did not develop among men of different castes who exchanged roles in religious dramas—a finding contrary to the holistic reasoning of social psychologist George H. Mead, who had generalized from Americans' playing of baseball.[14] But also disconfirming Durkheim's supposition that "individuals" cannot emerge in a "mechanical" caste system, I and others found most Hindus attributing highly differentiated and even multiple social identities to each other. Personal integration and consistency were not admired among senior Hindus, who were instead advised to develop flexible, disengaged personalities like those of American adolescents suffering from "identity diffusion." Assumptions and logics markedly different from those of the modern West thus seemed to underlie Hindu notions about persons and their social functioning. The problem now became how to investigate such fundamentals, rather than just to continue recording the puzzling behavior that they generated.

11. G. M. Carstairs, *The Twice-Born: Study of a Community of High-Caste Hindus* (London: Hogarth Press, 1957).

12. A. K. Ramanujan, "The Indian Oedipus," in *Oedipus: A Folklore Casebook*, ed. L. Edmunds and A. Dundes (New York: Garland, 1983), 234–66.

13. S. H. and L. I. Rudolph, "Rajput Adulthood: Reflections on the Amar Singh Diary," *Daedalus* 102 (1976): 145–67.

14. M. B. Singer, "The Radka-Krishna Bhajans of Madras City," *History of Religions* 2 (1963): 183–226.

Coping Constructively with Anomalies

Findings that contradict Western cultural expectations, as these do, continue to surprise social science researchers in non-Western societies around the world, but such findings have rarely been used to produce better theoretical paradigms. Relativist researchers, who are disinclined toward generalizing, and empiricist, humanist, and historicist researchers, who are skeptical about science, all profit by "exception hunting"—an industry whose products are incidentally required by that dual Western paradigm which postulates both ideal rules and deviant behaviors as necessary features of every situation. Strange behaviors are detailed by all these kinds of researchers, and are opposed in report after report, not only to "rules," but also to "theory," which suffers impoverishment thereby.

Nonrelativist researchers who are concerned with saving the present, would-be universal social sciences may either stretch the meanings of the Western categories to encompass their strange findings, or sweep those findings aside as distortions caused by poor data, utilitarian interests, ignorance, or the odd local idea. Few researchers have had the temerity to put observed oddities back on the table as data for theorizing. Most fear that by doing so they would destroy the prevailing imperial social scientific paradigms—paradigms for which they conceive no possible alternatives.

I would like to suggest, however, that alternative social sciences are potentially available in the materials of many non-Western cultures, and that their development is essential to serve in the many places now either left to ad hoc description or badly monopolized by social sciences borrowed from the West. An analogy for the present condition of social theory may be made with the centuries during which Europeans naively demanded, often with nonsensical results, that unrelated languages all over the world conform to Latin grammatical paradigms. Although thought to contain the most natural and perfect analytic scheme, Latin grammar then actually constituted a major obstacle to scientific advance. A general science of linguistics began to develop only with the writing of alternative grammars whose differing categories are efficient because they are appropriate to the material, having been derived from no language other than the one under study.

Social scientists could sensibly emulate the linguists: rather than continuing to endure the absurdities that come from applying just their own tribal paradigms to other peoples who do not share them, researchers might well seek to investigate, before they attempt to interpret behavior in another culture, the ontology of that culture. What are its realities? What is the particular system of categories by which the people of that culture understand each other? What are the terms in which they themselves produce, perceive, and interpret human nature? What are the implicit questions to which their institutions and behaviors are their manifest answers? What, in other words, is the actual or potential social science of that culture?

Sketches are offered here of my own and others' initial efforts to construct parts of alternative social sciences for three non-Western civilizations—those of Hindu India, Shinto-Buddhist Japan, and Muslim Morocco. I offer these three brief but positive examples in an order from greater to lesser development, and in summaries whose decreasing lengths correspond to my own degrees of present acquaintance with them.

In epitomizing the kinds of general theoretical concepts that appear to be especially needed for understanding each of these civilizations, I concentrate here on their own definitions of persons and interpersonal relations. Person concepts are basic features, usually essential preconceptions for the rest of any social science. Contrary to the naive supposition that people are understandable in the same terms everywhere, each of these civilizations prefers to define persons in terms of different media: Hindu civilization favors motile media that we might most readily understand as liquid, while Japanese civilization speaks of pneumatic operations in a gaseous medium, and Moroccan culture the play of light over crystalline aggregates. Reasoning further in their favored media, thought within these civilizations offers diverse understandings of interpersonal processes that might be called respectively hydrodynamic, aerodynamic, and photodynamic. All three sorts of dynamics are worth considering as general theoretical schemes because they contrast so thoroughly with each other as well as with the solid-vs.-nonsolid, skeletal-vs.-muscular, static-vs.-dynamic, structural-vs.-functional metaphors that are so often met in the social sciences of the dichotomizing West.

A Hydrodynamic Behavioral Science for Hindu India

Researchers working in India have not merely struggled with unsuitable Western categories, but have also repeatedly encountered more suitable indigenous ones. They have found in well-known Hindu texts of astrology, biology, and religion, as well as in the current words and routines of Indian daily life, numerous processual formulations that fit accurately with the wholly motile and dynamic realities of life that are of most concern to Hindus. Using such indigenous formulations as alternatives to those of the Western social sciences is proving also to be analytically more effective.[15]

The cultural ancestors of the Hindus—the authors of their own technology, sciences, and philosophy—lived mostly outdoors with the cycling seasons and wandering stars, as farmers on India's warm alluvial plains. Unlike the compartmentalized urban philosophers of cold northwestern Europe who founded the hard-vs.-soft, material-vs.-spiritual Western social and human sciences, and more like today's atomic physicists and molecular and ecological biologists, Hindu thinkers have for two millennia described their human world as a "confluence" (*saṁsāra*) of "substances in motion" (*dravya*). They came to conceive of all material substances as malleable, as moving through open channels and receptacles, like the soft materials of an irrigated field. They discuss openings, permeable passages, and shifting interpersonal networks; they express no confidence in the durability of anatomy, architecture, or institutions; they consider closed and stable personalities to be either saintly or pathological. The movements of substances are constrained by elemental "earth," which provides soluble loci and connections that are at best temporary. All entities are also penetrated and surrounded by "sky," or "ether," which allows spaces through which substances can circulate. The only perfectly indestructible, inherently nonmotile Hindu categories are also indescribable—the nonsubstantial souls of all beings that are capable of life and the universal oversoul.

A person or other Hindu entity consists mostly of three very moveable elements called "fire," "water," and "air." Constituting seasonal "humors" in foods and in the environment as well as "faults" in humans, these three elements become respectively translatable as "bile," "phlegm," and "wind." In the world of human "aims," a similar triad reappears as "attachment," "advantage," and "cohesion" (the avoidance of incohesion) respectively. Most generally and philosophically, the same triad of properties is known as the three processual qualities or constitutive "strands," whose names may be respectively translated as "passion," "goodness," and (incoherent) "darkness."

Such triads of motile properties are present for Hindus in all things and actions. Their presences may be diagnosed from perceptions of, for example, the degrees of "heat," "weight," and "dirt" or "untimeliness," which they respectively generate; but usually their variable incidences are known from their distinct kinetic processes. The three

---

15. A synthesis of some of the commonest Hindu formulations, with references to some of the many sources from which it was developed, will be found in *India through Hindu Categories* ed. McKim Marriott (Newbury Park, Cal.: Sage Publishers, 1990).

processes can be thought of in liquid terms respectively as "flow" (the quantity, velocity, or friction generated by a substance's movement), "fluidity" (the penetrating capacities, downward direction, or sequentiality of a substance's movement), and "flux" (pulsation, resistance, backward turbulence, or loss—processes that work against the other two).[16]

Such primary attention to dynamics closely resembles the thinking found in sciences such as hydrology and oceanography as they have developed in the West, but no concept quite like any one of the Hindu processual triads is commonly used in current social scientific descriptions of human behavior in the West. There conventional social-conceptual space remains largely occupied by dry metaphors dealing with "structures," "strata," "statuses," "rules," "enduring values," "concrete facts," and "character"—metaphors of fixity that carry forward the plane and solid geometry of Euclid. Western social science has necessarily supplemented its repertoire of static concepts with an expanding set of active forces, such as "function," "practice," "conflict," and "change." For the West, however, such dynamics are distinct from statics, and may be abnormal or adventitious, while for Hindu India, activity and process (*karma*) are normal and inherent in all things.

That the ubiquitous Hindu properties have many sets of names (each set corresponding to a different, interpenetrating layer of Hindu reality) should occasion no surprise, for they concern powerful ideas much like those that are in mathematics and symbolic logic called the "fundamental relational properties." Such properties underlie analytic thought in most fields of Western natural science, where they are similarly known by diverse names. Western exegetes usually state these properties in their order-generating forms as the three "equivalence relations"—"reflexivity," "symmetry," and "transitivity." The less abstract, more contentful and substantial Hindu lists of strands, aims, elements, and humors instead emphasize chaos-prone, "antiequivalence" ways of looking at three similar relational properties. The Hindu axioms can thus be stated abstractly as "nonreflexivity," "nonsymmetry," and "nontransitivity"—a triad that yields a realistic, if rather pessimistic-sounding description of those unstable conditions of substance which have been called "liquid" above.

Persons, like everything else in the human world of the Hindu sciences, are thought to be open and therefore changeable composites of these relational properties. Since such persons cannot avoid to some extent altering their contents by transactions in words, food, sight, touch,

16. In my more technical writings, I label these three liquid processes as "mixing," "marking," and "unmatching," respectively.

and so on, they are better considered as "dividuals," rather than as securely separate and indivisible "*in*dividuals." The changeable unities that they may develop and feel for each other are therefore also better described as "liquidarities," rather than as the "solidarities" of Durkheim. Substantial interpersonal influences such as those noted above (female irrepressibility, oedipal reversals, father-son mergers, and servant-master emulations) appear as logical entailments, rather than as anomalous developments, if one starts with Hindu assumptions about persons and processes. So do attempts to control liquidity, such as asceticism and caste barriers—attempts that might otherwise be mistakenly counted (by a Freudian) as indexes of irrational anxiety and (by a Weberian) as a traditionalistic clinging to a fixed past.

Since Hindu persons' components are heterogeneous, no one is expected to achieve personal integration. Persons in fact are expected to develop multiple voices, each being evaluated by different social criteria; and communities correspondingly maintain different rankings among different parts or aspects of the same persons. The soul (which by Hindu reckonings may have no characteristics at all) is the one component of a person that is to be kept unattached to other persons and other components, ready for death and rebirth in the next life: hence the equivalence of souls implied by interchanges of religious roles produces no equality of whole persons, as Singer and others have found. Many further behavioral implications of Hindus' liquid definitions of reality can be anticipated to unfold through empirical research.[17]

An Aerodynamic Social Science for Japan

In Japan, as in India, social-conceptual technologies imported from the West have been criticized as grossly defective. Efforts to state Japan's peculiarities have, however, been hampered by the fact that Japan, unlike both India and the West, lacks indigenous "Great Books" in biology, psychology, sociology, or cosmology whose authoritative formulations might assist theoretical development. Indeed, the Japanese tend to distrust or deny any such determinate verbal pronouncements. Researchers who, like myself, seek the Japanese realities from which a social science might be constructed have therefore had to derive their formulations from features of everyday Japanese life, from its linguistic usages, phys-

17. Examples will be found in E. V. Daniel, *Fluid Signs: Being a Person in Tamil Way* (Berkeley: University of California Press, 1984); A. G. Gold, *Fruitful Journeys: the Ways of Rajasthani Pilgrims* (Berkeley: University of California Press, 1988); G. G. Raheja, *The Poison in the Gift; Ritual, Prestation, and the Dominant Caste in a North Indian Village* (Chicago: University of Chicago Press, 1988); and M. Trawick, *Notes on Love in a Tamil Family* (Berkeley: University of California Press, 1990).

ical arrangements, and often silent gestures. Observed to be among the features of greatest Japanese concern are containers, spaces, and energy (understood best as movements of air), and these are accordingly postulated here as the categories most likely to prove useful for a Japanese social science.[18]

Pneumatic functioning—specifically abdominal breathing—activates a container that models and may be partly formative of Japanese feelings about persons and interpersonal relations. The personal center is conceived as a "belly" (*hara*), an elastic bag that flexes with pulmonary activity; or as a "heart," an even more inner container that responds sensitively to variations in surrounding pressures, as one's ears respond to sound. Many Japanese cherish memories of having been carried during early childhood, bound ventrally to the mother's or an older sister's back by her abdominal sash; in such close juxtaposition, much is known about each through the other's touch, respiration, and movements, without overt vocalization.

Unlike the invulnerability attributed to "individuals" in the West, and also unlike the vulnerability attributed to porous dividuals in Hindu India, Japanese usages imply that persons are normally impervious, but flexibly bounded and bonded. Japanese are much concerned with relative pressures and with controlling access to their personal containers—faces, rooms, houses, dyadic relationships, and groups. As they constantly readjust the boundaries of such containers, they redefine interpersonal spaces as relatively outer or inner, as public or private, as suitable for the freely expansive, or only for the compressed and disciplined uses of personal energy.

Uniform personal pronouns do not exist in Japanese language, persons being variously designated by terms defining their closeness and seniority relative to the speaker and others. Persons, their closeness and seniority, can all be discussed as sociospatial relationships between container and contained. Accordingly one's self may be called "[one's] own part" (*jibun*) of an implied group, its magnitudes or even its existence depending on whether there is space in the containing group for someone to "have" (that is, to inflate) his "belly" self.

The valued Japanese idea of "oneness" (*ittaikan*) means not the wholeness of single persons, but the unity of two or more persons. Such

18. Principal sources for these suggestions are T. S. Lebra, *Japanese Patterns of Behavior* (Honolulu: University of Hawaii Press, 1976), D. K. Kondo, *Crafting Selves* (Chicago: University of Chicago Press, 1990), and N. R. Rosenberger, "Dialectal Balance in the Polar Model of Self: The Japanese Case," *Ethos* 7 (1989): 88–113. The "pneumatic" interpretations are my own.

unity for Japanese is to be achieved not by Western solidarity and not by Hindu-like interchanges of personal substance, but by the reciprocal responsiveness of persons to mutual pressures within their shared air space.

One especially desirable state for the pneumatic Japanese person to achieve is internal emptiness, a state reinforced by and reinforcing the Buddhist ideal of the innermost self as a vacuum devoid of selfishness. A related desire for personal boundaries is flexibility, which is thought to be enhanced by suffering, much as a new piece of leather may be thinned and softened by kneading and distressing it. A well-developed, pneumatic personal container should be capable both of complete compression when interpersonal circumstances require, and also of sudden expansion, as when an automobile air bag inflates to fit the available space in an emergency.

Martial artists—exemplars of Japan's feudal past—and also today's corporate moral trainers say that the potential energy or "spirit" (*ki, tamashii*) develops in the belly best through breathing disciplines, which regulate air moving between inner and outer spaces. Literary artists similarly attend also to the heart's monitoring of the delicate breezes passing in and out of the person, since these are the materials of poetic inspiration.

Western and Indian definitions are both strained by claiming that the Japanese in using these notions have any contentful personal "psychology" in which to instruct us, so largely are they concerned with pressures and dynamics in the unfilled spaces between and within people. Thus the Japanese concept of anyone's "humanity" (*ningensi*) is not a list of traits or qualities so much as attention to interpersonal spaces and relatedness. The Japanese are similarly much concerned with the spaces between the sounds in their classical music, with the intermediate shades between definable colors, with the uncategorizable spaces between the fixed boxes of Western scientific paradigms, and generally with the indefinability of things Japanese.

By their own thinking about people in terms of air moving through variable spaces, the Japanese seem pointedly to avoid having both what Western social scientists would recognize as a well-defined theoretical system and what Hindu thinkers would call a substantial or coherent one. An exception, of course, is when Japanese address themselves to social scientists of Western type: then their own concepts may be obligingly mistranslated so as to fit the required space—the noncongruent, but standard Western categories of "ego," "psychology," "structure," "status," and "group," for example. Reciprocally, efforts by either Western or Hindu theorists to be as sensitive as is Japanese usage to variations of interpersonal relations might breathe new life into what the paradigms of their own social sciences have been saying—and not saying—about selves.

A Photodynamic Social Science for Morocco[19]

The Muslim Moroccan world contains persons who, unlike the Japanese, are sharply defined in some of their particulars, but who are also multifaceted, socially mobile, subject to contextual redfinition, and thus accustomed to negotiation. Presumed to be solid, but not homogeneous, the Moroccan person can be said to see and to show himself as a mosaic—a composite of many light-reflecting surfaces. How others appraise him will differ as they view the known specifics that are relevant to any immediate ethical context. Fixity in geographic or social space is not expected. A man (males are the only full persons) is partly his ethnic origins, partly his previous loci, partly his other relatednesses (of many kinds), both claimed and attributed. An adult person's names are therefore many: they multiply as he moves through the various contexts of his life, and are employed variously according to others' knowledge and points of view on his life history.

In each context, the person is seen by others in whatever light of reason is given to them by God. If God's light is strong and clear, the person may seem whole to his observers, all his relevant facets being evident. But if God's light is weak or clouded, some part may not show, and thus may fail to validate a person's claim or attribute. God is the source of all light, and his light, reflected in a person's ocular mirror, is the personal soul; only he knows the whole truth about persons, their souls, and their ultimate fates. Men are left to reason, speculate, debate, and bargain over all partial, uncertain human contingencies. Among humans, there is much opportunity for shifting views between near and far, for optical illusion, for false vision as well as true; there is also much need for reliance on divinity's illumination.

Moroccan folk sociologists and learned Muslim theorists, too, necessarily focus on single persons, since Moroccan tribes, classes, guilds, sects, and other associations tend to group multifaceted persons in cross-cutting ways that often cannot be neatly delineated. Analysts must therefore invert Durkheim's method, and begin from personal particulars, rather than from social generalities. Even clusters of persons allied by birth, marriage, and clientship take the forms of person-

---

19. I take evidence for my "kaleidoscope" largely from the ethnographic interpretations by C. Geertz, H. Geertz and L. Rosen, in *Meaning and Order in Moroccan Society: Three Essays in Cultural Analysis* (Cambridge: Cambridge University Press, 1979).

centered "stars" (H. Geertz), rather than regular genealogical "trees." Such clusters may alternatively be described as intaglios that are, like architectural arabesques, differently readable from various angles. Visually they are clusters of points among which beams of light are seen to be mutually reflected and refracted, the play of light varying with the mosaic surfaces of all the persons who are associated, and who thus provide each other's environments. But since Moroccan persons are also assumed to move about, the aggregates of their identities are perhaps best likened to the shifting crystalline images seen in a kaleidoscope.

That North African Muslim understandings of persons and groups take kaleidoscopic forms should not be surprising if one recalls that they were devised by desert-traveling traders and warriors not unlike the merchants who now dominate the Moroccan market places. In their mobility they may resemble some persons of the modern West, but they are very unlike the settled nineteenth-century philosophers of religion, the state, and revolution who shaped the static-vs.-dynamic Western social sciences. They are equally unlike those many generations of peoples whose commonsense realities are enshrined in the self-analytic cultures of either liquid India or pneumatic Japan.

Conclusions

Human behavior both in the West and in the wide variety of other civilizations, such as those of Morocco, Japan, and India, seems likely to be better understood only by developing an equally wide range of alternative sciences—sciences which can grasp and reason with mankind's diverse ways of perceiving and constructing reality. The presently limited, conventional Western ways of asking about "self," "culture," and "society" may be handicaps even to understanding our own changing selves, just as they are surely major obstacles to wider understanding. Only an enlarged repertoire of alternative, possible, scientific realities—hydrodynamic, aerodynamic, photodynamic, and many more, along with the mostly solid-vs.-nonsolid ontology that used to be presupposed in the West—can give us the diversity of questions that we must be ready to ask of ourselves, of the next culture, and of the next person whom we may meet.[20]

---

20. Social sciences have yet to be constructed upon more than a few of the many different possible understandings of persons. Biologically, for example, one people may draw its thought from cardiac functioning—M. Z. Rosaldo, *Knowledge and Passion; Ilongot Notions of Self and Social Life* (Cambridge: Cambridge University Press, 1980); another from auditory and olfactory functioning—A. Seeger, *Nature and Society in Central Brazil: The Suyá Indians of Mato Grosso* (Cambridge: Harvard University Press, 1981); and still

A program for fostering such a repertoire might begin by reconstructing the intellectual biographies of exemplary Western social science masters. Such reviews would not decontextualize the masters' theoretical achievements—the systems of questions devised by them—but would aim to discover the processes by which they devised their systems from the cultural materials and the particular social situations in which they worked. One might demonstrate the cogency of those systems by deploying them further in contexts similar to those from and for which they had been devised. One would not unwittingly mock those systems by universalizing them—by applying their concepts in socially and culturally alien contexts, as Soc 2's junketing seminarians did and as today's social scientists often still do.

For expanding the repertoire of alternative social science questions, one would then endeavor, among different social and cultural materials, not to recite the past masters' favored words, but to emulate their achievements in analytical concept-production and theoretical system-construction. One would respect the masters and enrich their sciences by developing, as they did, new systems of questions derived from, and thus capable of yielding, better understandings of the varied realities in whose terms the world's varied peoples live their lives.

Here is challenge enough for many coming generations of investigators. Only by abandoning the illusion of immediate theoretical transcendence, grasping the cultural and social materials from which the existing social sciences have grown, and learning to construct the many supplementary volumes of questions that are needed—only then will they make the sciences best suited to the next case, near or far, past or future.

NOTE. Trained in Japanese language and a long-time researcher in India, the author was a student in the Department of Anthropology from 1946 to 1955. He taught Soc 2 from 1958 to 1978, and South Asian Civilization from 1957 to 1981.

---

another from alimentary functioning—C. A. Lutz, *Unnatural Emotions: Everyday Sentiments on a Micronesian Atoll* (Chicago: University of Chicago Press, 1988). The actual range of variation in such understandings has yet to be defined.

Afterword

Ralph W. Nicholas

We have a custom, in the College of the University of Chicago, of talking about "the curriculum" as if it were disembodied and self-existent. The fallacy of that kind of discourse is dispelled by this book. By giving concrete reality to a single social sciences course as it was conceived and practiced at different times and in different generations of students and faculty, this set of reflections defines the limits of both change and continuity in our curriculum. It discussed this particular course in the voices of the faculty who have made and remade it throughout its existence. The whole of what we grandly refer to as "the curriculum" of the College has the same character. It was never a fixed entity; it was always the product of a faculty consensus; it has its existence in particular student generations in particular historical settings. Framed by such social and cultural influences, what is most surprising about Soc 2 is the extraordinary level of continuity over nearly sixty years. That continuity is expressed in certain texts, which do not lose their relevance under changing circumstances, and certain general problems—roughly, the organization of appetitive humans into ordered social groups defined by a continuing cultural tradition—that do not change with the times.

Many of us revere "the curriculum" as it was realized for a time during the presidency of Robert Maynard Hutchins in the 1940s. At a moment in a continuous flow we have chosen to freeze forever in our memories, that curriculum consisted of completely prescribed general education courses based on special paperbound volumes published by the Syllabus Division of the University of Chicago Press, presented in a combination of large lectures and small class sections devoted to discussion of the readings by the students. Student work assignments during the academic year were somewhat varied, though there were generally quarterly examinations intended to tell students how they were progressing. What counted was the comprehensive examination administered at the end of each course, in the spring, by the University Examiner's Office. In the opening chapter of this volume, David Or-

279

linsky explains how that extraordinary curriculum came into being. It was the product of exquisitely wrought faculty politics. High-minded ideology bent on bringing into reality a new conception of general education lay behind its establishment. However, in a familiar pattern of matching ends and means, the high-minded ideologues of the College faculty engaged in some raw politics and vote manipulation to get their way with the curriculum. That pedagogically splendid curriculum ultimately foundered on practical issues: fewer and fewer students came forward to enlist in its imaginative and demanding program. The administration that succeeded Hutchins believed—rightly or wrongly—that it was necessary to disband the College's distinctive faculty in order to remedy the malady of that brilliant but failing curriculum.

The disbanding of the College's faculty and the wrecking of the College's curriculum have often been confused one with the other. While "disbanding" and "wrecking" dramatically overstate the reality of what happened in this conservative and slow-to-change university, they fairly register the sentiment among both students and faculty about what happened in the fifties. It is not my purpose to try to chronicle what might be called the Kimpton years. Nor do I attempt to analyze the College structure designed by Edward Levi, although this is the institution which I have been privileged to serve as dean for the past four years. What needs to be said here is that continuity with the tradition and values of the "Hutchins College" is very strongly marked in the contemporary College; there is today a College faculty and a College curriculum. This current College's faculty is also a divisional faculty, but it is peculiarly different from the faculty of the divisions when issues affecting baccalaureate degrees are discussed. Today's College curriculum is quite unlike any other in America higher education; it is one which offers a truly integrated vision of knowledge, albeit without much of the Hutchins (or Adler) éclat.

The College curriculum now is, roughly speaking, half prescribed and half dependent upon a student's choice of concentration programs and elective courses. Among the courses in the prescribed half, there are alternatives, so that not all students in the College are expected to have read all of the same books, or selections from the great works. (In the Hutchins College, because so many bright students succeeded in passing placement tests in courses about which they knew very little, there were also many students who got B.A.'s without having read the set books.) It seems to me that the principal message of this book is that the faculty has never let go of what it thinks most important about learning and teaching, and we have found a way of presenting those values in such a way as to assure their continuing attractiveness to intellectually able students.

I was not a College student at Chicago and never took Soc 2 or anything even faintly resembling it when I was an undergraduate. I have only snippets of evaluation by students—both those who loved Soc 2, and those whose minds were elsewhere—from which to construct a student perspective on the course. However, I have been a member of the Soc 2 staff for twenty years and I was chairman of that staff for six years. I have had the opportunity to reflect often on many of the enduring parts of the reading list and to speculate on their persisting influence on me.

I do not know whether it is better for what Herbert Spencer called "cerebral hygiene" to teach Soc 2 for a few years and then move on to other courses and other works, or to do it as a steady diet. Those who passed through the course staff and on to other work tell of the lasting benefits they have incurred in meeting the challenging breadth of this course and in the intellectual encounter with the other members of the staff. Soc 2 has framed my way of understanding human activity to such an extent that I sometimes doubt my ability to gain any critical distance from its influence. The ways of thinking of Weber and Marx, of Durkheim and Freud are my ways of thinking. The *Entäusserung* of Marx and the anomie of Durkheim, the *Bewusstsein* of Marx and the *Unbewusstsein* of Freud spring into my consciousness at (usually) appropriate moments of my everyday life.

Although I must now be counted among the old hands of the Soc 2 staff at Chicago, it appears to me that the effect of teaching the course on my intellectual life is not so different from the influence it has had on others who have taught it—Michael Schudson, Lewis Coser, Joseph Gusfield, David Riesman, and Marc Galanter in this volume—then moved on to other institutional settings and other pedagogical paradigms. It is not just the individual authors or books that exert this influence: thousands of social scientists have read and intellectually interiorized all of the same things we have. It is the ensemble of works, orchestrated each year by a brilliant and critical faculty group, their conversation with one another carried out in the voices of successive generations of naive students, and the unity of the course over three interconnected quarters that has given this experience its special power.

It is difficult to know how far Soc 2 has influenced the thinking of the American public. Today, first-year students who take the course are already loaded with a vocabulary—for example, "charisma," "life style," and "patriarchalism"—that was once confined to the small group who had read more of Weber's writing than just *The Protestant Ethic and the Spirit of Capitalism*. However, the small significance they attach to such terms requires that they be reintroduced with appropriate gravity during the course. Some important books have no doubt made their way into public consciousness at least in part through the Soc 2 reading list, and the influential *The Lonely Crowd* was a product of David Riesman and the course staff.

It is no easy matter to get a book included in the Soc 2 syllabus. In the bygone days of syllabi that were lithographic copies—often of laboriously produced typescripts—varying the reading list from year to year was a difficult matter. Now, however, with thousands of good titles easily available and copying machines at the ready, decision making about the syllabus is the most difficult annual task of the course staff. The method by which agreement is achieved, establishing the contents of each year's reading list, guarantees that a book has been examined from several different perspectives before it is elected. By contrast with a "consensual" reading list in which each participating faculty member gets to name a personal choice, the Soc 2 method requires that a proponent defend a nominated work against the criticisms and claims of other faculty members. Thus, the debate about the importance of a book and its author's ideas is begun, each year, long before the first student is enrolled in the class. And it usually continues after the class is over, since a chosen work has to be selected again in each successive year. Soc 2 is a "staff-taught course," as we often say, not simply in that a number of faculty members are teaching the same things at the same time to different groups of students, but also in the deeper sense that the group has jointly agreed on its syllabus and the rationale for organizing the material in a certain pattern.

Throughout the long life of this course, members of the staff have carried with them the realities and concerns of the society in which they were living. The course was born during the Great Depression. The concerns of that epoch for social justice and for large, centrally administered programs of social welfare, as well as the turmoil in Europe that led into World War II, were clearly manifest in the reading list. The transformation of societies for the benefit of humanity at large, as well as the puzzling resistance to change of cultures, no matter how "simple," were issues in the syllabus after the war. There was a European bias in the reading lists from the 1930s and 1940s: Freud, Marx, Weber, and Durkheim were there throughout. However, the course was heavily influenced by anthropologists and by social science research carried out in settings then beyond major Euro-American influence. The causes and consequences of the spread of industrialism beyond its western European and North American origins were major areas of concern during the postwar years. A relativistic and high but not uncritical respect for the standards and values of cultural systems quite different from our own was implicit in the construction of Soc 2 from a very early period.

The 1947 syllabus includes a remarkable document which might

well be a part of one of the contemporary syllabi. This is Ruth Underhill's wonderful *Autobiography of a Papago Woman,* which was first
published in 1936 as a memoir of the American Anthropological Association. Underhill's work with the woman called Chona was conducted
between 1931 and 1935, when Chona was about ninety years of age.
Thus Chona's life and her recollections of what she learned from her
parents, extended back into the time before the "pacification" of the Indians of the Southwest, and before the establishment of major Anglo
influence on the lives of the native people in the region. Underhill
served as Chona's amanuensis while Chona served as Underhill's guide
to Papago culture; there was a strong mutuality between the brilliant
American anthropologist in the early stages of her new career and the
self-reliant old Indian woman. The product is easily identified, in the
1990s, with "feminist," "third-world," "multicultural," and "postmodern" discourse. Obviously, in 1947, this work was not selected for inclusion in the syllabus because of any of these contemporary concerns. It
was included because the course staff felt the importance of presenting,
as social science, the perspective of a woman whose culture contrasted
sharply with that of the College students. Although it was lodged in a
volume with selections from Bettelheim, Marx, and Weber, Chona's autobiography was unvarnished by any social scientific theory beyond the
general notion that the memories of a single individual constitute a
worthwhile record of human experience, and that the human person is
significantly constituted by her or his cultural system. Many of us today
would treasure a record of the discussion leading up to the inclusion of
this excellent study in a reading list otherwise so "classical" in character.
It was probably the same kind of knockdown argument which, in more
recent years, preceded the first inclusion of Claude Lévi-Strauss's *Savage Mind* in the list.

The fifties are remembered as a hard time for Soc 2 because they were
a hard time for the College. The end of the Hutchins years was distressing for both the students and the faculty of the College, but those times
had a distressing social character of their own that had little to do with the
University of Chicago. Students dropped out of the College in large
numbers, not simply because they were demoralized by the fate of the
College but because they shared the existential demoralization of the
"beat generation." Although it was exaggerated, there was a perception
that the environment in the College mirrored that of the society at large
during the McCarthy era. It is interesting, however, that the reading lists
from Soc 2 in those days are anything but pessimistic. The prospect of
worldwide nuclear conflict was approached as a soluble problem. Robert
Redfield's restudy of the Maya Indian community of Chan Kom, in Mexico, was included. He called it *The Village That Chose Progress;* the students

called it *The Little Village That Could*. David Riesman's last Soc 2 lectures, in 1957, dealt with leisure, which he correctly anticipated would soon be a social phenomenon of very large dimensions in American life.

Very few social scientists foresaw the social phenomena that came to dominate the sixties: the war in Indochina and its reflection in America, and the struggle to establish the civil rights of black Americans. The death of Senator Joseph McCarthy symbolized the end of an era of social conformity and political compliance that was often typified, as to the students, as the silent generation, and as to their elders as *The Man in the Gray Flannel Suit*. Throughout America, students of the sixties reacted against the ethos of conformity and compliance in a series of nearly spontaneous, collective symbolic acts with such ramifying social consequences that no one could any longer dispute the effectiveness of symbols.

At Chicago, the faculty of the College was divided over the actions of the students. The curriculum of the College, as an integral conception capable of surviving changes in the larger social and cultural environment, felt the influence of this era of activism very profoundly. A Soc 2 faculty stayed together, however, even when they could hardly agree on a common reading list. Having cultivated the practice of peaceable disagreement over a long period of time, the Soc 2 tradition survived the sixties. In the name of relevance, some startling curricular changes were made in many institutions during this tumultuous period. Relatively, the syllabus for Soc 2 remained rock solid. It is not that innovations were not made in the reading list, but rather that the innovations of the sixties were not noticeably different in character from those that were made both earlier and later. The enduring core of works by Weber and Marx, Durkheim and Freud, withstood the tide of moral and political indignation that marked that period. The current conception of political correctness in the academy is a lineal descendant of the political opinion and moralizing style of 1969, carried by those who were then students into today's universities. Its influence is nowadays exerted in meetings of the staff, just as its precursors were, and it has exercised its influence—now, as then—without destroying or distorting the general scheme of education in the social sciences that it embodies.

Teaching together, as we have done for so long in the Soc 2 staff, is quite unusual in America, or anywhere else for that matter. It has left all of us changed in certain ways that are suggested by Michael Schudson's strikingly insightful account of the recollections of the generations of teachers in Soc 2. Public examination of this experience is bound to look a little like navel contemplation. What we intended, however—as Schudson suggests—is more Talmudic (in the best sense) than it is Hindu. By recovering some of the most important debates and deliberations of nearly sixty intense years, we may be able to understand the true value of some of the masterpieces of social science and their relevance to analysis and action in the present. Teaching Soc 2 creates a genuine and deep acquaintance with important books about human beings, society, and culture. Part of this acquaintance is developed in staff meetings, which have taken very different directions with changes in our own society and America's role in the world. Another, and equally important, part of this acquaintance is cultivated through the repeated teaching of the same books to generations of students. While our historical and cultural contexts have changed, College students getting their first serious lessons in social science remain quite similar.

In our Talmudic dialogues, the role of the most learned rabbi passes frequently from one member of the staff to another. Thanks to the miracle of the nondisciplinary course, no one has a lock on the truth, and each participant—an accomplished specialized social scientist as well as generalist scholar—has a significant contribution to make to every discussion. Just as one faculty member sees the order and organization of the reading list apparently headed toward chaos, another discerns a fine synthesis emerging. These have been great conversations. It is important to recognize that they have made a substantial difference in the thought and work of so many of the outstanding social scientists of the last fifty years.

The community we have created in the staff of Soc 2 over a momentous sixty years has some of the characteristics common to all human communities. Members have left and new ones have been recruited; now none of the original members remains, yet the community is identifiably the same. The predominant interests and concerns of our community have reflected those of the wider society of which we are a part. But, at the same time, we possess something which distinguishes us from all the other elements of our society: an intellectual legacy based on the conception that a whole human being—a person with a sense of self—is both product and participant in a distinctive social and cultural system, a system of interaction and meaning which give form and significance to human life. Society and culture, not given in nature but created by human action, are what make us human persons. Implicitly, each teacher of Soc 2 has shared the belief that every student needs to understand not only this general idea, but also the enormous variety of forms in which is has been manifest throughout humankind and human history. We have found means of fulfilling this mission suitable to times of world war and peace, to times of domestic repression and liberty, and to times of tranquility and turmoil. This experience teaches us caution about anticipating the ways in which the course will adapt itself to the twenty-first century. It is tempting, however, to imagine a world in which superpower confrontation becomes a minor concern, in which enhanced facilities for communication and travel are matched by an en-hanced regard for cultural variety and social diversity, and where the eternal tension between equality and liberty is nearly in equilibrium. We are social scientists and we live in a world of social facts. We do not expect miracles nor do we think that sound education leads inexorably to a splendid world society. However, the character of the world's civili-zations and global social relations without the kind of education we have sought to offer is far less promising.

The Contributors

Bertram Cohler is William Rainey Harper professor in the Social Sciences Collegiate Division and professor in the departments of Psychology, Education, and Psychiatry at the University of Chicago. He is the author (with H. Grunebaum) of *Mothers, Grandmothers, and Daughters: Personality and Child Care in Three-Generation Families* (1981) and (with J. Musick) of *Intervention among Psychiatrically Disabled Parents and Young Children* (1987).

Lewis A. Coser is distinguished professor of sociology emeritus at the State University of New York-Stony Brook and adjunct professor of sociology at Boston College. His most recent books include *Refugee Scholars in America* (1984) and *A Handful of Thistles: Collected Papers in Moral Conviction* (1988).

Marc Galanter is the Evjue-Bascom professor of law and South Asian Studies and director of the Institute for Legal Studies at the University of Wisconsin—Madison. He is the author of *Competing Equalities: Law and the Backward Classes in India* (1984), *Cults: Faith, Healing, and Coercion* (1989), and (with T. Palay) *Tournament of Lawyers* (1991).

Robert Ginsberg is professor of philosophy, The Pennsylvania State University—Delaware County Campus. He is the author of *Welcome to Philosophy!* (1982) and *Gustav Vigeland: A Case Study in Art and Culture* (1984) and the editor of *The Philosopher as Writer: The Eighteenth Century* (1987).

Joseph R. Gusfield is professor emeritus of the Department of Sociology, University of California—San Diego. His books include *Communities* (1975); *The Culture of Public Problems* (1981); and *Kenneth Burke on Symbols and Society* (1989).

Donald N. Levine is Peter B. Ritzma professor in the Department of Sociology and the College, and former dean of the College at the University of Chicago. His books include *Wax and Gold: Tradition and Innovation in Ethiopian Culture* (1965); and *The Flight from Ambiguity: Essays in Social and Cultural Theory* (1985).

John J. MacAloon is associate professor in the Division of the Social Sciences and the College, the University of Chicago. His books include *This Great Symbol: Pierre de Coubertin and the Origins of the Modern Olympic Games* (1981) and *Brides of Victory: Gender and Nationalism in Olympic Ritual* (1992).

McKim Marriott is professor of anthropology and professor in the Social Sciences Collegiate Division, The University of Chicago. He is the editor of *Village India: Studies in the Little Community* (1955) and *India through Hindu Categories* (1990).

Ralph W. Nicholas is professor of anthropology and dean of the College, the University of Chicago. He is the author (with Ronald Inden) of *Kinship in Bengali Culture* (1977) and of numerous articles on South Asian politics and religion.

David E. Orlinsky is professor in the College and the Committee on Human Development, the University of Chicago. He is the author (with Kenneth Howard) of *Varieties of Psychotherapeutic Experience* (1975) and "Process and Outcome in Psychotherapy Research" (1986).

David Riesman is Henry Ford II professor of the social sciences emeritus at Harvard University. His works include *Constraint and Variety in American Education* (1956); (with N. Glazer and R. Denney) *The Lonely Crowd* (1961); and (with C. Jencks) *The Academic Revolution* (1977).

Michael Schudson is professor in the departments of Communication and Sociology at the University of California—San Diego. A MacArthur Fellow, his books include *Discovering the News* (1981) and *Advertising: The Uneasy Persuasion* (1986).

F. Champion Ward is a former dean of the University of Chicago College, Ford Foundation vice-president for education and research, and chancellor and acting dean of the graduate faculty of the New School for Social Research. His numerous publications on higher education include *The Idea and Practice of General Education* (ed., 1950) and "Principles and Particulars in Liberal Education" (1964).

Harold S. Wechsler is associate professor of education at the University of Rochester and former chair of the higher education program at the University of Chicago. His books include *the Qualified Student: A History of Selective College Admissions in America, 1870–1970* (1977) and (with S. Schlossman and M. Sedlak) *"The New Look": The Ford Foundation and the Revolution in Business Education* (1988).

Index of Names

A

Abel, Richard, 257
Abrams, M. H., 113
Abu-Lughod, Lila, 142
Adler, Mortimer, 35, 48n, 50–53, 227
Angell, J. R., 35
Antze, Paul, ix
Apter, Andrew, 132
Ashmore, Harry S., 48
Atherton, John, 204

B

Bakan, David, ix, 126, 145
Banfield, Edward, 192
Barr, Stringfellow, 35, 53
Bateson, Gregory, 124
Beaumont, Gustave, 200
Becker, Howard, 129, 133–36, 138, 143
Beer, Samuel, 202
Bell, Daniel, 8, 60, 77, 108, 120, 124, 127–28, 130, 133–34, 139, 142, 145, 166–67, 177, 187n, 189, 218
Bendix, Reinhard, 8, 108, 126, 128, 130–31, 146, 187n
Benedict, Ruth, 104, 120, 148, 158, 172, 183, 188, 195, 265
Benney, Mark, viii, 127, 150
Berelson, Bernard, 192
Berg, Ivar, 215
Berger, Bennett, 177
Bernstein, Haskell, 243
Bettelheim, Bruno, 120, 133, 150–51, 189n, 190n, 239, 283
Bidwell, Charles, 203
Blau, Peter, 137
Boas, Franz, 116
Boddy, Janice, 137

Booth, Wayne, 67–68
Boucher, Chauncey S., 41, 46–49
Boulding, Kenneth, 191
Bourdieu, Pierre, 142
Boyer, Ernest L., 7
Boyer, John, ix, 72
Bramson, Leon, 128, 133
Brandeis, Louis, 181
Brick, Howard, 142
Broder, David, 100
Brown, Richard, 176
Brumbaugh, Aaron J., 49, 54
Bruner, Jerome, 232, 234, 237–38
Bryan, Ashley, 153
Buchanan, Scott, 35, 45, 50–51, 53
Bulmer, Martin, 14n
Burghardt, Gordon, 15
Burke, Kenneth, 174
Burke, Martin, 142
Burton, Ernest DeWitt, 41, 43, 46

C

Cassidy, Sally, 135, 145, 192–93
Cayton, Horace, 193, 215
Chamberlin, T. C., 38
Chodorow, Nancy, 145
Chona, 283
Cohler, Bertram, ix–x, 10, 17–18, 125–126, 131, 134, 143–44, 146
Cohn, Morris, 257
Comte, Auguste, 114
Conant, James Bryant, 179
Cooley, C. H., 116
Coser, Lewis, 8, 16, 108, 127, 136, 167, 185, 281
Coser, Rose, 136, 185
Cott, Nancy, 142